TOEICテスト BEYOND 990 超上級リーディング 7つのコアスキル

テッド寺倉／ロス・タロック 共著

TOEIC is a registered trademark of Educational Testing Service (ETS). This publication is not endorsed or approved by ETS.

アルク

はじめに

　私は今までにTOEIC公開テストを36回受験し、29回満点を取得しました。満点取得率にすると8割です。そして私の知人には、私と同等かそれ以上の「TOEIC満点取得力」を持っている人が少なくとも10人はいます。その一方で、テスト対策にかなりの時間と労力を費やしているにもかかわらず、長い間、満点などの目標スコアに到達できないという人もいます。模試や問題集で膨大な量の問題を解いているのであれば、勉強量は十分足りているはずです。なぜ効率よくスコアアップできないのでしょうか。

原因1　模試の構造的問題
　模試は、テスト本番のシミュレーションや持久力向上という目的には適した教材です。しかし、860点以上のスコアを持つ上級者にとって、模試の問題の9割はすでに正解できる簡単な問題です。そういう人が模試を解くのは、極論すれば、自分が本当に取り組むべき1割の問題に出合うために、9割の不要な問題をも解き、学習時間を浪費していることになります。

原因2　1問あたりの学習効率の悪さ
　TOEICを制作するETSは、常に手加減してくれています。少し本気を出せば、もっと難易度が高い問題や、正解に近い不正解選択肢を増やすことは可能ですが、そこまではハードルを上げてきません。平均スコア580点前後（公開テスト）の受験者層にとって、難しすぎるテストは好ましくないからです。このTOEICを忠実に模倣した市販の問題集も、必然的に易しめにできています。これは、満点を目指すような上級者にとって良いことではありません。テスト本番レベルの薄められた易しい問題をたくさん解くことは、学習効率の面では理想的ではないからです。

原因3　不正解の理由の分析不足
　学習効率が上がらないもう1つの理由は、不正解した問題の分析と原因究明が十分でないことです。「解説を読めば理解できる」「時間さえかければ解けた」「うっかりミスだった」という結論で片付けてしまっている不正解の中に、実は重大なスキルの不足が潜んでいる可能性があります。

上級者の不正解を誘う問題には、おおよそのパターンがあります。そういった問題を体系化し、そこで求められるスキルを意識的かつ集中的に強化することが、本書の目的です。

　本書を制作するにあたり、まず公式問題集と公開テストを徹底的にリサーチし、上級者でも間違える可能性のある、難度の高い問題を抽出しました。次に、それらの問題について傾向や共通項を洗い出し、**正解を得るために必要な本質的能力とは何か**を考察しました。その結果得られた7つのスキルと難問パターンをベースに、TOEICを受験し研究し続けている英語ネイティブの著者、ロス・タロック氏とともに問題作成に取り組みました。そうして書き上げた問題を、満点取得者11人を含む合計35人によるモニタリングを経て、妥協のないクオリティーに磨き上げました。

以下が本書の主な特長です。
- TOEICで安定的に満点を取得するために不可欠な**7つのスキルを解明**
- それぞれのスキルを集中的に鍛えるための**オリジナルトレーニングを提供**
- 上級者向けに**高品質かつ高難度の問題を体系的に収録**
- 負荷を高める仕掛け・正解に近い不正解を盛り込み、**1問で数倍の学習効果を実現**
- 収録問題数を増やすために**和訳は紙面に掲載せず、ダウンロードで提供**

　上級者がさらに実力を伸ばすことに貢献する良質な問題だけを収録した本書を利用すれば、模試10冊にも相当する効果が得られると考えています。TOEICを完全攻略し、安定的に990点を取れる力を持つ"BEYOND 990er"になることを目指す人にとって、本書が一助となるを期待しています。

2015年10月
テッド寺倉

CONTENTS
目 次

はじめに ……………………………………………………………………… 2
本書の使い方 ………………………………………………………………… 6
弱点スキル診断テスト ……………………………………………………… 8

CHAPTER 1 精読力
PERUSING
➡ 拡大解釈・縮小解釈をしない力

精読力とは？ ………………………………………………………………… 18
 トレーニング Menu 1 ……………………………………………………… 22
     Menu 2 ……………………………………………………… 26
実践問題 ……………………………………………………………………… 33

CHAPTER 2 情報検索力
SCANNING
➡ 解答に必要なピンポイント情報を素早く見つける力

情報検索力とは？ …………………………………………………………… 58
 トレーニング Menu 1 ……………………………………………………… 62
     Menu 2 ……………………………………………………… 66
実践問題 ……………………………………………………………………… 74

CHAPTER 3 要約力
SUMMARIZING
➡ つながりとイメージをつかむ力

要約力とは？ ………………………………………………………………… 96
 トレーニング Menu 1 ……………………………………………………… 100
実践問題 ……………………………………………………………………… 110

CHAPTER 4 裏取り力
CORROBORATING
➡ 根拠をもって正解・不正解を証明できる力

裏取り力とは？ ……………………………………………………………… 134
 トレーニング Menu 1 ……………………………………………………… 139
     Menu 2 ……………………………………………………… 144
実践問題 ……………………………………………………………………… 150

CHAPTER 5　言い換え対応力
PARAPHRASING
➡ 「具体」から「抽象」に変換する力

- 言い換え対応力とは？ ……………………………………………………… 170
- トレーニング　Menu 1 ……………………………………………………… 174
- 　　　　　　　Menu 2 ……………………………………………………… 178
- 実践問題 ……………………………………………………………………… 184

CHAPTER 6　語法・語感力
SENSITIVITY TO WORDS / USAGE
➡ ディテールへの注意力

- 語法・語感力とは？ ………………………………………………………… 202
- トレーニング　Menu 1 ……………………………………………………… 206
- 　　　　　　　Menu 2 ……………………………………………………… 210
- 実践問題 ……………………………………………………………………… 215

CHAPTER 7　難語対応・忍耐力
ADVANCED VOCABULARY / ENDURANCE
➡ 持てる知識でベストを尽くせる力

- 難語対応・忍耐力とは？ …………………………………………………… 236
- トレーニング　Menu 1 ……………………………………………………… 240
- 　　　　　　　Menu 2 ……………………………………………………… 250
- 実践問題 ……………………………………………………………………… 258

コラム
- Ted's Talks：BEYOND対談（ロス・タロック、ヒロ前田、TEX加藤）…… 55、131、283
- Ted's Talks：TOEICを超越する人3タイプ ……………………………… 94、200、234
- Ted流TOEICの泳ぎ方 …………………………………… 45、123、127、161、183

弱点スキル診断テスト　解答一覧 ……………………………………………… 285

本書の使い方

本書はTOEICテストのリーディングセクション（Part 5、6、7）でハイスコアを取るために必要な7つのスキルを養成するための教材だ。構成・使い方は以下の通り。

弱点スキル診断テスト

20問のミニテスト。各問題は7つのスキル（精読力、情報検索力、要約力、裏取り力、言い換え対応力、語法・語感力、難語対応・忍耐力）に紐付けされている。どの問題を間違えたかによって、今の自分に不足しているスキルを簡易判定できる。

メインのページ（CHAPTER 1〜CHAPTER 7）

スキル解説

その章で扱うスキルの概要説明。「弱点スキル診断テスト」の問題を例に取り、該当スキルの不足によって起きるミスの典型例が解説されている。

トレーニング

それぞれのスキルを集中的に鍛えるための、特殊な高地トレーニングが1〜2種用意されている。制限時間を意識しながら取り組んでみよう。

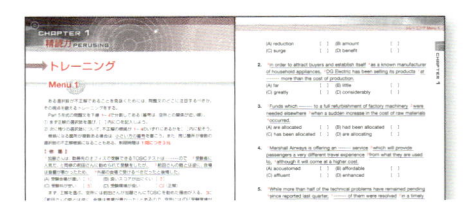

実践問題

仕上げに本番形式の問題を解く。上級者と超・上級者を分ける難問が多く含まれている。制限時間内に解き、スキルが身についたかどうかを確認しよう。

役立つ情報コラム

Ted's Talks──BEYOND対談
本書の主著者テッド寺倉が、共著者のロス・タロック、姉妹本『TOEIC®テスト BEYOND 990 超上級問題＋プロの極意』の著者であるヒロ前田、TEX加藤にインタビュー。

Ted's Talks──TOEICを超越する人3タイプ
TOEICテストで安定して満点を取るBEYOND 990ersを、英語学習歴やTOEICテストとの向き合い方から3タイプに分類。彼らを成功に導いた要因を分析する。

Ted流TOEICの泳ぎ方──長続きする英語自己学習法
TOEIC対策・英語学習は、「続けること」が最も難しい点。同じくなかなか続かない運動習慣（水泳）になぞらえて、自律的に学習を進めるコツを考察する。

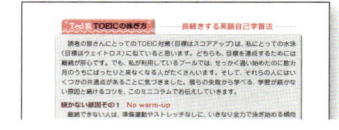

本書で使われている品詞のマーク

| 名 | : 名詞 | 代名 | : 代名詞 | 関代 | : 関係代名詞 | 動 | : 動詞 | 形 | : 形容詞 | 副 | : 副詞 |
| 接 | : 接続詞 | 前 | : 前置詞 |

※複数の品詞がある語については、本書の問題で使われている品詞や、TOEICでよく登場する品詞を掲載している。

ダウンロード特典のご案内

本書に収録した問題の和訳は、下記ウェブサイトからダウンロードできます。

ALC Download Center　ダウンロードセンター
http://www.alc.co.jp/dl/

● ダウンロード手順
上記の「ダウンロードセンター」にアクセス
➡ 『TOEIC®テスト BEYOND 990 超上級リーディング 7つのコアスキル』を選択
➡ 表示される「申し込みフォーム」に必要事項を記入して、送信
➡ メールにてダウンロード先のURLが届くので、そのURLからダウンロード

● 提供特典
• 診断テスト、トレーニング、実践問題の和訳（PDF）
※ダウンロードは必ずパソコンにて行ってください。
※ファイルはZIP形式で圧縮されています。解凍ソフトで展開の上ご利用ください。

弱点スキル診断テスト

　TOEICの開発元であるETSは、受験者のどのような能力を測ろうとしているのか。公式問題集や公開テストのリーディングセクションから、上級者でもミスする可能性のある難問を集め、出題ポイントを分析すると、その狙いが浮かび上がってくる。本書ではこの分析を通じて、リーディングセクションで常時満点を取るために必要な能力を以下の7つに分類した。

> 1. 精読力　2. 情報検索力　3. 要約力　4. 裏取り力
> 5. 言い換え対応力　6. 語法・語感力　7. 難語知識・忍耐力

　これらの「7つのコアスキル」について詳しく学ぶ前に、現在のあなたに不足しているスキルを、診断テストで割り出そう。

【 診断の仕方 】

- 右ページから始まる診断テスト（Part 5、6、7）の問題を一気に解こう。
  問題数は20問。解答目標時間は20分。
  目標時間内に終わらなかった場合は、なるべく急いで最後まで解答しよう。
- 正解だと思う選択肢の記号を、ページの右端あるいは左端の解答欄に記入しよう。
- 正解の根拠がはっきりわからず勘で答えた場合、あるいは少しでも解答に自信がない場合は、「勘マーク」の欄に✓を入れよう。
- 解答が終わったら、p. 16に進み、答え合わせをしよう。

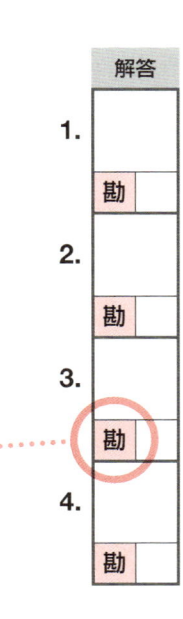

Part 5   空所に入る語句として、最も適切なものを1つ選ぼう。

1. The ------- of an empty space on the third floor into a conference room has made meetings far easier to arrange.
   (A) utilization
   (B) allocation
   (C) conversion
   (D) construction

2. The ------- among customers is that higher prices would be acceptable if product quality were also to improve.
   (A) decision
   (B) feeling
   (C) reputation
   (D) question

3. Research has shown that it is still ------- because of cultural differences that some kitchen appliances are selling better in northern states.
   (A) prime
   (B) primary
   (C) primarily
   (D) primed

4. It took technicians at the manufacturing facility several days to ------- the cause of a malfunction that had halted production.
   (A) establish
   (B) attribute
   (C) arrive
   (D) search

5. McClymont Books sells its publications more cheaply in Canada, ------- the fact that they are based in the United States results in significant additional costs.
(A) despite
(B) due to
(C) besides
(D) although

6. One of the secrets of operating a successful business is employing people who can be ------- on to work without direct supervision.
(A) encouraged
(B) trusted
(C) counted
(D) authorized

7. Since the customer service department was taken over by Ms. White, it has been far more ------- to requests for assistance from customers.
(A) helpful
(B) pleasant
(C) understanding
(D) responsive

8. The council decided to remove trees used in the ------- of the park boundaries because they were dropping leaves onto neighboring property.
(A) delineation
(B) mediation
(C) solidification
(D) consolidation

Part 6

空所に入る語句として、最も適切なものを1つ選ぼう。

Questions 9-11 refer to the following information.

Many sports fans are reluctant to buy a season pass because they are concerned that they may be unable to make full use of their purchase. Unexpected work commitment and interstate transfers are commonly ------- reasons for underutilized

9. (A) insisted
   (B) accessed
   (C) cited
   (D) neglected

passes, resulting in a huge waste of money. To put minds at ease, GameOne is offering an insurance package that ensures you get true value for money.

Should you be unable to use your ------- for an extended

10. (A) ticket
    (B) services
    (C) membership
    (D) policy

period, GameOne will refund the value of the unused portion.

The cost of this insurance is only 10 percent of the purchase price and could potentially save you hundreds of dollars. The terms and conditions and a detailed list of acceptable -------

11. (A) locations
    (B) circumstances
    (C) withdrawals
    (D) consequences

are included in the brochure.

Why not spend a little more to protect your investment and enjoy the coming season worry-free?

GameOneInsurance.com

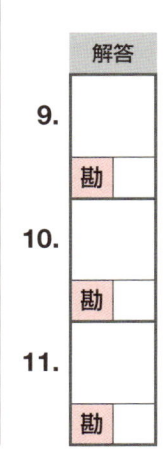

Part 7

文書に関する設問の解答として、最も適切なものを1つずつ選ぼう。

Questions 12-15 refer to the following article.

Dalton Air Finds New Direction

Sydney (August 10)—Since the leadership change in mid-May, there has been much speculation about how David Panetta, the new CEO, will make his mark on Australia's largest international airline.

The first hint of what the future holds came this week, when Dalton Air purchased 14 additional aircraft, albeit used, from Borden Aerospace. The company released a statement on Thursday saying that it would add eight destinations in Asia and Europe by next spring and is considering expanding the workforce accordingly. However, public relations manager, Joe Walker, acknowledged in an interview with the press that the latter piece of news would still require approval at the general meeting of shareholders next month.

Mr. Walker also mentioned that the undertaking might be achieved by merging with a smaller airline. Many experts in the industry speculate that because there is little time for them to hire and train staff before the first flights, it would be a logical step for the rapidly growing company. In that scenario, the new chief's business contacts from his time leading two other aviation companies might come in handy in finding an ideal partner.

12. What is NOT indicated about Dalton Air?
(A) It has new management.
(B) It is partnered with Borden Aerospace.
(C) It is expanding its service.
(D) It operates in foreign countries.

13. According to the article, what will most likely happen in September?
(A) New routes will be launched.
(B) An airline will be acquired.
(C) A meeting will take place.
(D) A number of employees will be hired.

14. What do industry experts predict for Dalton Air?
(A) Some of its employees will be retrained.
(B) A plan will be unanimously approved.
(C) Additional offices will be opened.
(D) The number of personnel will increase.

15. According to the article, what is Mr. Panetta expected to do?
(A) Use his personal ties
(B) Extend a deadline
(C) Adopt a new practice
(D) Appoint a board member

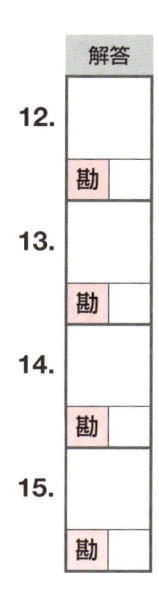

Questions 16-20 refer to the following advertisement and e-mail.

Boston's largest advertising agency, Gauguin Advertising and Media (GAM) is looking to hire a new associate producer in its media division. The position will provide Web site consultation services to clients worldwide. It is a unique and exciting position full of challenges and opportunities to explore foreign countries.

We are seeking self-starters who keep abreast of the latest Web standards and technologies. Applicants must hold a degree in marketing from an accredited university or have extensive experience in the marketing department of a major corporation. Other necessary qualifications include some data analysis experience and an up-to-date portfolio of previous creative work.

Please be advised that only suitable applicants will receive a reply. Applications will be replied to either by phone or by e-mail. Please specify which you would prefer and be sure to provide the relevant details with your résumé.

Send all applications to Mark Weinberg at Human Resources by March 3.

mweinberg@gam.com

E-Mail Message

From: Joe Hope <jhope@geoline.com>
To: Mark Weinberg <mweinberg@gam.com>
Date: Tuesday, February 22
Subject: Position (associate producer)
Attachment: Résumé_JHope.doc

Dear Mr. Weinberg,

I have long been interested in working for Gauguin Advertising and Media and this is the second time I have applied for a position at your firm.

I am applying because of my strong desire to be involved in the creation of innovative marketing strategies for market leaders. My portfolio as a product marketing coordinator, which is included with my résumé, is rather limited in variety because I have been working at De La Care Corporation which is exclusively a cosmetics company. However, I am able to swiftly grasp the needs of specific industries.

I am a competent computer user and will take any courses needed to bring me up-to-speed on the software GAM uses. As I mention in the attached résumé, I am also an expert photographer having won a number of local awards. My degree in international business had a marketing component and that, combined with my five years' experience at De La Care, makes me well suited to this position.

As I am about to switch my mobile phone subscription, I would like to opt for the second contact option. I look forward to hearing from you soon.

Sincerely,
Joe Hope

16. What is suggested about the position?
  (A) Continuous training will be provided.
  (B) Some overseas travel is required.
  (C) A license as a data analyst is preferable.
  (D) Applications will be acknowledged on receipt.

17. What is indicated about Mr. Hope?
  (A) He has interviewed with GAM before.
  (B) He is undertaking a course in Internet marketing.
  (C) He is eager to take on creative challenges.
  (D) He is sending his portfolio by regular mail.

18. What requirement for the position does Mr. Hope mention in his e-mail?
  (A) Competency in photography
  (B) A degree in international business
  (C) Computer programming skills
  (D) Relevant examples of work

19. In the e-mail, the word "component" in paragraph 3, line 4, is closest in meaning to
  (A) element
  (B) prospect
  (C) certificate
  (D) ingredient

20. How would Mr. Hope prefer to be contacted?
  (A) By phone
  (B) By fax
  (C) By mail
  (D) By e-mail

弱点スキル診断テスト 解答

【 採点の仕方 】

- pp. 9〜15の解答欄を見て、自分が選択した記号を下表の「あなたの解答」欄に記入する。
- 不正解の場合は、「不正解」の欄に ✓ を入れる。正解した場合でも、「勘」マークに ✓ を入れていた場合は、「正解だが勘」の欄に ✓ を入れる。
- ✓ の入った行の★マークすべてを〇で囲む。
- 「該当コアスキル」の列ごとに、〇のついた★の数を数え、最下行に記入する。

　★の数が多かったスキルが、あなたの現在の「不足スキル」となる。該当する章は、重点的に学習しよう。全問正解した人も、本文ではさらに難度の高い、さまざまなパターンの問題を収載しているので、気を抜かず挑んでほしい。

	問題	正解記号	あなたの解答	不正解	正解だが勘	該当コアスキル 1 精読力	2 情報検索力	3 要約力	4 裏取り力	5 言い換え対応力	6 語法・語感力	7 難語対応・忍耐力
記入例	0	(B)	(A)	✓			㊀		㊀			
Part 5	1	(C)					★				★	
	2	(B)				★					★	
	3	(C)				★			★			
	4	(A)							★		★	
	5	(D)				★			★			
	6	(C)					★					
	7	(D)				★						
	8	(A)										★
Part 6	9	(C)							★		★	
	10	(A)					★	★				
	11	(B)					★					★
Part 7 SP	12	(B)					★		★			
	13	(C)					★	★				
	14	(D)					★					★
	15	(A)					★			★		★
Part 7 DP	16	(B)					★	★				
	17	(C)					★	★				
	18	(D)				★			★			
	19	(A)				★			★	★		
	20	(D)					★					
	〇をした★の合計：					/7	/7	/7	/7	/4	/7	/5

※2、6、16、20番以外は、その問題で問われるコアスキルの章で解説されている。
　上記4問の解説と、各問題の解説があるページの一覧は、pp. 285〜287を参照のこと。

CHAPTER 1

精読力
PERUSING

このスキルが足りない人は…

- [ ] リーディングセクションのスコアが420〜450点で伸び悩んでいる

- [ ] スコアを見るとミスしたようだが、間違えた自覚がない

- [ ] 解答の根拠があやふやなまま答えてしまう

CHAPTER 1
精読力
PERUSING

➤ 拡大解釈・縮小解釈をしない力
必要になるパート：Part 5／6／7

　一般的に精読とは、「細かいところまで丁寧に読むこと」ですが、TOEICのリーディングセクションで必要な「精読力」とは、**「英文に忠実に読み、拡大解釈・縮小解釈をしない力」**であると言えます。

　Part 7の問題を例に考えてみましょう。レストランの広告の文書に、We offer catering for conferences and workshops.（会議や研修にケータリングいたします）という記述があったとします。そして、設問が「このレストランについて述べられていることは何か」だったとします。これに対し、It delivers food.（食事を配達する）という選択肢は、記述の内容と重なるので正解です。しかし、It offers home catering services.（家庭向けのケータリングサービスを提供している）という選択肢は、記述の意味する範囲とズレているので不正解と判断しなければなりません。「会社にケータリングできるなら、一般家庭にも配達できるのではないか」という**拡大解釈は禁物**です。

　次にPart 5、6の語彙問題の例を見てみましょう。We will hold a ------- to celebrate the restaurant's third anniversary. という問題文では、partyやprize draw（抽選会）は空所に挿入可能な語の範囲内ですが、price reduction（割引）やrenovation（改装）はhold（～を開催する）の目的語になれないので、範囲外となります。

　TOEICでコンスタントに満点を取る人（以下、「BEYOND 990er」と呼びます）は、この**「範囲内」と「範囲外」の線引きが明確**です。彼らは問題文を精読するこ

とで、選択肢を見る前に、正解になる語句の範囲をある程度想定できています。そして、いざ選択肢に目を移すと、正解だけが浮き上がって見えるのです。

　精読力を問う問題は難度が高い問題です。リーディングセクションの420〜450点辺りで壁にぶつかり、そこから伸び悩んでいるという方は、この力が不足している可能性があります。診断テストの設問を例にとって、精読力不足によって起きるミスのパターンと防止法を見ていきましょう。

【Part 5】 p. 9, 3（色字の選択肢が正解）

3. Research has shown that it is still ------- because of cultural differences that some kitchen appliances are selling better in northern states.
(A) prime　　　　形 主要な
(B) primary　　　形 最初の、主要な
＊(C) primarily　　副 主として
(D) primed　　　動 入れ知恵された

Part 5、6：空所に入る語句の範囲を思い込みで狭めない

　Part 5、6の文法問題には、文法の知識だけでは正解にたどり着けないものがあります。上の問題はその一例です。空所とその前後のつながりは、「it is 形容詞 that」（that以下は〜だ）と「it is 副詞 because of ... that」（that以下は〜に…によるものだ）の両方の可能性があり、どちらが適切かは文意から確定しなければなりません。「it isときたら形容詞しかない」と、**空所の可能性を"縮小解釈"してしまうのが典型的なミスのパターン**です。

　Part 5や6の文法問題は、文構造の把握や品詞の区別だけでもかなりの確率で正解できますが、万全を期すならば文意を精査するプロセスも外せません。満点を目指すなら、**「型」で正解候補を選んだ後、「意味」でダブルチェックする**ことを習慣にしましょう。そうすれば縮小解釈のワナにはまることはありません。

　次に、Part 7で精読力が必要なケースを見てみましょう。

【Part 7】 p. 14, 18 (抜粋)

広告

> We are seeking self-starters who (C)keep abreast of the latest Web standards and technologies. Applicants must hold a degree in marketing from an accredited university or have extensive experience in the marketing department of a major corporation. Other necessary qualifications include (C)some data analysis experience and an up-to-date portfolio of previous creative work.

メール

> My portfolio as a product marketing coordinator, which is included with my résumé, is rather limited in variety because I have been working at De La Care Corporation which is exclusively a cosmetics company. However, I am able to swiftly grasp the needs of specific industries.
>
> (C)I am a competent computer user and will take any courses needed to bring me up-to-speed on the software GAM uses. As I mention in the attached résumé, (A)I am also an expert photographer having won a number of local awards. (B)My degree in international business had a marketing component and that, combined with my five years' experience at De La Care, makes me well suited to this position.

18. What requirement for the position does Mr. Hope mention in his e-mail?
  (A) Competency in photography
  (B) A degree in international business
  (C) Computer programming skills
  ＊(D) Relevant examples of work

Part 7：一致・不一致の線引きを厳密に行う

　この問題は、まず設問を精読する必要があります。設問は「Hope氏がメールの中で言及している応募要件は何か」を問うています。よって、①広告にある応募要件、②メールでHope氏がアピールしていること、③選択肢、の3つの範囲が重なる部分、すなわち、3つに共通する情報を探す必要があります。

　(A)「写真撮影が上手なこと」、(B)「国際ビジネスの学位」は、メールでしか述べられていない情報なので簡単に排除できます。(C)の「コンピュータープログラミングのスキル」はどうでしょうか。広告には「最新のウェブ規格や技術に精通していること」や「データ分析の経験」という要件が書かれていますが、これらを「コンピュータープログラミングのスキル」と同等とするのは拡大解釈であり不適切です。メールにも、「コンピューターを使うのは得意」とは書かれていても、「プログラミングができる」とまでは書かれていません。正解は、両文書で述べられているportfolio（作品集）を言い換えた(D)「（応募する職に）関連のある作品例」です。

　このような「ちりばめられた情報を関連付ける」問題は、解答に時間がかかります。そこで我慢して精読できず、「きっとこういう意味なんじゃないかな」と本文を曲解してしまうのが不正解のパターンです。BEYOND 990erも、こういう問題はある程度時間をかけて慎重に解いています（その分、易しい問題を速く解き、時間を稼いでいます）。

　精読力を磨くには、4択問題の正解を選ぶだけでなく、問題文を細かい単位に分割して精査し、正しく理解できているかどうかをチェックすることが有効です。2種類のトレーニングを用意したので、チャレンジしてみてください。

POINT
- 拡大・縮小解釈は厳禁。選びたい選択肢のために解釈を曲げないこと。
- Part 5、6の文法問題は、「型」で絞り込み「文意」でダブルチェック。
- Part 7の「ちりばめられた情報を関連付ける」問題は時間をかけて慎重に解く。

CHAPTER 1
精読力 PERUSING

→トレーニング

Menu 1

　ある選択肢が不正解であることを見抜くためには、問題文のどこに注目するべきか。その視点を鍛えるトレーニングをする。
　Part 5形式の問題文を下線1〜4で分割してある（番号は、空所との関係が近い順）。
① まず正解の選択肢を選び、[　]内に○を記入しよう。
② 次に残りの選択肢について、不正解の根拠が1〜4のいずれにあるかを[　]内に記そう。
　根拠になる箇所が複数ある場合は、小さい方の番号を書こう。また、同じ箇所が複数の選択肢の不正解根拠になることもある。制限時間は**1問につき3分**。

【 例 題 】
¹ 加藤さんは、勤務先のオフィスで受験できるTOSICテストは-------ので　² 受験者に人気だ、と同僚の前田さんに勧められて受験をしたが、　³ 前田さんの話とは逆に、会場は音響が悪かったため、　⁴ 外部の会場で受けるべきだったと後悔した。
(A) 受験会場が遠い　[1]　　(B) 良いスコアが出にくい　[2]
(C) 受験料が安い　　[3]　　(D) 受験環境が良い　　　　[○]（正解）

　まず、正解を選ぶ。空所には前田さんが加藤さんにTOSICを勧めた理由が入る。3に「前田さんの話とは逆に、会場は音響が悪かった」とあるので、空所には(D)「受験環境が良い」が入る。よって、(D)は○とする。
　次に、残りの選択肢が不正解である根拠を検討する。1に「勤務先のオフィスで受験できる」とあるので会場は近い。これが(A)「受験会場が遠い」が不正解となる根拠なので、(A)には1を記す。同様に、(B)には2（「良いスコアが出にくい」は「受験者に人気」に反する）、(C)には3（「受験料が安い」は「会場の音響が悪い」の「逆」にはならない）を記す。

──● 各3分

1. ⁴ According to insiders, ¹ the ------- of spending on research and development　² has come about　³ as a result of improved practices and outsourcing.

トレーニング Menu 1

(A) reduction	[ ]	(B) amount	[ ]
(C) surge	[ ]	(D) benefit	[ ]

2. ³ In order to attract buyers and establish itself ⁴ as a known manufacturer of household appliances, ² DG Electric has been selling its products ¹ at ------- more than the cost of production.

(A) far	[ ]	(B) little	[ ]
(C) greatly	[ ]	(D) considerably	[ ]

3. ¹ Funds which ------- to a full refurbishment of factory machinery ² were needed elsewhere ³ when a sudden increase in the cost of raw materials ⁴ occurred.

(A) are allocated	[ ]	(B) had been allocated	[ ]
(C) has been allocated	[ ]	(D) are allocating	[ ]

4. ¹ Marshall Airways is offering an ------- service ² which will provide passengers a very different travel experience ³ from what they are used to, ⁴ although it will come at a higher cost.

(A) accustomed	[ ]	(B) affordable	[ ]
(C) affluent	[ ]	(D) enhanced	[ ]

5. ³ While more than half of the technical problems have remained pending ⁴ since reported last quarter, ¹ ------- of them were resolved ² in a timely manner.

(A) one	[ ]	(B) most	[ ]
(C) the rest	[ ]	(D) very few	[ ]

6. ⁴ As the leading authority on the subject, ¹ Jeff Yamato is going to ------- a series of introductory workshops ² on doing business in Japan ³ during his visit to the United States in June.

(A) attend	[ ]	(B) appear	[ ]
(C) miss	[ ]	(D) lead	[ ]

CHAPTER 1

23

Menu 1の解答・解説

※問題文の訳文は紙面では省略（訳文の入手方法はp. 7をご覧ください）。

1. [4] According to insiders, [1] the ------- of spending on research and development [2] has come about [3] as a result of improved practices and outsourcing.

- come about 実現する、起こる ● practices 業務、慣行 ● outsourcing 外部委託、業務の外注

(A) reduction　名 減少　　［○］　　(B) amount　名 量　　［2］
(C) surge　　　名 急上昇　［3］　　(D) benefit　名 利益　［2］

解説 ▶ 3「改善された業務と外部委託の結果」として、「研究開発への支出」は「減少」するべきだ。よって、正解は(A) reduction。(B) amountと(D) benefitは、2のcome about（起こる）を動詞に取れないので不適。「量（利益）が起こる」という訳から考えても不適切だと気づくはずだ。(C) surgeは「急上昇」という意味で、3の結果としては不適切というのが不正解の理由だ。

2. [3] In order to attract buyers and establish itself [4] as a known manufacturer of household appliances, [2] DG Electric has been selling its products [1] at ------- more than the cost of production.

- establish oneself as ~ ～としての地位を確立する ● household appliances 家電製品

(A) far　　　　副 はるかに　［3］　　(B) little　　　　　副 ほとんど～ない　［○］
(C) greatly　　副 大いに　　［1］　　(D) considerably　副 かなり、相当に　［3］

解説 ▶ 3「購入者を引き付けるため」という目的に合うのは、「製造原価をほとんど超えない値段」なので、(B) littleが正解。(A) farは3の目的に反するので不正解だ。(C) greatlyは比較級を修飾できないので、1で不正解が確定。(D) considerablyは、比較級を強調することはできるが、製品価格が製造コストより「かなり」高い値段、という意味になり、3と合わない。

3. [1] Funds which ------- to a full refurbishment of factory machinery [2] were needed elsewhere [3] when a sudden increase in the cost of raw materials [4] occurred.

- refurbishment 改修 ● raw material 原料

(A) are allocated　　　　　［2］　　(B) had been allocated　　［○］
(C) has been allocated　　［1］　　(D) are allocating　　　　　［1］

解説 ▶ 2や3で述べられていることより先に「資金は割り当てられていた」とする必要があるので、正解は過去完了形の(B)。(A)は現在形で、過去形の2や4と時制が合わないことが不正解の根拠（番号が小さい2を正解とする）。(C)はhasが複数主語のFundsに一致せず、(D)はare allocatingの目的語がなく不適切なので、いずれも1の時点で不正解。

4. [1] Marshall Airways is offering an ------- service [2] which will provide passengers a very different travel experience [3] from what they are used to, [4] although it will come at a higher cost.

(A) accustomed　形 慣れた　[2]　　(B) affordable　形 手頃な　　[4]
(C) affluent　　形 裕福な　[1]　　(D) enhanced　　形 向上した　[○]

解説 ▶ 4「料金が高くなる」と2「非常に異なる旅行経験を提供する」という記述から「向上した」サービスが文意に合うとわかり、正解は(D) enhanced。(A) accustomedは2の「異なる」という記述に反するので不適。(B) affordableは4で値上げが示唆されていることが不正解の理由。(C) affluentは「裕福な」という意味の形容詞で「サービス」を修飾できないので、1で不正解が確定。

5. [3] While more than half of the technical problems have remained pending [4] since reported last quarter, [1] ------- of them were resolved [2] in a timely manner.
　● pending 未決の

(A) one　　　　代名 1つ　　　　[1]　　(B) most　　　代名 大部分　　　　　[3]
(C) the rest　残りのもの　[○]　　(D) very few　代名 ほとんどが〜ない　[3]

解説 ▶ 3「技術的な問題の半分以上が未解決」という情報が「対比」の接続詞Whileによって導かれているので、「『残りの』問題は解決された」とする(C)が正解。(A) oneは単数扱いなのでwereが合わず、1で不正解が確定。空所に(B) mostを補うと「大部分は解決された」、また(D)を補うと「ほとんどが解決されていない」となり、いずれも3との対比が成立せず、それが不正解の理由となる。

6. [4] As the leading authority on the subject, [1] Jeff Yamato is going to ------- a series of introductory workshops [2] on doing business in Japan [3] during his visit to the United States in June.
　● authority 権威者、大家　● introductory workshop 入門講習会

(A) attend　動 〜に出席する　[4]　　(B) appear　動 現れる　　　　　[1]
(C) miss　　動 〜を逃す　　　[4]　　(D) lead　　動 〜を指導する　　[○]

解説 ▶「一連の入門講習会」を目的語に取り、4「その件に関する第一人者として」という記述に合う(D) leadが正解。(A)は「受講者として出席する」という含意があるので4が不正解の根拠。(B) appearは自動詞で、後ろに前置詞atが必要なので1で不正解が確定。自動詞・他動詞の区別を問う問題では、フレーズで記憶しているかどうかが試される。(C) missは4と合わない。

Menu 2

Part 7の文書の記述内容と選択肢の情報が合致するかどうかを判断する訓練を行う。

ボックス内には、ある文書から抜き出した3〜5文がある。それらの情報と、(A) 〜 (D) または(E)の内容が合致するかどうかを判断し、合致するなら [　] に〇を、合致しなければ×を記入しよう。制限時間は**1セットにつき4分**。

● 各4分

1.

> [1] A new stretch of road between Whitehall and the state's capital will be opened on Monday.
>
> [2] Construction began some 18 months ago and it cost the local government as much as $60 million to reach all the way to Jonestown.
>
> [3] Many in the community were in opposition to the project initially, but now there is great excitement because of the convenience it promises.

(A) Jonestown is the state's capital city.　　　　　　　　　　　　[　]
(B) The construction was carried out at the state's expense.　　[　]
(C) The project had support from the whole community.　　　　[　]
(D) People expect that the new road will reduce traffic.　　　　 [　]

2.

> [1] The Boston city transport authority is launching a jingle competition for local musicians.
>
> [2] The winning submission will be used in advertisements for municipal trains, buses and ferries.
>
> [3] Prizes include a cash reward as well as one year of unlimited travel on Boston public transport.
>
> [4] The competition is exclusive to local residents and only one piece of music per person will be accepted.

(A) The city of Boston is offering a new service.　　　　　　　　　　　　　　[　]
(B) Musicians are encouraged to submit their music for use in advertising.　[　]
(C) There is a monetary incentive to enter the contest.　　　　　　　　　　[　]
(D) Only people who live in Boston will be considered.　　　　　　　　　　[　]

3.

[1] Unless otherwise specified, Nileways Online ships all orders using RedHat Transport.

[2] Our special relationship with RedHat Transport enables us to send goods at substantially discounted rates and pass on the savings to you.

[3] People who live in remote areas are welcome to select another courier if RedHat does not operate in your area.

[4] In such cases, Nileways' parcel insurance and next day delivery guarantee do not apply.

(A) RedHat Transport is owned by Nileways Online.　　　　　　　　　[ ]
(B) Nileways Online offers reduced shipping charges when using RedHat Transport.　　　　　　　　　[ ]
(C) Customers can decide which transport company to use.　　　　　[ ]
(D) Nileways Online requires that customers pay for insurance.　　[ ]

4.

[1] Harridan's Cinema is now offering weekly and monthly pass cards which should benefit frequent visitors.

[2] Cards of various colors, which entitle holders to different levels of service, are available.

[3] The standard blue card allows one person to watch up to four movies a week for only $25, whereas the green card allows the holder to see the same number of movies with a friend for only $5 more.

[4] The orange and purple cards cost $40 and $50 respectively and are valid for a whole month, meaning that holders can watch up to 16 movies for this low price.

[5] Cards can only be purchased during the month of August while stocks last.

(A) Purchasers should choose cards of their favorite color.　　　　　　[ ]
(B) A companion of a green card holder is not charged for admission.　[ ]
(C) Purple cards cost $40.　　　　　　　　　　　　　　　　　　　　　　　[ ]
(D) Harridan's Cinema shows 16 movies a month.　　　　　　　　　　　[ ]
(E) There are a limited number of cards available for purchase.　　　[ ]

5.

> [1] *The Stanton Times* is launching its new online service to provide residents of Stanton access to local news in a more convenient way.
>
> [2] The publisher stated that although she expects to lose some sales revenue when people stop buying the printed version, the environmental benefits make it worthwhile.
>
> [3] The profits, on the other hand, are expected to receive a boost from the reduced costs, online advertisements and paid content limited to registered online members.
>
> [4] Other benefits mentioned in the press release include more updates to content and a customizable front page.

(A) *The Stanton Times* is a newly established news source. [ ]
(B) Online subscriptions are priced equally to printed papers. [ ]
(C) The decision to start the online service has financial advantages. [ ]
(D) Some of the newspaper's online content will only be available for purchase.
[ ]
(E) The headlines may differ depending on the selected newspaper format.
[ ]

6.

> [1] Formosa Coffeehouse is opening its 100th café in Britain this week in the Craigie Mall in downtown Glasgow.
>
> [2] For the past five years, the chain has been enjoying great popularity, among young people in particular.
>
> [3] Owner Ralph Chang spoke from his headquarters in Brooklyn, New York about the latest café, saying that he was so grateful to the people of Britain for making Formosa Coffeehouse such a success.
>
> [4] Many people believe the secret of the company's success lies in the cheerful decor and swift service.

(A) A significant portion of Formosa Coffeehouse clientele is youthful. [ ]
(B) Formosa Coffeehouse originated in New York. [ ]
(C) The owner expressed appreciation to city officials in Britain. [ ]
(D) Formosa Coffeehouse's popularity is partly attributed to its interior design.
[ ]

Menu 2の解答・解説

1.

[1] A new stretch of road between Whitehall and the state's capital will be opened on Monday.
[2] Construction began some 18 months ago and it cost the local government as much as $60 million to reach all the way to Jonestown.
[3] Many in the community were in opposition to the project initially, but now there is great excitement because of the convenience it promises.

● stretch 区間、範囲 ● all the way to ~ ～までずっと ● in opposition to ~ ～に反対して
● convenience 利便性 ● promise ～を約束する、請け合う

解説 (A) Jonestown is the state's capital city. ［○］：[1]「Whitehallと州都間」と[2]「Jonestownまで道を延ばす」を考え合わせると、「州都」＝「Jonestown」が成り立つので○。／ (B) The construction was carried out at the state's expense. ［○］：[2]「地元自治体は6000万ドルもの費用を負担した」とあるので○。／ (C) The project had support from the whole community. ［×］：[3]「コミュニティーの人々の多くは当初そのプロジェクトに反対していた」とあるので「コミュニティー全体の支持を得た」は×。／ (D) People expect that the new road will reduce traffic. ［×］：[3]住民は「利便性（の向上）」が見込まれることにわくわくしている」のであり、「交通量が減ることを期待している」わけではないので×。「交通量が減れば運転しやすくなって利便性が高まるのでは」と考えるのは拡大解釈だ。

2.

[1] The Boston city transport authority is launching a jingle competition for local musicians.
[2] The winning submission will be used in advertisements for municipal trains, buses and ferries.
[3] Prizes include a cash reward as well as one year of unlimited travel on Boston public transport.
[4] The competition is exclusive to local residents and only one piece of music per person will be accepted.

● transport authority 交通局 ● jingle ジングル ※ラジオなどで使われる、コマーシャル用の短い音楽。
● competition コンテスト ● the winning submission 受賞作 ● municipal 地方自治体の、市の
● cash reward 賞金 ● exclusive to ~ ～限定の

解説 (A) The city of Boston is offering a new service. [×]：[1]「ジングル音楽コンテスト」は市交通局が提供する「サービス」とは言えないので×。／ (B) Musicians are encouraged to submit their music for use in advertising. [○]：[1]「地元のミュージシャンのためのジングル音楽コンテスト」と[2]「受賞作は宣伝で使われます」という情報を考え合わせて○。／ (C) There is a monetary incentive to enter the contest. [○]：[3]「賞品は現金やボストン公共交通機関1年間乗り放題パスを含む」を言い換えた「コンテストに参加する金銭的な動機がある」は○。／ (D) Only people who live in Boston will be considered. [○]：[1]でこのコンテストはボストンで行われることがわかり、[4]「コンテスト（参加）は地元住民に限られている」の記述と考え合わせると「ボストンに住んでいる人々だけ」がコンテストに参加できると導けるので○。

3.

[1] Unless otherwise specified, Nileways Online ships all orders using RedHat Transport.

[2] Our special relationship with RedHat Transport enables us to send goods at substantially discounted rates and pass on the savings to you.

[3] People who live in remote areas are welcome to select another courier if RedHat does not operate in your area.

[4] In such cases, Nileways' parcel insurance and next day delivery guarantee do not apply.

● unless otherwise specified 特別の指定がない限り　● substantially かなり、相当　● discounted rates 割引価格　● pass on ~ ~を渡す　● remote area 遠隔地　● courier 宅配便業者　● operate 営業する

解説 (A) RedHat Transport is owned by Nileways Online. [×]：[1]「Nileways Onlineはすべての注文品を、RedHat運輸を使って発送する」とあるが、これは会社の所有関係とは関係ないので×。／ (B) Nileways Online offers reduced shipping charges when using RedHat Transport. [○]：[2]にNileways OnlineはRedHat運輸との特別な関係から得た「経費節減分をあなたに還元する」とあり、「減額配送料金を提供する」と解釈できるので○。／ (C) Customers can decide which transport company to use. [○]：[3]「自由に別の宅配便業者を選ぶことができる」とあるので○。RedHat運輸を選択することによる顧客へのメリットは説明されているが、選択する義務についての記述はない。[1]のUnless otherwise specified（特別の指定がない限り）の部分も、顧客が宅配業者を指定できることを示唆している。／ (D) Nileways Online requires that customers pay for insurance. [×]：[4]にRedHat運輸以外を指定すると「Nilewaysの荷物保険は適用されない」とはあるが、「保険に加入することを要求している」という記述はないので×。

4.

[1] Harridan's Cinema is now offering weekly and monthly pass cards, which should benefit frequent visitors.
[2] Cards of various colors, which entitle holders to different levels of service, are available.
[3] The standard blue card allows one person to watch up to four movies a week for only $25, whereas the green card allows the holder to see the same number of movies with a friend for only $5 more.
[4] The orange and purple cards cost $40 and $50 respectively and are valid for a whole month, meaning that holders can watch up to 16 movies for this low price.
[5] Cards can only be purchased during the month of August while stocks last.

- benefit 〜に利益をもたらす ● frequent visitor 常連客 ● entitle A to B B を受け取る権利を A に与える
- holder 所有者 ● whereas 〜に対して、〜の一方で ● respectively それぞれ ● valid for 〜 〜の間有効である ● while stocks last 在庫がある限り

解説 (A) Purchasers should choose cards of their favorite color. [×]：[2]「色ごとに異なるサービスを提供するカード」とあり、「好きな色のカード」を選ぶわけではないので×。／ (B) A companion of a green card holder is not charged for admission. [○]：[3]「ブルーカードでは1人週に4本まで映画を見る」ことができ、グリーンカードはそれに「追加5ドルだけで同じ数の映画をご友人1人と一緒に見ることができる」とあるので、「グリーンカードの同伴者は入場料を請求されない」は○。／ (C) Purple cards cost $40. [×]：[4]「オレンジとパープルのカードはそれぞれ40ドルと50ドル」とある。つまりパープルカードは50ドルなので×。／ (D) Harridan's Cinema shows 16 movies a month. [×]：[4]「この低価格で16本まで映画を見ることができる」とあるが、これはカードの特典についての記述で、映画館が月に何本上映しているかについての情報はないので×。拡大解釈を誘う問題だ。／ (E) There are a limited number of cards available for purchase. [○]：[5]「在庫がある限り」と述べられているので○。

5.

[1] *The Stanton Times* is launching its new online service to provide residents of Stanton access to local news in a more convenient way.
[2] The publisher stated that although she expects to lose some sales revenue when people stop buying the printed version, the environmental benefits make it worthwhile.
[3] The profits, on the other hand, are expected to receive a boost from the reduced costs, online advertisements and paid content limited to registered online members.
[4] Other benefits mentioned in the press release include more updates to content and a customizable front page.

- revenue 収入 ● environmental benefits 環境面での利点 ● worthwhile その価値はある ● boost 増加
- customizable カスタマイズ可能な

解説 (A) *The Stanton Times* is a newly established news source. [×]：[1]「新しいオンラインサービスを始めます」とあるが、*The Stanton Times* 紙自体が新しいとは書いていないので×。「新しいかどうか」または「新しいのは何か」は設問に絡むことが多いので、注目すべき情報。／ (B) Online subscriptions are priced equally to printed papers. [×]：新聞の印刷版とオンライン版の購読価格の比較についてはどこにも述べられていないので×。／ (C) The decision to start the online service has financial advantages. [○]：[3]にオンライン版を導入することによって「利益が上がると期待されています」とあることから、「財政的な利点」はあると言えるので○。／ (D) Some of the newspaper's online content will only be available for purchase. [○]：[3]に「登録オンライン会員限定の有料コンテンツ」があると述べられているので、「オンラインコンテンツのいくつかは購入でのみ入手可能」は○。／ (E) The headlines may differ depending on the selected newspaper format. [○]：[4]「カスタマイズ可能なトップページ」とあり、オンライン版は印刷版とは異なる見出しを持つ可能性があると判断できるので○。

6.

[1] Formosa Coffeehouse is opening its 100th café in Britain this week in the Craigie Mall in downtown Glasgow.

[2] For the past five years, the chain has been enjoying great popularity, among young people in particular.

[3] Owner Ralph Chang spoke from his headquarters in Brooklyn, New York about the latest café, saying that he was so grateful to the people of Britain for making Formosa Coffeehouse such a success.

[4] Many people believe the secret of the company's success lies in the cheerful decor and swift service.

- popularity 人気　● in particular 特に　● headquarters 本社　● latest 一番新しい　● lie in ~ ~にある
- decor 装飾　● swift 迅速な

解説 (A) A significant portion of Formosa Coffeehouse clientele is youthful. [○]：[2]「特に若者の間で大変人気があります」とあり、「客層のかなりの部分は若者である」と推測できるので○。／ (B) Formosa Coffeehouse originated in New York. [×]：[3]「ニューヨークのブルックリンにある本社」とはあるが、これをもってニューヨークで創業したとは言えないので×。拡大解釈を誘うトラップだ。なお、企業などの拠点、支店の有無、家族経営かどうかは設問で問われやすい情報項目だ。／ (C) The owner expressed appreciation to city officials in Britain. [×]：[3]「オーナーは成功させてくれたイギリスの人々にとても感謝している」とあるが、「イギリスの市職員」に感謝しているとは言えないので×。／ (D) Formosa Coffeehouse's popularity is partly attributed to its interior design. [○]：[4]で「店の成功の秘訣」の1つとして「明るい内装」が挙げられているので、「人気の一因は内装デザイン」は○。

CHAPTER 1 精読力 PERUSING

実践問題

仕上げに、本番形式の難問にチャレンジ。正解と不正解の境界線を精読力で見極めて解こう。

Part 5

空所に入る語句として、最も適切なものを1つ選ぼう。(解答・解説はpp. 42〜44)

⏱ 3分

1. Despite the growing cost of shipping raw materials around the world, the price of manufactured goods is steadily -------.
   (A) decreasing
   (B) minimizing
   (C) rising
   (D) dividing
   Ⓐ Ⓑ Ⓒ Ⓓ

2. If production is likely to get ------- schedule, it is the job of managers to inform retailers so that they can give customers advance notice on late delivery.
   (A) ahead of
   (B) on with
   (C) behind
   (D) through
   Ⓐ Ⓑ Ⓒ Ⓓ

3. The success of the product launch is ------- dependent on the timing of the release, as well as the amount of advertising beforehand.
   (A) separately
   (B) less
   (C) solely
   (D) largely

   Ⓐ Ⓑ Ⓒ Ⓓ

4. The highly successful social networking service provider Friendspage ------- has a popular line of game consoles selling well around the world.
   (A) unlikely
   (B) also
   (C) similarly
   (D) instead

   Ⓐ Ⓑ Ⓒ Ⓓ

5. ------- applying himself in every project the marketing division has undertaken, Mr. Miller has quickly become an indispensable member of the team.
   (A) Energy
   (B) Energetic
   (C) Energetically
   (D) Energized

   Ⓐ Ⓑ Ⓒ Ⓓ

6. The quality of the reviews is ------- makes *City Dining* magazine a worthwhile read rather than simply a collection of advertisements.
   (A) something
   (B) whichever
   (C) what
   (D) either

   Ⓐ Ⓑ Ⓒ Ⓓ

7. Brochures for the C56 Laundry Wizard highlight the ------- of the machine such as its ability to both wash and dry.
   (A) functioning
   (B) functional
   (C) function
   (D) functions   Ⓐ Ⓑ Ⓒ Ⓓ

8. As all word processing software features error detection -------, there is no excuse for submitting documents with spelling mistakes.
   (A) capably
   (B) capable
   (C) capabilities
   (D) capableness   Ⓐ Ⓑ Ⓒ Ⓓ

9. The complexity of the photocopier's manual has led directly to the increased number of requests for assistance ------- received by the service department.
   (A) are
   (B) being
   (C) were
   (D) is   Ⓐ Ⓑ Ⓒ Ⓓ

Part 6

空所に入る語句として、最も適切なものを1つずつ選ぼう。(解答・解説はpp. 46~49)

Questions 10-12 refer to the following advertisement. 1分30秒

Introducing the Edson Hawk

Preorder soon or miss out! The Edson Hawk is our 30th-anniversary, limited release off-roader, which has the features and engineering people that have come to expect of an Edson. Revealed for the first time last month at the Yokohama Recreational Vehicle Motor Show, it was ------- by critics for its beautiful styling and innovative design.

    10. (A) judged
        (B) disregarded
        (C) praised
        (D) produced Ⓐ Ⓑ Ⓒ Ⓓ

Go! Magazine test driver, Mark Willis, wrote that the Hawk was one of the most ------- cars he had ever driven. "It easily travels over the roughest

    11. (A) dependable
        (B) actionable
        (C) economical
        (D) liable Ⓐ Ⓑ Ⓒ Ⓓ

terrain with its huge four-liter engine. What it lacks in fuel efficiency, it more than makes up for in looks and power."

Edson is ------- producing 3,000 of this very special model. Please visit the

    12. (A) still
        (B) only
        (C) seldom
        (D) clearly Ⓐ Ⓑ Ⓒ Ⓓ

members-only section of the Web site to discover more about the Hawk because this exciting new vehicle will not be on display in any of our showrooms.

Questions 13-15 refer to the following article.

New York - A brand of coffee costing only $3 a packet ------- the International

13. (A) may win
(B) has won
(C) is winning
(D) could have won

Ⓐ Ⓑ Ⓒ Ⓓ

Coffee Federation (ICF) Coffee of the Year Competition. The coffee was considered best by a panel of five judges, all of whom have earned the prestigious ICF five-star rating as baristas. It was a shock to everyone, not least of all the company that produced the coffee.

Sterling Coffee of Hawaii does not actually grow coffee beans. It just buys excess beans from the growers in the region, blends them together, and sells the output at remarkably ------- prices.

14. (A) reasonable
(B) vague
(C) inflated
(D) compromised Ⓐ Ⓑ Ⓒ Ⓓ

Tom Sterling, the owner of Sterling Coffee, was reportedly thrilled with the news, although he wishes he had ------- the production capacity

15. (A) evened
(B) outsourced
(C) evaluated
(D) raised   Ⓐ Ⓑ Ⓒ Ⓓ

as the demand is likely to rise dramatically as the news spreads.

Part 7

文書に関する設問の解答として、最も適切なものを1つずつ選ぼう。

(解答・解説はpp. 50〜54)

Questions 16-19 refer to the following e-mail.

⏰ **4分**

E-Mail Message

To: Rui Matos <rmatos@gth.co.uk>
From: Zoe Chamran <zchamran@gth.co.uk>
Date: April 17
Subject: Bookings for GTH charity

Hello Rui,

Jill Murray from the Cleminson Hotel in Leeds called with regard to the GTH charity benefit to be held there in May. Since Mr. Smythe is in Dublin on business, I thought you might be the best person to handle the following issue. She would like to verify exactly how many guests we will be inviting. She said that our current booking is precisely the minimum number of guests for the ₤70 per head rate. If there is even one cancellation, the rate will rise to ₤75 per head.

I have calculated the cost based on the room-rate table and it turns out that if we have 47 or more guests, we should not cancel any rooms, as the total invoiced amount will still be lower that way. It would be cheaper to cancel rooms if we have 46 or fewer guests. At present, we have 46 confirmed guests and we are expecting four more to reply. This number includes Ms. Wendy Wu and Mr. Victor Tyler, who are regular patrons at our events. Judging from previous years, I think it is safe enough to go with the current booking of 50.

Do you agree with my assessment? Ms. Murray said that she would wait until the end of the day to hear from us about any changes. After that, cancellation fees will be incurred in accordance with their reservation policies. Mr. Smythe is taking a flight back via Liverpool immediately after his meeting. Although it's a fiscal matter, perhaps we should give a quick reply now, and inform him when he gets back to Hull.

Regards,
Zoe Chamran

16. What is the e-mail mainly about?
 (A) Choosing accommodation options
 (B) Finding an event venue
 (C) Arranging guest passes
 (D) Confirming a reservation　　Ⓐ Ⓑ Ⓒ Ⓓ

17. Who most likely is responsible for financial decisions?
 (A) Mr. Matos
 (B) Ms. Chamran
 (C) Mr. Smythe
 (D) Mr. Tyler　　Ⓐ Ⓑ Ⓒ Ⓓ

18. What does Ms. Chamran suggest?
 (A) Relying on a prediction
 (B) Canceling some hotel rooms
 (C) Paying some penalty fees
 (D) Expediting replies from guests　　Ⓐ Ⓑ Ⓒ Ⓓ

19. What did Ms. Murray say she would do on April 17?
 (A) Fix a price
 (B) Return a call
 (C) Stand by for a flight
 (D) Cancel a reservation　　Ⓐ Ⓑ Ⓒ Ⓓ

Questions 20-24 refer to the following announcement and e-mail.

(DC) The Duchamp College of Art Annual Portrait Contest

The Duchamp College of Art holds its annual portrait contest in December each year. The competition is open to students of Duchamp College of Art whether they be currently enrolled or graduates. It should be made clear, however, that graduates who have competed before will not be considered for first prize if they have competed before.

School tradition dictates that when a head of the college retires, his or her image is to be the subject of all entries. This started 90 years ago when, at the age of 80, the school's founder, Edward Duchamp, retired to his home country of France. He had dedicated most of his life to the school, and the students held an impromptu competition to show their appreciation.

This year, Dr. Bonnard is taking retirement and so we intend to observe the tradition. Winning portraits of retired deans are displayed permanently in the waiting room in front of the dean's office. This is a great honor and past winners include Randolph Goodwin and Rebecca Moore, both of whom went on to have hugely successful careers in art and publishing. All other entries will be exhibited at the entrance hall for 90 days after the competition.

E-Mail Message

To: Danielle Waters <dwaters@dcoa.com>
From: Max Williams <mwilliams@williamsart.com>
Date: 19 November
Subject: Annual Portrait Contest

Dear Ms. Waters,

Thank you for sending me the updated information on the annual portrait contest.

I would like to ask that the organizers reconsider one of the conditions of entry. I have entered the contest several times in the past, and to learn that I am now ineligible for first prize is very disappointing. I can understand that having the same person win year after year would be bad for the competition, but this limitation seems too severe. In the past, I have been asked to be a judge of the competition but turned down the offer because I thought it would affect my eligibility.

Though I am indebted to Dr. Bonnard for his wonderful encouragement, I cannot say at this time whether I will be submitting an artwork. If you are seeking people to fill the role I previously rejected, please let me know, because I feel that that may be the best way for me to contribute.

Best regards,
Max Williams

20. What is indicated about the Duchamp College of Art?
(A) It is located in France.
(B) It employs its graduates.
(C) It is over 100 years old.
(D) It has received many awards.

21. Who most likely is Dr. Bonnard?
(A) A school administrator
(B) A founder of a college
(C) A judge of a competition
(D) A successful artist

22. Where will the winning entry be exhibited?
(A) In a waiting room
(B) In the entrance hall
(C) In the founder's home
(D) In a school publication

23. What is suggested about Mr. Williams?
(A) He has never met Dr. Bonnard.
(B) He is a graduate of the Duchamp College of Art.
(C) He has won the portrait competition before.
(D) He can no longer attend the annual contest.

24. What does Mr. Williams ask Ms. Waters to do?
(A) Hold an additional competition
(B) Open a contest to the public
(C) Reconsider the portrait subject
(D) Allow him to evaluate submissions

実践問題の解答・解説

※問題文の訳文は紙面では省略（訳文の入手方法はp. 7をご覧ください）。

Part 5

1. Despite the growing cost of shipping raw materials around the world, the price of manufactured goods is steadily -------.

   * (A) decreasing　動 下がっている
   (B) minimizing　動 〜を最小化している
   (C) rising　動 高くなっている
   (D) dividing　動 分かれている

   ● manufactured goods 製品　● steadily 着々と

   解説 「原料の輸送コスト」が高まっていることが逆接のDespiteで導かれているので、カンマの後のthe price of manufactured goods（製品の価格）は反対に下がっているとすべき。よって、正解は(A) decreasing。

2. If production is likely to get ------- schedule, it is the job of managers to inform retailers so that they can give customers advance notice on late delivery.

   (A) ahead of　〜の先に
   (B) on with　〜と一緒に
   * (C) behind　前 〜に遅れて
   (D) through　前 〜を通して

   ● production 生産　● retailer 小売店　● advance notice 事前の通知

   解説 形だけを見れば、scheduleの前の空所には(A) ahead ofと(C) behindを入れることができる（それぞれ「計画より前倒しで」、「計画より遅れて」の意味になる）。どちらが文意に適切かを判断するには、カンマ以降を精読しなければならない。give customers advance notice on late delivery（配送の遅れを顧客に事前に通知する）とあることから、前半のif節は「計画より遅れた場合」とするべきなので、(C) behindが正解だ。

3. The success of the product launch is ------- dependent on the timing of the release, as well as the amount of advertising beforehand.

   (A) separately　副 別々に
   (B) less　副 より少なく
   (C) solely　副 単独で
   * (D) largely　副 大いに

   ● as well as 〜 〜と同様に　● the amount of 〜 〜の量　● beforehand 事前に

   解説 (B) lessはthanを伴う比較対象がないので排除できるが、その他の選択肢は問題文全体を精読して絞り込む必要がある。(A) separatelyは「別々に」が指す対象がないので不適。(C) solelyはas well as（と同様に）以下があるので「単独で」とは言えず不正解。正解は「大いに」の意味のlargely。

4. The highly successful social networking service provider Friendspage ------- has a popular line of game consoles selling well around the world.

(A) unlikely　形 ありそうもない
*(B) also　副 〜もまた
(C) similarly　副 同等に、類似して
(D) instead　副 その代わりに

● popular line 人気商品、ラインアップ　● game console ゲーム機

解説 主語と動詞の間にある空所には副詞が入る。(A) unlikelyは形容詞なので不可。ソーシャルネットワーキングサービスで「非常に成功している」Friendspageが、他の分野でも「人気商品ラインアップ」を持っているというつながりから、「追加」の意味を持つ(B) also（もまた）が正解。(C) similarlyは「同様に」、(D) insteadは「代わりに」の意味だが、いずれも文意に不適切。

---

5. ------- applying himself in every project the marketing division has undertaken, Mr. Miller has quickly become an indispensable member of the team.

(A) Energy　名 精力
(B) Energetic　形 精力的な
*(C) Energetically　副 精力的に
(D) Energized　動 活性化された

● undertake 〜を請け負う　● indispensable 不可欠な

解説 文頭が空所だと(A) Energyのような名詞が主語として入る可能性を検討しなければならないが、applying以下がそれを意味的に修飾できないことと、カンマの後の節とつながらなくなることから不適。applyingが現在分詞で、分詞構文であると捉えると、himselfは主語Mr. Millerを指すことになり、文意が通る。よって、空所にはapplyingを修飾する副詞の(C) Energeticallyが入る。

---

6. The quality of the reviews is ------- makes *City Dining* magazine a worthwhile read rather than simply a collection of advertisements.

(A) something　代 何か
(B) whichever　関代 〜するどちらでも
*(C) what　関代 〜するもの
(D) either　代 どちらか一方

● worthwhile（時間、労力、費用分の）価値がある　● read 読み物

解説 空所にはThe quality 〜 isの節の補語になり、かつmakesの主語になることができる語が入る。関係代名詞で「〜するもの」という意味の(C) whatが正解。このwhat節は「*City Dining*誌を、単なる広告の寄せ集めではなく、価値がある読み物にするもの」という意味になる。(B) whicheverも関係代名詞だが、「〜するどちらでも」という意味なので不適。(A) somethingは代名詞なのでsomething thatのように関係代名詞が後ろに必要。(D) either（どちらか一方）は、それが指せる2つの選択肢がないので不可。

7. Brochures for the C56 Laundry Wizard highlight the ------- of the machine such as its ability to both wash and dry.

(A) functioning 　動 機能すること
(B) functional 　形 機能的な
(C) function 　名 機能
＊(D) functions 　名 機能（複数）

● highlight 〜を強調する

解説 theとofの間にある空所には名詞が入るが、名詞として機能する選択肢は動名詞の(A) functioningも含めると3つある。着目すべきはsuch as（例えば〜）で、これは、its ability to both wash and dryは単なる一例で、C56という洗濯機が他にいくつもの「機能」を持っていることを示唆している。よって、複数形の(D) functionsが正解。

8. As all word processing software features error detection -------, there is no excuse for submitting documents with spelling mistakes.

(A) capably 　副 有能に
(B) capable 　形 有能な
＊(C) capabilities 　名 機能、性能
(D) capableness 　名 有能さ

● feature 〜を備える　● detection 検出

解説 副詞の(A) capablyを空所に入れると動詞featuresを修飾し、「有能に備える」という不自然な意味になるので(A)は不適切。正解は「エラー検出機能」という意味の複合名詞を作る(C) capabilities。(D) capablenessは「機能」のような具体的な意味はなく、「有能さ」という抽象的な意味なので、文意に合わない。

9. The complexity of the photocopier's manual has led directly to the increased number of requests for assistance ------- received by the service department.

(A) are
＊(B) being
(C) were
(D) is

● complexity 複雑さ　● lead to 〜につながる

解説 主語The complexityに対応する動詞はhas ledなので、空所に入るbe動詞と後ろの過去分詞receivedは本動詞を作ることができない。よって、空所前のrequests for assistance（支援要請）を修飾する句を作る現在分詞の(B) beingが正解。このbeingが省略され、receivedの動詞の形を問う問題も定番だ。進行中の意味を強調するbeing＋過去分詞のパターンもあることを押さえておこう。

Ted流TOEICの泳ぎ方　………長続きする英語自己学習法………

　読者の皆さんにとってのTOEIC対策（目標はスコアアップ）は、私にとっての水泳（目標はウェイトロス）に似ていると思います。どちらも、目標を達成するためには継続が肝心です。でも、私が利用しているプールでは、せっかく通い始めたのに数カ月のうちにぱったりと来なくなる人がたくさんいます。そして、それらの人にはいくつかの共通点があることに気づきました。彼らの失敗から学べる、学習が続かない原因と続けるコツを、このミニコラムでお伝えしていきます。

続かない原因その1　No warm-up

　継続できない人は、準備運動やストレッチなしに、いきなり全力で泳ぎ始める傾向があります。体が慣れていない状態で無理をすると、必要以上にしんどく感じてしまいます。TOEIC対策なら、長文よりも短文から取り組んだり、まずは音読で頭を英語モードに切り替えたりして、メニューの組み立てを工夫しましょう。

Part 6

問題 10-12 は次の広告に関するものです。

Introducing the Edson Hawk

Preorder soon or miss out! The Edson Hawk is our 30th-anniversary, limited release off-roader, which has the features and engineering that people have come to expect of an Edson. Revealed for the first time last month at the Yokohama Recreational Vehicle Motor Show, it was ------- by critics for its beautiful styling and innovative design.

10. (A) judged
(B) disregarded
(C) praised
(D) produced

Go! Magazine test driver, Mark Willis, wrote that the Hawk was one of the most ------- cars he had ever driven. "It easily travels over the roughest

11. (A) dependable
(B) actionable
(C) economical
(D) liable

terrain with its huge four-liter engine. What it lacks in fuel efficiency, it more than makes up for in looks and power."

Edson is ------- producing 3,000 of this very special model. Please visit the

12. (A) still
(B) only
(C) seldom
(D) clearly

members-only section of the Web site to discover more about the Hawk because this exciting new vehicle will not be on display in any of our showrooms.

● limited release 限定発売　● off-roader オフロード車　● terrain 地形

10. (A) judged 動 批判された、判断された
(B) disregarded 動 無視された
＊(C) praised 動 称賛された
(D) produced 動 生み出された

解説 Edson社の新しい限定販売車に対する評論家(critics)たちの評の理由に注目する。its beautiful styling and innovative design(美しい形と革新的なデザイン)のようにポジティブなポイントが挙げられていることから、(C) praisedが適切。(A) judgedや(B) disregardedはネガティブな評価なので、for以下の理由と合わず、不適切。

11. ＊(A) dependable 形 信頼できる
(B) actionable 形 実行可能な
(C) economical 形 省エネの、経済的な
(D) liable 形 責任がある

解説 テストドライバーがEdson Hawkについて、どのような車だと評しているかを判断する。直後で引用されている彼の発言がヒントだ。「the roughest terrain(荒れた地面)も物ともせずに走る」とあるので、(A) dependableが適切。「燃費の良さはないが、それを補ってあまりあるルックスとパワー」とも述べているので、(C) economicalは不正解。残りの2つの選択肢は車の描写にふさわしくない。

12. (A) still 副 まだ
＊(B) only 副 だけ
(C) seldom 副 めったに～ない
(D) clearly 副 明確に

解説 is producing(製造しようとしている)を修飾する副詞を選ぶ。第1段落で、Preorder soon or miss out!(チャンスを逃したくなければ予約注文はお早めに)と促していることや、limited release off-roader(限定発売のオフロード車)と述べられていることから、この特別なモデルは3000台「だけ」の少数生産であると推測できるので、(B) onlyが正解となる。(C) seldomのような頻度を表す副詞は、進行形と共には用いられないので不可。

問題 13-15 は次の記事に関するものです。

New York - A brand of coffee costing only $3 a packet ------- the International

13. (A) may win
(B) has won
(C) is winning
(D) could have won

Coffee Federation (ICF) Coffee of the Year Competition. The coffee was considered best by a panel of five judges, all of whom have earned the prestigious ICF five-star rating as baristas. It was a shock to everyone, not least of all the company that produced the coffee.

Sterling Coffee of Hawaii does not actually grow coffee beans. It just buys excess beans from the growers in the region, blends them together, and sells the output at remarkably ------- prices.

14. (A) reasonable
(B) vague
(C) inflated
(D) compromised

Tom Sterling, the owner of Sterling Coffee, was reportedly thrilled with the news, although he wishes he had ------- the production capacity

15. (A) evened
(B) outsourced
(C) evaluated
(D) raised

as the demand is likely to rise dramatically as the news spreads.

- packet 袋、小さな包み ● a panel of ～ ～の一団 ● prestigious 一流の ● excess 余分な
- reportedly 報道によれば ● thrilled 興奮した ● production capacity 生産能力

13. (A) may win
　＊(B) has won
　(C) is winning
　(D) could have won

解説 コーヒー品評会に関する記事。**13**は時制問題で、この品評会がすでに行われたのか、これからなのかが、正しい時制を判断するポイントになる。空所は冒頭の文にあるので続きを読む。直後の文がThe coffee was considered ...と過去時制なので、品評会は終わっている。結果が人々を「驚かせた」とあることからも、安価なコーヒーが「優勝した」ことを表す完了形の(B) has wonが正解。(D) could have wonは「優勝できたかもしれない」という仮定法過去完了だが、直後の文が述べる「最高と評価された」という事実と合わない。

14. ＊(A) reasonable　形 手頃な
　(B) vague　形 あいまいな
　(C) inflated　形 やたらと高い
　(D) compromised　動 低下した、悪化した

解説 コーヒーの値段については、記事の冒頭でonly $3 a packet（1袋たったの3ドル）と書かれている。また、第2段落の空所の手前に書かれている、その値付けができる理由（地元の生産業者から余剰の豆を購入しブレンドする）からも、(A) reasonable（手頃な）しかない。(C) inflatedは反対に「暴騰した」の意。(D) compromisedは過去分詞、つまり受け身になっているので、ここでは他動詞のcompromise（〜を損なう、傷つける）の活用形だ。よって、意味的にprices（価格）を修飾できない。

15. (A) evened　動 〜を平坦にした
　(B) outsourced　動 〜を外部に委託した
　(C) evaluated　動 〜を評価した
　＊(D) raised　動 〜を上げた

解説 品評会後の急激な需要の増加に対する、オーナーの気持ちを表すのに適した語を選ぶ。production capacity（生産能力）を「上げておけばよかった」とすると文意が通るので、正解は(D) raised。(B) outsourced（〜を外部に委託した）は、第2段落で「Sterling Coffee社はもともとコーヒー豆を自社で生産していない」と述べられているので不適。

Part 7

問題 16-19 は次のメールに関するものです。

E-Mail Message

To: Rui Matos <rmatos@gth.co.uk>
From: Zoe Chamran <zchamran@gth.co.uk>
Date: April 17
Subject: Bookings for GTH charity

Hello Rui,

Jill Murray from the Cleminson Hotel in Leeds called with regard to the GTH charity benefit to be held there in May. ¹Since Mr. Smythe is in Dublin on business, I thought you might be the best person to handle the following issue. She would like to verify exactly how many guests we will be inviting. She said that ²our current booking is precisely the minimum number of guests for the £70 per head rate. If there is even one cancellation, the rate will rise to £75 per head.

I have calculated the cost based on the room-rate table and it turns out that if we have 47 or more guests, we should not cancel any rooms, as the total invoiced amount will still be lower that way. It would be cheaper to cancel rooms if we have 46 or fewer guests. At present, we have 46 confirmed guests and we are expecting four more to reply. This number includes Ms. Wendy Wu and Mr. Victor Tyler, who are regular patrons at our events. ³Judging from previous years, I think it is safe enough to go with the current booking of 50.

Do you agree with my assessment? ⁴Ms. Murray said that she would wait until the end of the day to hear from us about any changes. After that, cancellation fees will be incurred in accordance with their reservation policies. Mr. Smythe is taking a flight back via Liverpool immediately after his meeting. ⁵Although it's a fiscal matter, perhaps we should give a quick reply now, and inform him when he gets back to Hull.

Regards,
Zoe Chamran

- with regard to ~ ～に関して
- verify ～を確認する
- precisely まさに
- per head 1人当たり
- patron 常連客
- assessment 判断、査定
- be incurred 発生する
- in accordance with ~ ～に従って

16. What is the e-mail mainly about?
(A) Choosing accommodation options
(B) Finding an event venue
(C) Arranging guest passes
∗ (D) Confirming a reservation

解説 第1段落に「チャリティー会場となるホテルの担当者から、招待者数の確認の電話があった」と書かれていることから、(B)「イベント会場を見つける」と(C)「ゲストパスを手配する」は正解候補から外れる。メール送信者は第2段落3で宿泊予約人数に関する提案をしており、第3段落冒頭でそれに対する同意を受け手に求めている。従って、(D)「予約を確認する」が正解。宿泊料金のシステムについては述べているが、ホテルや部屋のタイプなどのオプションを選ぶ話ではないので(A)は不適切。

---

17. Who most likely is responsible for financial decisions?
(A) Mr. Matos
(B) Ms. Chamran
∗ (C) Mr. Smythe
(D) Mr. Tyler

解説 (C)のSmythe氏は第1段落1に「出張中」とある。不在のSmythe氏にわざわざ言及している点に引っ掛かりを感じたら、この人物の情報をさらに探そう。第3段落5に「財務の問題ですが、今すぐに返事をして、Smythe氏には彼がHullに戻ってきてから知らせるべきだと思います」とある。2つの情報から、財務に関する決定の責任を負うのは本来はSmythe氏だと推測できるので、(C)が正解。(A) Matos氏はメールの受け手で、送信者の(B) Chamran氏が今回の緊急対応をすべきだと判断した人物。設問文は、財務に関するさまざまな決定について「常時」責任があるのは誰かと問うているので(is responsibleと現在形で、financial decisionsと複数形であることからわかる)、それをMatos氏とするのは誤り。

---

18. What does Ms. Chamran suggest?
∗ (A) Relying on a prediction
(B) Canceling some hotel rooms
(C) Paying some penalty fees
(D) Expediting replies from guests ● expedite 迅速に処理する

解説 第1段落2から、現在の予約人数は宿泊料金が1人当たり70ポンドになる最少人数であること、第2段落3のthe current booking of 50から、それが50人であることがわかる。Chamran氏は同じ第2段落で、参加者が47人以上だと、50人での予約を維持した方が支払額が低くなるが、46人以下だとキャンセルした方が安いと試算しており、さらに、「現在、出席確認が取れているのは46人だが、前年までの実績から考えても、予約は現状の50人のままにしておいても差し支えないだろう」と書いている。すなわち、彼女は「予測を当てにすること」を提案していると言えるので、(A)が正解。Chapter 3で触れる「要約力」も問われる問題だ。

19. What did Ms. Murray say she would do on April 17?
(A) Fix a price
(B) Return a call
(C) Stand by for a flight
(D) Cancel a reservation

解説 ▶ April 17はメールの送信日。メールには、ホテルの担当者Murray氏が参加人数の確認の電話をしてきて（第1段落冒頭）、「本日中」は予約人数の変更を受け付けるが、その後の変更にはキャンセル料がかかると言った、と書かれている（第3段落4）。宿泊料金は予約人数で変動するので、予約人数が決まれば料金も決まる。従って、Murray氏がこの日しようとしているのは(A)「料金を決める」こと。

問題 20-24 は次の案内とメールに関するものです。

DC The Duchamp College of Art Annual Portrait Contest

The Duchamp College of Art holds its annual portrait contest in December each year. The competition is open to students of Duchamp College of Art whether they be currently enrolled or graduates. ¹It should be made clear, however, that graduates who have competed before will not be considered for first prize if they have competed before.

²School tradition dictates that when a head of the college retires, his or her image is to be the subject of all entries. ³This started 90 years ago when, at the age of 80, the school's founder, Edward Duchamp, retired to his home country of France. He had dedicated most of his life to the school, and the students held an impromptu competition to show their appreciation.

⁴This year, Dr. Bonnard is taking retirement and so we intend to observe the tradition. ⁵Winning portraits of retired deans are displayed permanently in the waiting room in front of the dean's office. This is a great honor and past winners include Randolph Goodwin and Rebecca Moore, both of whom went on to have hugely successful careers in art and publishing. All other entries will be exhibited at the entrance hall for 90 days after the competition.

E-Mail Message

To: Danielle Waters <dwaters@dcoa.com>
From: Max Williams <mwilliams@williamsart.com>
Date: 19 November
Subject: Annual Portrait Contest

Dear Ms. Waters,

Thank you for sending me the updated information on the annual portrait contest.

I would like to ask that the organizers reconsider one of the conditions of entry. ⁶I have entered the contest several times in the past, and to learn that I am now ineligible for first prize is very disappointing. I can understand that having the same person win year after year would be bad for the competition, but this limitation seems too severe. ⁷In the past, I have been asked to be a judge of the competition but turned down the offer because I thought it would affect my eligibility.

Though I am indebted to Dr. Bonnard for his wonderful encouragement, I cannot say at this time whether I will be submitting an artwork. ⁸If you are seeking people to fill the role I previously rejected, please let me know, because I feel that that may be the best way for me to contribute.

Best regards,
Max Williams

[案内] ● be enrolled 在籍する ● dictate 〜を指示する ● dedicate 〜をささげる ● impromptu 即興の
● observe the tradition 伝統を守る ● dean 学長 ● permanently 恒久的に
[メール] ● condition 条件 ● ineligible 資格がない ● turn down 〜を辞退する ● eligibility 適格性
● be indebted to 〜 〜に恩義がある ● reject 〜を断る ● contribute 貢献する

20. What is indicated about the Duchamp College of Art?
 (A) It is located in France.
 (B) It employs its graduates.
 ＊(C) It is over 100 years old.
 (D) It has received many awards.

解説 Duchamp美術学校について述べられていることを選ぶ問題。案内の3で「このコンテストは90年前、創立者が80歳で引退した際に始まった」、さらに「創立者は人生の大半を学校にささげた」と述べている。90年という年月に、80歳の人の人生の大半に相当する年月を加えれば100年を超えるのは妥当な推測だ。従って、(C)「100年を超える歴史がある」が正解。(A)のフランスは学校創立者の出身地で、学校の所在地ではない。

21. Who most likely is Dr. Bonnard?
 ＊(A) A school administrator
 (B) A founder of a college
 (C) A judge of a competition
 (D) A successful artist

解説 正解の根拠になる情報はちらばっている。案内の第3段落4に「Bonnard氏が引退するので、その伝統を守ろうと考えている」とある。伝統とは、第2段落2の「学長が引退するときは、学長の肖像がコンテストのテーマになる」だ。これらを統合すると、Bonnard氏は現在の学長だとわかる。「学長」は案内の中でもhead、deanと2種類の表現が用いられ、正解の選択肢の(A)でもadministrator（管理者、理事）と言い換えられている。

22. Where will the winning entry be exhibited?　● winning entry 優勝作品
　＊(A) In a waiting room
　(B) In the entrance hall
　(C) In the founder's home
　(D) In a school publication

解説 ▶ 受賞作が飾られる場所はどこかという設問。第3段落5に、「引退した学長たちの肖像画の優勝作品は待合室にずっと飾られる」とある。今回の優勝作品も同じ場所に展示されると推測できるので、(A)が正解だ。

---

23. What is suggested about Mr. Williams?
　(A) He has never met Dr. Bonnard.
　＊(B) He is a graduate of the Duchamp College of Art.
　(C) He has won the portrait competition before.
　(D) He can no longer attend the annual contest.

解説 ▶ 両文書を参照させる問題。案内の1に「以前にコンテストに参加したことがある卒業生は1等賞の対象にならない」とある。メールの6で、Williams氏は「1等賞を取る権利がないことは残念だ」と述べている。よって、Williams氏は「Duchamp美術学校の卒業生」と推測でき、(B)が正解。(D)「毎年恒例のコンテストには、もう出席できない」は拡大解釈にあたる。

---

24. What does Mr. Williams ask Ms. Waters to do?
　(A) Hold an additional competition
　(B) Open a contest to the public
　(C) Reconsider the portrait subject
　＊(D) Allow him to evaluate submissions

解説 ▶ メールの中の依頼表現に注目する。第3段落8に、「私が前に断った役割を担う人材を探しているなら知らせて」と書かれている。前に断った役割とは、第2段落7にある「コンテストの審査員」のことだ。つまり、Williams氏は審査に参加させてほしいと頼んでいる。be a judgeをevaluate submissions（提出物の評価をする）と言い換えた(D)が正解。(C)「肖像画の対象となる人物を再検討する」は、第2段落1行目の「エントリー条件の1つを再検討してほしい」という依頼で使われているreconsiderという語を用いた不正解選択肢だ。

Ted's Talks ❶
BEYOND対談 —— 共著者 ロス・タロック

問題作成者だからこそわかる、TOEICが仕掛ける罠とは？

Ted ： TOEICの英語は、英語ネイティブの目にはどのように映りますか。

Ross ： とても丁寧に書かれていて、おかしな表現や意味が不明瞭な文は見受けられません。また、登場人物は非常にロジカルに行動します。現実の世界は残念ながら、そんなにパーフェクトではないですよね。また、TOEICには使用できる語彙に制限があります。模擬問題の作成者としては、TOEICの世界に存在しない語句を使わないように注意しなければなりません。

Ted ： 本書を作るにあたっては、その点について何度も話し合い、ギリギリのラインを探りましたね。TOEICで使われる語句や言い換え表現には、何らかの法則性は見いだせますか。

Ross ： はい。まず、イギリス英語の表現はめったに使われません。解釈が分かれる可能性のある表現も避けられています。現実の世界では文脈に従って解釈できれば問題ありませんが、TOEICでは文脈から独立しても1つしか意味を持たない表現が使われています。例えば、ongoingという形容詞には「進行中の」と「継続している」という2つの意味があります。よって、The contract is ongoing. という文は「契約は発効している、有効期間中である」と「契約は継続的だ、(何もない限り)ずっと続く」の両方の解釈が可能となり、TOEICでは避けるべき表現ということになります。

Ted ： 問題作成も奥が深いですよね。ロスさんは多くのTOEICの問題を見てきたと思いますが、TOEICというテストは何を測定していると思いますか。

Ross ： 実は、TOEICで700点くらいしか取れなかった英語ネイティブに会ったことがあるので、TOEICには英語の知識以外も必要だと思います。単純に記憶力や知能を試すような問題は出題されませんが、推論力を問うような問題はよく出題されます。Part 6の文脈依存型問題やPart 7のちりばめられた情報を関連付ける問題では、いくつかの事実から推論する力が必要になります。それに、Part 5では注意深さが必要ですね。問題文を

Ted's Talks ❶

最後まで読まなかったために、罠にはまってしまうこともあるので。

Ted ： 逆に、TOEICがきっとやらないだろうと言えることはありますか。

Ross： TOEICを制作するETSはフェアな出題をします。例えば、本文にMediatech requires some of its employees to work on Sunday.（Mediatech社は何人かの従業員に日曜出勤を求める）という記述があり、What is mentioned about Mediatech employees?（Mediatech社の従業員について何が述べられているか）という設問があったとしましょう。これについて、They are required to work on weekends.（彼らは週末に出勤することを求められている）という選択肢が不正解で、その理由が「Theyは『何人かの従業員』ではなく『すべての従業員』を指すから」というものであれば、それはフェアではありません。そのような問題はおそらく出ないでしょう。

Ted ： 本書にまとめた7つのスキルの中で、すでに高い英語力を持つ人がTOEICでコンスタントに満点を取るためには、どれが最も重要だと思いますか。

Ross： まず「忍耐力」は必要です。先ほど触れた、満点が取れなかった英語ネイティブには、それが欠けていたのでしょう。「要約力」と「言い換え対応力」もとても大切です。問題作成者にとっても、それらは武器なんです。答えを見つけにくいようにキーを文書中にちりばめて、同義語を使って隠すのです。素早く答えを見つけたかったら、そういった仕掛けに対応できないといけません。

ただ、990点とそれ以外のスコアとの差は、「語法・語感力」だと思います。いかに速く読めて論理力があっても、単語の意味と用法を知らなければ正解できません。語法を極めたい方には、私とヒロ前田さんの共著、「**TOEICテスト究極のゼミPART 5語彙・語法【超上級編】**」をお薦めします。

CHAPTER 2

情報検索力
SCANNING

このスキルが足りない人は…

- ☐ 解答のキー（正解を特定する情報）を見逃してミスする
- ☐ 不正解を誘うトラップにまんまとはまる
- ☐ 問題文・文書を何度も読み直すはめになり、時間をロスする

CHAPTER 2
情報検索力
SCANNING

➡ **解答に必要な
ピンポイント情報を
素早く見つける力**

必要になるパート：Part 5／6／7

　TOEICで求められる「情報検索力」とは、**解答に必要なピンポイントの情報を素早く的確に見つける力**です。Part 5、6で言えば、前置詞や時を表す表現など、キーとなる語句さえ見つけられれば解答できるような問題で、このスキルが求められます。Part 7でも、人物の役職や店の営業時間などの短い語句が解答のキーになる問題は、情報検索力を駆使することで解答時間を大幅に短縮できます。

　リーディングセクションを効率よく解くためには、問題に応じて精読モードと情報検索モードを切り替える必要があります。「精読モード」では、文意や前後関係などの細部に目を配り、狭く深く読み進めますが、「情報検索モード」では、それとは対照的に、**文書全体に広く浅く目を通して、キーだけをピックアップ**します。

　コンスタントに満点を取り続けるBEYOND 990erの中には、飛ばし読みをせず、英文をすべて読んで解く「全部読み」派が少なくありません。しかし、そのような人にとっても、解答の過程で、確認のために文中のキーを再度検索する作業は必要です。部分的に読んでキーを頼りに素早く解く「部分読み」派や、パートによって読み方を使い分ける「ハイブリッド」派は、情報検索をさらに多用しています。**時間的制約が厳しいTOEICテストにおいて、情報検索力は、どのようなレベル・タイプの受験者**にとっても要のスキルの1つなのです。

　それでは診断テストの設問を例にとって、このスキルの発揮の仕方を確認しましょう。

【Part 5】 p. 9, 1（色字の選択肢が正解）

1. The ------- of an empty space on the third floor into a conference room has made meetings far easier to arrange.
   (A) utilization　　名 利用
   (B) allocation　　名 割り当て
　＊(C) conversion　　名 改造
   (D) construction　名 建設

Part 5：空所から離れたところにあるキーを見逃すな

　an empty space（空きスペース）やa conference room（会議室）という語の意味を手掛かりに解こうとした人は、なかなか正解を絞り込めなかったはずです。この問題はconvert A into B（AをBに改造する）というセットフレーズの知識を問うもので、解答するためにはintoというキーの存在を素早く察知する必要があります。このように、**キーが空所から離れていればいるほど、問題の難度は上がります。**

　上級者の多くはPart 5を解くとき、問題文を返り読みせず、一筆書きのように解いています。文頭から読んでいき、空所に到達するころには、正解となる語句のアタリがついていて、すんなり正解を選ぶことができるからです。

　しかし、この問題のように空所が文頭近くにあったり、空所のかなり後ろにキーが登場したりする場合は、空所に至った時点では正解が特定できません。**普段返り読みをしない上級者ほど、この「キー後出し」タイプの問題で早とちりをしがち**ですから、注意が必要です。

　次に、Part 6、7で情報検索力がカギになる問題パターンを見てみましょう。

【Part 6】 p. 11, 10（抜粋）

Many sports fans are reluctant to buy a season pass because they are concerned that they may be unable to make full use of their purchase. Unexpected work commitments and interstate transfers are commonly cited reasons for underutilized passes, resulting in a huge waste of money. To put minds at ease, GameOne is offering an insurance package that ensures you get true value for money.

Should you be unable to use your ------- for an extended period,

    10. * (A) ticket
      (B) services
      (C) membership
      (D) policy

GameOne will refund the value of the unused portion.

Part 6：ピンポイント情報の文脈型問題に注意せよ

　Part 6に出題される語彙問題には、いわゆる「文脈型」の問題というものがあります。これは、空所を含む文とは別の箇所にキーとなる情報がある問題です。**文脈型問題のキーは、それが文書の本筋にとって重要ではない情報だったり、他の設問を解く上で必要ではない情報だったりすると、見逃してしまいがち**です。

　この問題も、空所を含む文だけでは正解が特定できません。また、文書の概要（未使用分相当額を払い戻してくれる保険がある）を理解していても、正解を確定させるのは難しいでしょう。冒頭の2文に戻って、2カ所に登場するpass（入場許可証≒ticket）というキーを確認することで、ようやく他の選択肢に惑わされず、自信を持って正解が選べます。

【Part 7】 p. 12, 13（抜粋）

Sydney (August 10)—Since the leadership change in mid-May, there has been much speculation about how David Panetta, the new CEO, will make his mark on Australia's largest international airline. (中略)

... However, public relations manager, Joe Walker, acknowledged in an interview with the press that the latter piece of news would still require approval at the general meeting of shareholders next month.

13. According to the article, what will most likely happen in September?
 (A) New routes will be launched.
 (B) An airline will be acquired.
 ＊(C) A meeting will take place.
 (D) A number of employees will be hired.

Part 7：欠けたピースの存在に気づき、パズルの空白を埋めよ

　Part 7には、**複数のキーを見つけ、情報を統合することが求められる問題**があります。例えば、上の「9月に何があるか」という問題では、設問文中のSeptemberというキーワードは文書には登場しません。そこで、時期に関する他の表現を検索すると、第2段落の最後にnext monthが見つかります。また、この時期にmeeting of shareholders（株主総会）があるということもわかります。さらに「next monthとは何月か」を導くために情報検索をすると、冒頭の記事の日付（August 10）が見つかります。これで、「来月は株主総会」＋「今は8月」＝(C)「9月には会議がある」とわかります。TOEICに特有のこのパズルのような問題は、**欠けている情報の存在を意識し、その情報に関連する箇所を検索しながら読む**ことで攻略できます。

　この「情報検索力」を身につけるために、問題文が通常よりも長めのPart 5と、他の要素を排除して本文引用だけで解くPart 7を、高地トレーニングとして用意しました。ゲーム感覚で挑んでみてください。

●POINT
- [ ] Part 5の空所から離れたキーの見逃しは、上級者にも多い失点パターン。
- [ ] Part 6、7の文書の本筋に絡まないキー情報は、設問を起点として検索する。
- [ ] Part 7定番のパズル系問題は、「欠けたピース」の存在に気づけるかがカギ。

CHAPTER 2
情報検索力 SCANNING

➡ トレーニング

Menu 1

実際のPart 5より語数が多めの問題を解き、正解のキーとなる情報を素早く見つける練習をしよう。

空所に入る語句として最も適切なものを(A)～(D)から選ぼう。**制限時間は4分**。

● 4分

1. To ------- the terms and conditions of sale as outlined on the first page of this document, sign your name in the box provided at the bottom of the form.
   (A) prove
   (B) meet
   (C) agree
   (D) accept   Ⓐ Ⓑ Ⓒ Ⓓ

2. Designers of EVO purifying air conditioners at GMD Electronics ------- more features into the latest line had the research and development budget been a little less restrictive.
   (A) would incorporate
   (B) would have incorporated
   (C) were incorporating
   (D) have incorporated   Ⓐ Ⓑ Ⓒ Ⓓ

3. The CEO of Cooper Publicity has announced that he is looking to ------- its range of services first by assessing and restructuring the radio and television advertising business starting this June.
   (A) promote
   (B) broaden
   (C) reexamine
   (D) administer

4. On the members-only Web site, customers can ------- reviews of products they have purchased from Delware Online Shopping, but they will only become visible to other members upon approval.
   (A) contribute
   (B) distinguish
   (C) assess
   (D) view

5. ------- from numerous sources, *The Peterman Global Review* on retailers and consumers is highly sought after as it is one of the most important publications for marketing firms in the United States.
   (A) Compiled
   (B) Compiles
   (C) Compiling
   (D) Compile

6. According to a survey conducted at the conclusion of David Townsend's seminar, participants felt that it gave them a ------- understanding of financial planning than they had expected.
   (A) fullness
   (B) full
   (C) fully
   (D) fuller

Menu 1の解答・解説

※問題文の訳文は紙面では省略（訳文の入手方法はp.7をご覧ください）。

1. To ------- the terms and conditions of sale as outlined on the first page of this document, sign your name in the box provided at the bottom of the form.

   (A) prove 動 〜を証明する
   (B) meet 動 〜を満たす
   (C) agree 動 同意する
   ＊(D) accept 動 〜を承諾する

   ● terms and conditions 取引条件、諸条件

   解説 カンマ後ろのsign your name（署名してください）という行為の目的を考えると、the terms and conditions（取引条件）を「承諾するため」が適切なので、正解は(D) accept。(C) agreeは意味的には合うが、「取引条件」のような名詞を後ろに取るためにはtoが必要なので文法的に不可。(B) meetを入れると「取引条件を満たす」となるが、カンマ以降と意味がつながらず不適切。

2. Designers of EVO purifying air conditioners at GMD Electronics ------- more features into the latest line had the research and development budget been a little less restrictive.

   (A) would incorporate
   ＊(B) would have incorporated
   (C) were incorporating
   (D) have incorporated

   ● purify 〜の汚れを取り除く ● incorporate 〜を組み込む ● restrictive 制限のある

   解説 仮定法過去完了のhad beenが倒置法で用いられているので、時制が一致する(B) would have incorporatedが正解。had以下をifが導く節にすると、if the research and development budget had been ...だ。頻度は低いが、過去完了や倒置の問題は過去に出題されたことがあるので、押さえておこう。

3. The CEO of Cooper Publicity has announced that he is looking to ------- its range of services first by assessing and restructuring the radio and television advertising business starting this June.

   (A) promote 動 〜を宣伝する
   (B) broaden 動 〜を拡大する
   ＊(C) reexamine 動 〜を見直す
   (D) administer 動 〜を運営する

   ● assess 評価する

   解説 by以下の「広告ビジネスを評価して再編成する」という手段で何を行うのかを考えると、サービス範囲を「見直す」が適切なので、正解は(C) reexamine。(B) broadenや(A) promoteは、its range of services（サービス範囲）との組み合わせは問題ないが、by以下が「拡大」や「宣伝」のための手法ではないことから不適切。コロケーションだけで誤判断するミスを誘う問題だ。

64

4. On the members-only Web site, customers can ------- reviews of products they have purchased from Delware Online Shopping, but they will only become visible to other members upon approval.

* (A) contribute 動 〜を投稿する
(B) distinguish 動 〜を区別する
(C) assess 動 〜を評価する
(D) view 動 〜を見る

解説 but以下の「他の会員の目に触れるようになる」ものとは、客がウェブサイト上に「投稿」することができる、商品の評価のことだと解すると意味が通る。よって、正解は(A) contribute。but以下がwillを用いた未来時制なので、それらの評価はまだ見られない状態ということになる。(C) assess（評価する）や(D) view（見る）はまだできないはずの行為なので、空所には不適切だ。

---

5. ------- from numerous sources, *The Peterman Global Review* on retailers and consumers is highly sought after as it is one of the most important publications for marketing firms in the United States.

* (A) Compiled
(B) Compiles
(C) Compiling
(D) Compile

● compile 〜を（資料をまとめて）編集する　● numerous 非常に多くの　● be sought after 求められている

解説 選択肢はすべて動詞compile（編集する）の活用形。文や節の頭の部分が空所で、そこに動詞の活用形を補わせる問題の場合、分詞構文である可能性が高い。空所を含む節の意味上の主語は、*The Peterman Global Review*という出版物なので、多くの情報源から「編集される」と受け身を意味する過去分詞にするべきだ。よって、正解は(A) Compiled。(C) Compilingという現在分詞を入れると、出版物が「編集する」側になり、かつ目的語がないので不適切。

---

6. According to a survey conducted at the conclusion of David Townsend's seminar, participants felt that it gave them a ------- understanding of financial planning than they had expected.

(A) fullness 名 十分なこと
(B) full 形 十分な
(C) fully 副 十分に
* (D) fuller 形 より十分な

● at the conclusion of 〜 〜の終わりにあたり

解説 前に冠詞a、後ろに名詞understandingがあるので、空所には形容詞が入るとわかる。さらに、後方にthanがあるので、形容詞の比較級(D) fullerが正解。空所前後だけを見て(B) fullを選んでしまった人は、テスト本番でも同様のミスを犯している可能性がある。1問でもミスを減らしたいなら、正解を見つけたと思っても、他の選択肢に目を通すべきだ。

Menu 2

Part 7の文書で問題解答のキーとなる語句をピンポイントで見つける練習をする。

シングルパッセージを読み、設問に答えよう。**解答は文書の中から、答えとして適切な語句を引用する形で行うこと**。Part 7の文書は普段「全部読み」するという人も、ここではあえて情報検索・拾い読みに挑戦してほしい。**1パッセージにつき制限時間5分以内**で解くようにしよう。

5分

Questions 1-6 refer to the following e-mail.

E-Mail Message	
To:	Manuel Sanchez <msanchez@hacademy.biz>
From:	Rebecca Gregory <rgregory@bigstarone.com>
Date:	January 27
Subject:	Cancellations

Dear Mr. Sanchez,

I consulted you in person in late November regarding the spring course in introductory spreadsheets at Hammersmith Academy. I was informed that there were no more vacancies in the course and that I would only be offered a place if there was a cancellation.

I am sorry to bother you with this issue once again, but I would just like to check whether or not there have been any cancellations. I will be required to use spreadsheets as part of my work from March, and I am afraid that I am not familiar enough with them to perform adequately. My employer requires that I take part in a course at a vocational college like yours, and as far as I have researched,

Hammersmith offers the best courses of this kind in Bristol. Unfortunately, I will not be able to attend lessons in the afternoon, when there are still some seats left. This is because of my commitments at work.

I apologize if you have told me to contact another person for scheduling matters. I do understand from your business card that you are a learning advisor and probably do not directly handle the student enrollment process. If this is the case, please forward my e-mail to the person in charge.

Thank you very much for your assistance and I really hope I will be able to secure a place in the course.

Sincerely,
Rebecca Gregory

---

1. What type of business is Hammersmith Academy?

   A (v_____) (c_____)

2. At what level does Ms. Gregory want to take a course?

   (_____)

3. When will Ms. Gregory start using spreadsheets at work?

   In (_____)

4. For when are there vacancies still available?

   (_____) the (a_____)

5. In which city is the course held?

   (_____)

6. Who most likely is Mr. Sanchez?   A (l_____) (a_____)

Questions 7-13 refer to the following article.

Photography Standing Strong as a Pastime

Photography, a pastime whose growth stagnated at the end of the last century, when personal computers and video games preoccupied many minds, has seen a rise in popularity. Surveys conducted by the Rhodes Institute of Technology have shown that more and more of the population is spending longer and longer taking photos. While this is not like traditional photography using expensive cameras with complicated settings and additional equipment, it is still in its essence, the same activity. Most modern smartphones have extremely high grade lenses that rival those of professional cameras. Some might even argue that this new form of photography is purer, with people spending longer enjoying and sharing their images than discussing how they took them.

One of the reasons for the higher numbers of photos being taken is doubtlessly the fact that almost every adult carries their phone within reach 24 hours a day. This, coupled with the growth of social media, where photos are shared after being taken, has made photography a part of life for many people. The abundance of storage space, both in digital devices and online, enables anyone to take and save virtually as many photos as they wish at almost no cost.

It may be argued that the subject matter today is more often shots of meals taken in restaurants or quick snaps of interesting observances rather than carefully framed wildlife or natural beauty, which are the usual subjects for traditional photographers. Nevertheless, beauty is in the eye of the beholder and it looks as though this hobby is here to stay.

7. What caused photography to lose popularity?

　　　　　　　　　　(P　　　　) (　　　　　　) and (v　　　) (g　　　　)

8. Who conducted surveys about photography?

　　　　　　　　　　　　The (　　　) (I　　　　　) of (T　　　　　　)

9. What do most modern smartphones feature?

　　　　　　　　　　　　　　　　　　(H　　　) (g　　　　) (I　　　　)

10. What do people today often do after taking photos?

　　　　　　　　　　(S　　　　) (th　　　　) on (　　　　　) (　　　　　)

11. What has made it possible to save many photos?

　　　　　　　　　　　The (a　　　　　) of (s　　　　　) (s　　　　　)

12. What is the subject matter of traditional photography?

　　　　　　　　　　　　(W　　　　　) and (n　　　　　) (　　　　　)

13. Where are many photographs taken today?

　　　　　　　　　　　　　　　　　　　　　　　　　In (r　　　　　)

Menu 2の解答・解説

※文書中の色字＋下線部は、同じ番号の問題の正解根拠。

問題 1-6 は次のメールに関するものです。

E-Mail Message

To: Manuel Sanchez <msanchez@hacademy.biz>
From: Rebecca Gregory <rgregory@bigstarone.com>
Date: January 27
Subject: Cancellations

Dear Mr. Sanchez,

I consulted you in person in late November ²regarding the spring course in introductory spreadsheets at Hammersmith Academy. I was informed that there were no more vacancies in the course and that I would only be offered a place if there was a cancellation.

I am sorry to bother you with this issue once again, but I would just like to check whether or not there have been any cancellations. ³I will be required to use spreadsheets as part of my work from March, and I am afraid that I am not familiar enough with them to perform adequately. My employer requires that I take part in a course at ¹a vocational college like yours, and as far as I have researched, ⁵Hammersmith offers the best courses of this kind in Bristol. Unfortunately, I will not be able to attend ⁴lessons in the afternoon, when there are still some seats left. This is because of my commitments at work.

I apologize if you have told me to contact another person for scheduling matters. I do understand from your business card that ⁶you are a learning advisor and probably do not directly handle the student enrollment process. If this is the case, please forward my e-mail to the

> person in charge.
>
> Thank you very much for your assistance and I really hope I will be able to secure a place in the course.
>
> Sincerely,
> Rebecca Gregory

- introductory 入門の ● spreadsheets 表計算ソフト ※会計処理用のソフトウエア。 ● perform adequately 適切に業務を執り行う ● take part in ~ ~に参加する ● vocational college 職業訓練学校 ● commitment at work 職場での義務 ※ここでは「契約上、午後は勤務時間となっている」ということ。 ● enrollment process 入学手続き ● secure ~を確保する

1. What type of business is Hammersmith Academy?
Hammersmith Academyの業種は何か。 —— **A vocational college**（職業訓練学校）

2. At what level does Ms. Gregory want to take a course?
Gregory氏はどのレベルのコースを受講したいのか。 —— **Introductory**（入門）

3. When will Ms. Gregory start using spreadsheets at work?
Gregory氏が仕事で表計算ソフトを使い始めるのはいつか。 —— **In March**（3月）

4. For when are there vacancies still available?
まだ空席があるのはいつか。 —— **In the afternoon**（午後）

5. In which city is the course held?
コースはどの都市で開催されるか。 —— **Bristol**（ブリストル）

6. Who most likely is Mr. Sanchez?
Sanchez氏はどんな人物であると考えられるか。 —— **A learning advisor**（学習アドバイザー）

解説 設問文中のキーワードを起点とし、その関連情報を文書中に探し求める解き方をした場合、**1**、**5**、**6**の問題は複数の箇所を参照しなければならなかったはずだ。例えば、**1**ではHammersmith Academyという学校名がキーワードだが、第1段落ではこの学校がspreadsheetsの入門コースを提供していることしかわからず、業種まではわからない。さらに情報を検索すると、第2段落でa vocational college like yours（貴校のような職業学校）というキーが見つかり、正解が導ける。**ほしい情報のイメージ**（この問題では「どんなタイプの学校か」）を明確に持つことが、素早く情報検索をするコツだ。

問題 7-13 は次の記事に関するものです。

Photography Standing Strong as a Pastime

[7] Photography, a pastime whose growth stagnated at the end of the last century, when personal computers and video games preoccupied many minds, has seen a rise in popularity. [8] Surveys conducted by the Rhodes Institute of Technology have shown that more and more of the population is spending longer and longer taking photos. While this is not like traditional photography using expensive cameras with complicated settings and additional equipment, it is still in its essence, the same activity. [9] Most modern smartphones have extremely high grade lenses that rival those of professional cameras. Some might even argue that this new form of photography is purer, with people spending longer enjoying and sharing their images than discussing how they took them.

One of the reasons for the higher numbers of photos being taken is doubtlessly the fact that almost every adult carries their phone within reach 24 hours a day. This, coupled with [10] the growth of social media, where photos are shared after being taken, has made photography a part of life for many people. [11] The abundance of storage space, both in digital devices and online, enables anyone to take and save virtually as many photos as they wish at almost no cost.

It may be argued that [13] the subject matter today is more often shots of meals taken in restaurants or quick snaps of interesting observances [12] rather than carefully framed wildlife or natural beauty, which are the usual subjects for traditional photographers. Nevertheless, beauty is in the eye of the beholder and it looks as though this hobby is here to stay.

- stand strong 強さを保つ ● pastime 娯楽、気晴らし ● stagnate 成長が止まる、活気がなくなる
- preoccupy ～を夢中にさせる、～の心を奪う ● in its essence 本質的に ● rival ～に匹敵する
- within reach 手の届くところに ● coupled with ~ ～に加えて ● social media ソーシャルメディア、SNSサイト ● abundance 豊富なこと ● storage space 保管する場所、保存領域 ● virtually 事実上
- subject matter 素材、主題 ● observance 観察、観測 ● beauty is in the eye of the beholder 美は見る人の目の中にある、人の好みはさまざま

7. What caused photography to lose popularity?
写真撮影が人気を失った原因は何か。
―― Personal computers and video games（パソコンとテレビゲーム）

8. Who conducted surveys about photography?
誰が写真撮影について調査を行ったか。
―― The Rhodes Institute of Technology（Rhodes工科大学）

9. What do most modern smartphones feature?
最近のスマートフォンの多くは何を特徴にしているか。
―― High grade lenses（高品質のレンズ）

10. What do people today often do after taking photos?
最近の人々は、写真を撮ってからよく何をするか。
―― Share them on social media（ソーシャルメディアで共有する）

11. What has made it possible to save many photos?
多くの写真を保存することを可能にしたのは何か。
―― The abundance of storage space（豊富な保存領域）

12. What is the subject matter of traditional photography?
従来の写真撮影の題材は何だったか。
―― Wildlife and natural beauty（野生生物や自然美）

13. Where are many photographs taken today?
最近は写真の多くはどこで撮られるか。
―― In restaurants（レストランで）

解説 ▶ 記事や評論の読解が難しい理由の1つに、文書中のどこにどういう情報があるのかがわかりにくいということがある。対策として、まずはタイトルや第1段落の冒頭部分をチェックし、その文書の主旨を理解しよう。また、各段落のトピックセンテンス（段落の主題を述べる文。段落冒頭に置かれることが多い）を読み、全体の構造を大まかに把握すれば、情報検索のスピードアップに役立つ。例えば第2段落1文目を読めば、この段落で「近年写真が再流行している理由」が述べられていることがわかる。そうすると、**10**や**11**のような、現在の写真人気を下支えしているものに関する情報は、この段落を検索すれば見つかるだろうと推測できる。

CHAPTER 2 情報検索力 SCANNING

実践問題

仕上げに、本番形式の難問にチャレンジ。情報検索力を十分に発揮して解くようにしよう。

Part 5

空所に入る語句として、最も適切なものを1つ選ぼう。(解答・解説はpp. 82〜83)

🕐 ● 1分40秒

1. The sales presentation met with a very ------- response, with only a few clients expressing doubts about the product's marketability.
   (A) deliberate
   (B) enthusiastic
   (C) proportional
   (D) negative   Ⓐ Ⓑ Ⓒ Ⓓ

2. ------- the cost of production is unaffected by outside influences, there should be no fluctuations in retail price in the coming year.
   (A) Provided that
   (B) Even if
   (C) Although
   (D) Despite   Ⓐ Ⓑ Ⓒ Ⓓ

3. Reporting a larger than expected ------- in value in the final quarter, Durabond pleased investors at the shareholders' meeting yesterday.
   (A) progress
   (B) drop
   (C) gain
   (D) decline

4. Pride Industries has decided to ------- a printing factory in Westhaven as part of its expansion policy.
   (A) acquire
   (B) close
   (C) preserve
   (D) rename

5. Kling Stationery has ------- from its catalog several of the items which made it famous due to the fact that they have become outdated.
   (A) improved
   (B) selected
   (C) advertised
   (D) removed

Part 6

空所に入る語句として、最も適切なものを1つずつ選ぼう。(解答・解説はpp. 84〜87)

Questions 6-8 refer to the following letter. 1分30秒

October 11

Dear Ms. Randolph,

Regretfully, the Orlando City Council is not able to ------- your application

                      6. (A) adopt
                         (B) locate
                         (C) process
                         (D) identify Ⓐ Ⓑ Ⓒ Ⓓ

for a license to operate a charity carwash in Dole Park. The reason is that your application is missing some important items. In order to continue with evaluation and licensing, we need to see the following documents: your registration as a charity, a map of the area you plan to use, and your plan with regards to the cleanup after the event.

------- your application, I can see that you had intended to hold the carwash

7. (A) Viewing
   (B) Following
   (C) Complying
   (D) Regarding Ⓐ Ⓑ Ⓒ Ⓓ

on October 25. It is very important that the outstanding documents are delivered to this office by October 15 at the latest if you still need to have the application approved for that date.

It is possible to make changes to your application and discuss a project already under consideration. In such cases, please do not ------- to call or visit the Orlando City Council.

                      8. (A) attempt
                         (B) hesitate
                         (C) manage
            Ⓐ Ⓑ Ⓒ Ⓓ (D) request

Questions 9-11 refer to the following e-mail.

1分30秒

To: Maurine Doherty <mdoherty@pollockengineering.com>
From: Claude Ferguson <cferguson@cezannecatering.com>
Date: May 19
Subject: Event catering

Dear Ms. Doherty,

Thank you for your kind words following the special event on Saturday. I would like to take this opportunity to explain our fail-safe operating policy. We ------- for events days in advance. However, raw ingredients are not

9. (A) prepare
 (B) prepared
 (C) have prepared
 (D) will prepare   Ⓐ Ⓑ Ⓒ Ⓓ

delivered to us until noon on the day before so as to ensure maximum freshness.

Unfortunately, our supplier experienced an unforeseeable mishap in the lead up to your event. As a result, we had to ------- our backup plan. As

10. (A) rely on
 (B) cancel
 (C) reconsider
 (D) scrap   Ⓐ Ⓑ Ⓒ Ⓓ

soon as we learned of the problem, we contacted various producers and had staff travel around the region collecting ingredients.

It took longer than ------- and it was not until 10 P.M. the night before that

11. (A) acquired
 (B) anticipated
 (C) allowed for
 (D) agreed upon   Ⓐ Ⓑ Ⓒ Ⓓ

we got everything together. While this incident is somewhat embarrassing to us, I hope it serves to show the lengths we will go to in ensuring customer satisfaction.

I hope you will call on Cezanne Catering for your next special event.

Sincerely,

Claude Ferguson

Part 7

文書に関する設問の解答として、最も適切なものを1つずつ選ぼう。

(解答・解説はpp. 88~93)

Questions 12-15 refer to the following information. 4分

Join the Annual Riverdale Junior Marathon

The annual Riverdale Junior Marathon will be held on Sunday, October 15. Entry is limited to people between the ages of 10 and 18. Exceptions are made for adults who are accompanying minors under the age of 12 but such arrangements must be made in advance by contacting the organizing committee. In cases where such accommodations are made, entrants will be required to purchase and wear an identifying T-shirt.

Only entrants between the ages of 15 and 18 are eligible for the full marathon and younger entrants should join the ten-, five- or three-kilometer events. Registration is already underway and the deadline is September 29.
You can sign up by visiting the Web site or filling out an application form at the Riverdale Junior Marathon Information Center. Entry is $30 regardless of age or distance. The center is unable to accept cash, so a credit card will be required.

All race distances follow a circuit run course starting at the Riverdale Town Square at 9 A.M. sharp. Full marathon runners will wind their way through the city streets past the Riverdale Museum and Douglas University, before finishing at where they started sometime before 1:30 P.M. Runners who have not finished by that time will be required to forgo finishing and make way for traffic which will resume at 2:00 P.M.

A stage by the finishing line will be used to announce the winners for each distance approximately 15 minutes after the third-placed runners arrive. There are cash prizes for people who place first, second and third in each event, as well as special age group prizes. Further details of these are available from the Web site. Prizes will be allocated after the official adjudication process is complete, which will take two full days from the end of the race. Results will be published in the Riverdale Times newspaper on Friday, October 20 and prizes will be sent by registered mail. Additionally, all finishers will be given a small gift in recognition of their participation when they report to the race organizer's tent at the finish line.

www.riverdalejuniormarathon.com

12. What is indicated about the marathon?
(A) People over 18 years of age cannot take part.
(B) All entrants are required to wear an official T-shirt.
(C) There are four distance events available to enter.
(D) 15- to 18-year-olds must enter the full marathon.

13. Where does the full marathon end?
(A) The Information Center
(B) Riverdale Town Square
(C) Riverdale Museum
(D) Douglas University

14. What will occur at 2:00 P.M.?
(A) Streets will reopen to cars.
(B) The stage will be dismantled.
(C) Winners will be announced.
(D) A closing speech will be made.

15. When will prizes be awarded to event winners?
(A) On September 29
(B) On October 15
(C) On October 17
(D) On October 20

Questions 16-20 refer to the following advertisement and e-mail.

Ps PRIME STAR

Prime Star is Bermuda's largest provider of subscription video channels. We have over 30 channels to choose from and there are also package options designed to save you money. Individual channels are priced at $14 per month, or you can get a package of three or more for just a few extra dollars.

Music and Entertainment	**Sports and Leisure**
Entertainment News Music Box (nonstop music videos) Rock and Pop Aficionado! (news and documentaries on rock and pop music) $20 per month	Sports World The Travel Channel Extreme Sports This Sporting Life (documentaries) $20 per month
Arts and Science	**Film and Drama**
The Science Channel History of the World Music History $20 per month	The Drama Channel Movies 4 You World Movies $25 per month
Family	**News and Current Affairs**
Movies 4 You Music Box (nonstop music videos) This Sporting Life (documentaries) Sitcoms (comedy programs) Animation All Day $30 per month	News of the World South American News World Events Local Current Affairs Chat Shows $20 per month

Ultimate Package
Movies 4 You
The Drama Channel
Music Box (nonstop music videos)
Sports World
News of the World
$50 per month

Order online at www.primestar.com to receive a starter kit including the receiver.

E-Mail Message

To: Pierre Rousseau <prousseau@whiteswan.com>
From: Kate Robinson <krobinson@primestar.com>
Date: August 6
Subject: Your subscription

Dear Mr. Rousseau,

I am writing in reply to your request to change your subscription. From the questionnaire you took on our Web site, we understand that you wanted access to the movie channel and the music channel in particular and not much of the rest of the package. As you noted, it would be cheaper to order them separately than to continue to subscribe to the current package.

We are pleased to inform you that this month we are running a special campaign which entitles anyone signing up for a package or a minimum of two individual channels to choose one more channel for free. Current customers who wish to switch their subscription are also eligible. Therefore, even if you request the news channel, which you occasionally watch, on top of your two favorite channels, you will get almost the same level of service at a much lower price.

There are some conditions which apply when changing the content of your service. The first is that there is a waiting period. The waiting period is one month in addition to the outstanding portion of the current month, unless the contract was scheduled for renewal at the end of the month in which the change was requested. In cases where a less expensive service option is chosen, there is a one-time handling fee of $20. Depending on the age of your system, you may be required to swap your current hardware for a new tuner, because many of the older systems are less flexible when it comes to package selection. We will contact you and let you know whether or not this will be necessary after your application has been processed.

Unfortunately, as the process is rather complicated, alterations to the packages cannot be handled via the Web site. Please call one of our friendly staff to discuss your account.

Sincerely,

Kate Robinson
Customer Service
Prime Star

16. What kind of company is Prime Star?
(A) A production company
(B) A ticket broker
(C) A broadcaster
(D) A publisher

17. What package is Mr. Rousseau most likely subscribed to?
(A) Family
(B) Film and Drama
(C) Music and Entertainment
(D) Ultimate Package

18. What is NOT a condition of making a change to service content?
(A) The contract must be renewed.
(B) An administration charge is applicable.
(C) There is a delay before changes are enacted.
(D) System hardware may need to be replaced.

19. In the e-mail, the word "outstanding" in paragraph 3, line 3, is closest in meaning to
(A) superior
(B) remaining
(C) unpaid
(D) distinguished

20. How is Mr. Rousseau asked to contact Prime Star?
(A) By e-mail
(B) By telephone
(C) By accessing the Web site
(D) By visiting in person

実践問題の解答・解説

※問題文の訳文は紙面では省略（訳文の入手方法はp.7をご覧ください）。

Part 5

1. The sales presentation met with a very ------- response, with only a few clients expressing doubts about the product's marketability.

   (A) deliberate　形 慎重な
   *(B) enthusiastic　形 熱心な、乗り気な
   (C) proportional　形 釣り合った、比例した
   (D) negative　形 否定的な

   ● marketability 市場性

   解説▶ 空所にはプレゼンテーションに対してどのようなresponse（反応）があったかを表す語が入る。後ろにwith only a few clients expressing doubts（疑問を呈したのはごくわずかな顧客のみだった）とあるので、(B) enthusiastic（熱心な）を入れると意味が通る。(D) negativeを入れるとwith以降と意味が合わなくなるので不適切。

2. ------- the cost of production is unaffected by outside influences, there should be no fluctuations in retail price in the coming year.

   *(A) Provided that　接 〜だとすれば
   (B) Even if　接 たとえ〜だとしても
   (C) Although　接 〜にもかかわらず
   (D) Despite　前 〜にもかかわらず

   ● fluctuation 変動

   解説▶ 空所後は節なので、まず前置詞(D) Despiteを消去。「生産コストが影響を受けない」ことは「小売価格に変動がないこと」の条件なので、(A) Provided thatを入れ、「生産コストが影響を受けないならば、小売価格に変動はない」とすると意味が通る。(B) Even ifや(C) Althoughは逆接を意味する接続詞なので、カンマ前後の2つの節を論理的に結ぶことができない。

3. Reporting a larger than expected ------- in value in the final quarter, Durabond pleased investors at the shareholders' meeting yesterday.

   (A) progress　名 進歩
   (B) drop　名 落ち込み
   *(C) gain　名 増加
   (D) decline　名 減少

   ● the final quarter 第4四半期

   解説▶ カンマの後の主節にDurabond pleased investors（Durabond社は投資家たちを喜ばせた）とあるので、空所にはポジティブな意味の単語が入る。それに該当するのは(A) progressと(C) gain。(A)はin valueとの相性が悪く、「価値の進歩」という意味も不適切。よって、「価値の増加」というフレーズを作る(C)が正解。

82

実践問題の解答・解説

4. Pride Industries has decided to ------- a printing factory in Westhaven as part of its expansion policy.

　＊(A) acquire　動 ～を買収する
　(B) close　動 ～を閉鎖する
　(C) preserve　動 ～を保存する
　(D) rename　動 ～を改名する

● expansion 拡張

解説 文末にas part of its expansion policy（拡大方針の一環として）とあることから、Pride Industries社が事業の拡大をもくろんでいることがわかる。(A) acquireを空所に入れるとa printing factoryを目的語に取って「印刷工場を買収する」となり、文意が通る。よって、(A)が正解。その他の選択肢は「拡大」と意味が合わないため不適切。

5. Kling Stationery has ------- from its catalog several of the items which made it famous due to the fact that they have become outdated.

　(A) improved　動 ～を改良した
　(B) selected　動 ～を選んだ
　(C) advertised　動 ～を宣伝した
　＊(D) removed　動 ～を削除した

● outdated 旧式の、古い

解説 選択肢はすべて動詞の過去分詞。several of the itemsが空所に入る動詞の目的語だが、which節を伴い長い句になっているため、通常、目的語の後ろに置かれるfrom its catalogが前に来ている。due to以下に、Kling Stationeryが空所に入る動詞の動作をした理由は「古くなったから」だと書かれているので、空所には(D) removed（～を削除した）が適切。remove A from Bで「AをBから削除する、取り除く」の意。(B) selectedもselect A from B（AをBから選ぶ）の形を取るが、due to以下により排除される。

Part 6

問題 6-8 は次のレターに関するものです。

October 11

Dear Ms. Randolph,

Regretfully, the Orlando City Council is not able to ------- your application

6. (A) adopt
(B) locate
(C) process
(D) identify

for a license to operate a charity carwash in Dole Park. The reason is that your application is missing some important items. In order to continue with evaluation and licensing, we need to see the following documents: your registration as a charity, a map of the area you plan to use, and your plan with regards to the cleanup after the event.

------- your application, I can see that you had intended to hold the carwash

7. (A) Viewing
(B) Following
(C) Complying
(D) Regarding

on October 25. It is very important that the outstanding documents are delivered to this office by October 15 at the latest if you still need to have the application approved for that date.

It is possible to make changes to your application and discuss a project already under consideration. In such cases, please do not ------- to call or visit the Orlando City Council.

8. (A) attempt
(B) hesitate
(C) manage
(D) request

- regretfully 残念なことに ● charity 形慈善目的の 名慈善団体 ● evaluation 評価、査定 ● licensing ライセンス供与 ● registration 登録 ● with regards to ~ ~に関して ● outstanding 未処理の

6. (A) adopt 動 ～を採用する
   (B) locate 動 ～を探し当てる
   ＊(C) process 動 ～を処理する
   (D) identify 動 ～を突き止める

解説 手紙の受取人であるRandolph氏は、チャリティー目的の無料洗車を行うための申請書(application)をオーランド市に送ったようだ。この文書は、それに対する市職員からの返事。「重要な書類のいくつかが不足している」という第2文にある理由から、is not able to を伴って「～を処理することができない」という意味を作ることができる(C) processが正解。(A) adoptは「(意見や技術などを)取り入れる、採用する」という場合に使うので、applicationとは意味が合わない。

7. ＊(A) Viewing ～を見て
   (B) Following ～にならって
   (C) Complying ～に従って
   (D) Regarding ～に関して

解説 空所後にI can see that ... (…がわかる)とあり、市職員が申請書の内容について述べていることから、「～を見たところ」という意味の(A) Viewingが正解。これは分詞構文で、主節の理由を表している。この手紙自体がRandolph氏の申請書に関する内容なので、この時点で(D) Regarding (「あなたの申請書に関して」)とあらためて述べるのは文脈に合わない。(D)に違和感を持たなかった人は、文書のトピックを把握する力を養う必要がある。Chapter 3「要約力」のトレーニングを活用してほしい。

8. (A) attempt 動 (＋to doで)～することを試みる
   ＊(B) hesitate 動 (＋to doで)～することをためらう
   (C) manage 動 (＋to doで)なんとか～する
   (D) request 動 (＋to doで)～することを要求する

解説 Please do not hesitate to ~ (ご遠慮なく～してください)はビジネス通信文の定型表現。上級者であれば一瞬で解きたい問題だ。意味の面から考えたとしても、(A)、(C)、(D)のいずれを入れても「電話するな、要求するな」という市役所にあるまじき態度を意味することになってしまう。Please do not attempt to ~ (～しないでください)は警告文の定型表現。

問題 9-11 は次のメールに関するものです。

To: Maurine Doherty <mdoherty@pollockengineering.com>
From: Claude Ferguson <cferguson@cezannecatering.com>
Date: May 19
Subject: Event catering

Dear Ms. Doherty,

Thank you for your kind words following the special event on Saturday. I would like to take this opportunity to explain our fail-safe operating policy. We ------- for events days in advance. However, raw ingredients are not

9. (A) prepare
   (B) prepared
   (C) have prepared
   (D) will prepare

delivered to us until noon on the day before so as to ensure maximum freshness.

Unfortunately, our supplier experienced an unforeseeable mishap in the lead up to your event. As a result, we had to ------- our backup plan. As

10. (A) rely on
    (B) cancel
    (C) reconsider
    (D) scrap

soon as we learned of the problem, we contacted various producers and had staff travel around the region collecting ingredients.

It took longer than ------- and it was not until 10 P.M. the night before that

11. (A) acquired
    (B) anticipated
    (C) allowed for
    (D) agreed upon

we got everything together. While this incident is somewhat embarrassing to us, I hope it serves to show the lengths we will go to in ensuring customer satisfaction.

I hope you will call on Cezanne Catering for your next special event.

Sincerely,

Claude Ferguson

● fail-safe 絶対確実な ● raw ingredients 材料、生の素材 ● ensure 確かに〜をする ● unforeseeable 予見不可能な、予想外の ● mishap 不幸な出来事、災難 ● in the lead up to 〜 〜に至るまでの間に ● the lengths we will go to 何としてでもするという私たちの覚悟

9. ＊(A) prepare
   (B) prepared
   (C) have prepared
   (D) will prepare

解説 土曜日の特別イベントのために行ったケータリングサービスに関して、ケータリング業者の Ferguson 氏が Doherty 氏に送ったメールである。**9** は動詞の正しい時制を選ぶ問題。前の文に「私たちの絶対確実な運営方針について説明させてほしい」とあるので、空所を含む文以降はその説明だ。会社の方針などの習慣的な事柄は現在形で表す。よって、現在形の (A) prepare が入る。次の文の are not delivered が現在形で書かれていることも裏付けになる。

10. ＊(A) rely on   〜に頼る
    (B) cancel   動 〜をキャンセルする
    (C) reconsider   動 〜を再検討する
    (D) scrap   動 〜を廃棄する

解説 単文を見るだけでは解けない、文脈依存型の語彙問題。仕入れ先で unforeseeable mishap（予想外の出来事）があり、As a result（その結果として）、Ferguson 氏の会社は backup plan（代替案）に「頼る」ことになった、とすると文意が通る。よって正解は (A) rely on。他の選択肢はすべて backup plan を打ち消してしまうことになるので、この文脈には不適切。

11. (A) acquired   形 入手した
    ＊(B) anticipated   形 予想されていた
    (C) allowed for   許されていた
    (D) agreed upon   合意されていた

解説 空所を含む文は「〜より時間がかかり、前夜 10 時に、かろうじてすべての材料がそろった」という意味なので、空所に (B) anticipated（予想されていた）を入れると、「『予想されていた』より時間がかかって」となり、文意が通る。(A) acquired は「入手した」という意味が不適。(C) allowed for（許された）と (D) agreed upon（合意された）はいずれも空所を含む文だけで考えると不具合はないが、「許可」や「合意」に関する記述がメール中にないので、文脈から不正解となる。

Part 7

問題 12-15 は次の情報に関するものです。

Join the Annual Riverdale Junior Marathon

The annual Riverdale Junior Marathon will be held on Sunday, October 15. Entry is limited to people between the ages of 10 and 18. ¹Exceptions are made for adults who are accompanying minors under the age of 12 but such arrangements must be made in advance by contacting the organizing committee. ²In cases where such accommodations are made, entrants will be required to purchase and wear an identifying T-shirt.

³Only entrants between the ages of 15 and 18 are eligible for the full marathon and younger entrants should join the ten-, five- or three-kilometer events. Registration is already underway and the deadline is September 29. You can sign up by visiting the Web site or filling out an application form at the Riverdale Junior Marathon Information Center. Entry is $30 regardless of age or distance. The center is unable to accept cash, so a credit card will be required.

⁴All race distances follow a circuit run course starting at the Riverdale Town Square at 9 A.M. sharp. Full marathon runners will wind their way through the city streets past the Riverdale Museum and Douglas University, before finishing at where they started sometime before 1:30 P.M. Runners who have not finished by that time will be required to forgo finishing and ⁵make way for traffic which will resume at 2:00 P.M.

⁶A stage by the finishing line will be used to announce the winners for each distance approximately 15 minutes after the third-placed runners arrive. There are cash prizes for people who place first, second and third in each event, as well as special age group prizes. Further details of these are available from the Web site. ⁷Prizes will be allocated after the official adjudication process is complete, which will take two full days from the end of the race. ⁸Results will be published in the Riverdale Times newspaper on Friday, October 20 and prizes will be sent by registered mail. Additionally,

all finishers will be given a small gift in recognition of their participation when they report to the race organizer's tent at the finish line.

www.riverdalejuniormarathon.com

- exception 例外 ● minor 未成年者 ● accommodation 調整 ● entrant (競技などの) 参加者
- forgo 〜なしで済ます、〜 (権利など) を失う ● adjudication 判定 ● registered mail 書留郵便

12. What is indicated about the marathon?
(A) People over 18 years of age cannot take part.
(B) All entrants are required to wear an official T-shirt.
∗ (C) There are four distance events available to enter.
(D) 15- to 18-year-olds must enter the full marathon.

解説 下線部3から、種目としてはフルマラソンの他、10キロ、5キロ、3キロレースがあることがわかるので、(C)が正解。同じ文に「フルマラソンへの参加資格があるのは15歳から18歳まで」とあるが、must enter (参加しなくてはならない) とは書かれていないので、(D)は誤り。1に、例外的に大人も参加できる場合について書かれているので、(A)も不適切。2では1の内容を受け、「(例外に該当する)参加者はTシャツの購入と着用を求められる」と述べられている。よって、(B)も誤り。第1、第2段落に情報が分散しているので、素早い情報検索力が必要となる。

13. Where does the full marathon end?
(A) The Information Center
∗ (B) Riverdale Town Square
(C) Riverdale Museum
(D) Douglas University

解説 下線部4によると、すべてのレースはRiverdale Town Squareからスタートする。そして、フルマラソンはcircuit run course (周回走行コース) に沿って進み、「スタートした地点でフィニッシュする」とある。よって、(B) Riverdale Town Squareが正解。(A) The Information Centerは大会参加手続きが行える場所、(C) Riverdale Museum、(D) Douglas Universityはコース沿いにある建物である。

14. What will occur at 2:00 P.M.?

　＊(A) Streets will reopen to cars.
　(B) The stage will be dismantled.　● dismantle ～を取り壊す、解体する
　(C) Winners will be announced.
　(D) A closing speech will be made.

解説　設問のキーワード2:00 P.M.を本文で探すと、下線部5にある。「午後2時に交通規制が解除される」とあるので、それを言い換えた (A) Streets will reopen to cars. が正解。(B) の「ステージが解体される」という記述は本文にないので不適切。レースの勝者発表に関する記述は6にあるが、正確な時間は書かれていないので(C)も誤り。(D)についての言及はない。

15. When will prizes be awarded to event winners?
　(A) On September 29
　(B) On October 15
　＊(C) On October 17
　(D) On October 20

解説　下線部7に「レース終了2日後に賞金が配当される」と書いてある。大会は10月15日にあるので、答えは(C)の10月17日。設問のawarded(～を与える)が本文allocated(～を割り当てる)の言い換え。(A)の9月29日は大会参加の申し込み締め切り日、(B)の10月15日は大会開催当日。下線部8から(D)の10月20日は大会結果が新聞に掲載される日。

問題 16-20 は次の広告とメールに関するものです。

Ps PRIME STAR

[1]Prime Star is Bermuda's largest provider of subscription video channels. We have over 30 channels to choose from and there are also package options designed to save you money. Individual channels are priced at $14 per month, or you can get a package of three or more for just a few extra dollars.

Music and Entertainment
Entertainment News
Music Box (nonstop music videos)
Rock and Pop Aficionado! (news and documentaries on rock and pop music)
$20 per month

Sports and Leisure
Sports World
The Travel Channel
Extreme Sports
This Sporting Life (documentaries)
$20 per month

Arts and Science
The Science Channel
History of the World
Music History
$20 per month

Film and Drama
The Drama Channel
Movies 4 You
World Movies
$25 per month

Family
Movies 4 You
Music Box (nonstop music videos)
This Sporting Life (documentaries)
Sitcoms (comedy programs)
Animation All Day
$30 per month

News and Current Affairs
News of the World
South American News
World Events
Local Current Affairs
Chat Shows
$20 per month

Ultimate Package
Movies 4 You
The Drama Channel
Music Box (nonstop music videos)
Sports World
News of the World
$50 per month

Order online at www.primestar.com to receive a starter kit including the receiver.

```
===================== E-Mail Message =====================
To:       Pierre Rousseau <prousseau@whiteswan.com>
From:     Kate Robinson <krobinson@primestar.com>
Date:     August 6
Subject:  Your subscription
```

Dear Mr. Rousseau,

I am writing in reply to your request to change your subscription. From the questionnaire you took on our Web site, we understand that ²you wanted access to the movie channel and the music channel in particular and not much of the rest of the package. As you noted, it would be cheaper to order them separately than to continue to subscribe to the current package.

We are pleased to inform you that this month we are running a special campaign which entitles anyone signing up for a package or a minimum of two individual channels to choose one more channel for free. Current customers who wish to switch their subscription are also eligible. Therefore, even if you request ³the news channel, which you occasionally watch, on top of your two favorite channels, you will get almost the same level of service at a much lower price.

There are some conditions which apply when changing the content of your service. ⁴The first is that there is a waiting period. The waiting period is one month in addition to the outstanding portion of the current month, unless the contract was scheduled for renewal at the end of the month in which the change was requested. In cases where a less expensive service option is chosen, ⁵there is a one-time handling fee of $20. ⁶Depending on the age of your system, you may be required to swap your current hardware for a new tuner, because many of the older systems are less flexible when it comes to package selection. We will contact you and let you know whether or not this will be necessary after your application has been processed.

Unfortunately, as the process is rather complicated, alterations to the packages cannot be handled via the Web site. ⁷Please call one of our friendly staff to discuss your account.

Sincerely,

Kate Robinson
Customer Service
Prime Star

[広告] ● ultimate 究極の
[メール] ● in reply to ~ 〜への返事として ● entitle A to B AにBする資格を与える ● occasionally 時々 ● on top of ~ 〜に加えて ● swap 〜を交換する ● alteration 変更 ● handle 〜を処理する

16. What kind of company is Prime Star?
(A) A production company   (B) A ticket broker
＊(C) A broadcaster   (D) A publisher

解説 ▶ Prime Star社の業種を問う問題。広告の下線部**1**に、この会社はBermuda's largest provider of subscription video channelsだとある。subscriptionは「(本や雑誌の)定期購読」の他に、「お金を払って受けられる一定期間のサービス」という意味もある。よって、Prime Star社は有料チャンネルを配信する会社だとわかるので、答えは(C) A broadcaster（放送会社）。

17. What package is Mr. Rousseau most likely subscribed to?
(A) Family
(B) Film and Drama
(C) Music and Entertainment
∗ (D) Ultimate Package

解説 メールの受取人のRousseau氏が現在加入しているパッケージを選ぶ問題。メールの2（映画と音楽チャンネルが見たかった）と、3（ニュースチャンネルも時々見る）から、現在加入中のパッケージは映画と音楽、ニュースを見ることができるものだとわかる。この条件に合うものを広告の表から探すと、Movies 4 You（映画）とMusic Box（音楽）、News of the World（ニュース）をすべて含む(D) Ultimate Packageとなる。

---

18. What is NOT a condition of making a change to service content?
∗ (A) The contract must be renewed.
(B) An administration charge is applicable.　● applicable 適用される
(C) There is a delay before changes are enacted.　● enact　実行する
(D) System hardware may need to be replaced.

解説 メールの第3段落に、今回のプラン変更に関する条件が述べられている。更新のタイミング等に関しての記述はあるが、(A)「契約は更新されなければならない」とは書かれていないので、(A)が正解。(B)は下線部5の「20ドルの1回限りの手数料がかかる」と合致する。administration chargeは本文のhandling feeの言い換えだ。(C)は4の「待機期間がある」に当てはまる。(D)は6で述べられているチューナー交換の可能性と合致する。

---

19. In the e-mail, the word "outstanding" in paragraph 3, line 3, is closest in meaning to
(A) superior　∗ (B) remaining　(C) unpaid　(D) distinguished

解説 同義語問題は、前後の文脈を手掛かりにして判断する。outstandingを(B) remaining「残りの」で置き換えると「今月の残りの日数分に加えて」となり文意が通るので、これが正解。outstandingには(C)「未払いの」や(D)「傑出した」という意味もあるが、この文脈では同義語にならない。

---

20. How is Mr. Rousseau asked to contact Prime Star?
(A) By e-mail
∗ (B) By telephone
(C) By accessing the Web site
(D) By visiting in person　● in person 直接会って

解説 連絡手段に関する情報は、文書の終盤にあることが多い。メールの7に「アカウントに関して相談するには、スタッフに電話してください」とあるため、(B) By telephoneが正解。直前に「手続きが複雑なので、ウェブサイト上ではパッケージの変更処理はできない」という説明があるので、(C)は不適切。

Ted's Talks ❷

TOEIC を超越する人3タイプ ── 1. Hobbyist（愛好家）

> ***They love TOEIC. They gamify English.***
> （TOEIC大好き。英語はゲームだ。）

　TOEICが持つゲーム性や、努力がスコアとなって反映される点に魅力を感じ、TOEIC愛好家になって満点を取り続ける人がいます。一度何かにハマったら熱中しやすい、凝り性な人に多いタイプです。彼らが成功する要因を大きく3つにまとめてみます。

● 楽しさ

　TOEIC受験者の大半は、就職や転職、会社から目標スコア達成を求められているといった事情から、やむなくTOEICに接しています。彼らにしてみれば、TOEICが大好きな人がこの世に存在するというのは、にわかには信じがたいことでしょう。しかし、テスト勉強を楽しみに変えることができれば、努力は苦しみでなくなり、テストはそれ以上の喜びや価値を与えてくれるものに変わります。

● 執着

ゲームというのは一度ハマると完全攻略したくなるもの。TOEICも同じで、いったんハマると頻出問題から難問の類いまで徹底的に調べたくなります。スコアが伸びないと悔しいので、再度挑戦を試みるでしょう。TOEICをゲームとして捉えることで、スコアへのこだわりと、目標達成まであきらめない気持ちが得られるのです。

● 協力

　同じ趣味を持つ仲間が集まれば、情報をシェアしたり、お互いに教え合ったり、時には競争したりすることができます。頑張っている人を見て鼓舞されたり、自分の頑張りを褒められたりすると、良い仲間意識ができ、さらに学習に打ち込もうという気持ちになるでしょう。

　TOEICを部分的にでも楽しみ、それを原動力に変えるということは、すべてのTOEIC受験者が参考にできるポイントです。また、同じ興味を持つ人が集まり、助け合うということは、社会的な生き物である私たち人間が持つ本能にも合っています。このアフリカのことわざも、仲間を得ることのメリットを説いています。

If you want to go fast, go alone. If you want to go far, go together.
（速く行きたいなら独りで行け。遠くまで行きたいなら共に行け）

CHAPTER 3

要約力
SUMMARIZING

このスキルが足りない人は…

- [ ] 語数の多い英文は、目が滑るばかりで意味が頭に入らない

- [ ] Part 7は、設問ごとに文書を読み直さなければ解けない

- [ ] 選択肢がどれもしっくりこないことがたまにある

CHAPTER 3
要約力
SUMMARIZING

➡ つながりとイメージをつかむ力
必要になるパート：Part 6／7

　「要約」とは、**「文章の要旨を短くまとめ、端的に把握すること」**です。Part 7 では、狭い範囲の精読や、短い語句を探す情報検索だけでは解けない高難度の問題が出題されます。要約力は、そうした上級レベルの問題を攻略するために必要なスキルです。

　要約のプロセスは、通常の読解と同じように、文字情報を意味に変換するところから始まります。フレーズや文といった小さい単位で取り込まれた情報は、頭の中で組み合わさって、意味のかたまりとして蓄積されていきます。個々の具体的な意味のかたまりは、次第に関連付けられ、抽象化され、より大きなトピックにまとまります。そして、最終的にはイメージとして記憶にとどまります。文章を一言一句覚えようとすると、細かい部分が邪魔をして、全体のつながりやイメージがつかめなくなりますが、要約モードの読み方では逆に**元の文言は思い出せないが、全体のつながりとイメージは頭に残っているという状態**になります。

　この「情報のつながりとイメージを頭に残す力」は、Part 6 の文脈型問題や、Part 7 の「～について何が述べられているか」といった問題を解く上で非常に重要です。文書を要約しながら読んでいけば、内容がイメージ化されて頭に残るので、設問と選択肢を見た瞬間に正解の候補が選べます。つまり**選択肢を文書の内容と照合する手間が減り、解答時間が大幅に短縮できる**わけです。

　要約力が求められるタイプの問題は、近年のTOEICで数多く出題されており、このスキルを磨くことはますます重要になってきています。診断テストの設問を例にとって、要約力が必要なパターンを見ていきましょう。

【Part 6】 p.11, 10（色字の選択肢が正解）

Many sports fans are reluctant to buy a season pass because they are concerned that they may be unable to make full use of their purchase. Unexpected work commitments and interstate transfers are commonly cited reasons for underutilized passes, resulting in a huge waste of money. To put minds at ease, GameOne is offering an insurance package that ensures you get true value for money.

Should you be unable to use your ------- for an extended period,
10. ＊(A) ticket
(B) services
(C) membership
(D) policy
GameOne will refund the value of the unused portion.

Part 6：いきなり空所周辺を見ず、文書のつながりを把握せよ

　Part 6では、空所前後だけでなく文脈を読み取らなければ解けない文脈型問題が、1文書に少なくとも1問はあります。昨今は2問入っていることも珍しくないので、設問ごとに文書内にキーを探しに行く解答法では、時間がかかりすぎます。要約モードで文書を読み、効率のいい解答を目指しましょう。

　上の問題の例を見てください。文書を冒頭から読んでいき、空所にたどり着くまでに「仕事や転勤で、スポーツ観戦のシーズンパスが使えなくなったときのための保険商品」というイメージを頭に残します。これができていれば**10**の「何が使えない場合にGameOne社は返金してくれるのか」という問いに対する答えはすでに(A)に絞り込めているはずです。しかし、他の選択肢を排除しきれない場合は、自分の選択が正しいという確証を得るために、キーを再検索しましょう。**優れた要約力と情報検索力が合わさって初めて、全問正解レベルの読解力となる**のです。

【Part 7】 p.12, 14

Sydney (August 10)—Since the leadership change in mid-May, there has been much speculation about how David Panetta, the new CEO, will make his mark on Australia's largest international airline.

The first hint of what the future holds came this week, when Dalton Air purchased 14 additional aircraft, albeit used, from Borden Aerospace. The company released a statement on Thursday saying that it would add eight destinations in Asia and Europe by next spring and is considering expanding the workforce accordingly. However, public relations manager, Joe Walker, acknowledged in an interview with the press that the latter piece of news would still require approval at the general meeting of shareholders next month.

Mr. Walker also mentioned that the undertaking might be achieved by merging with a smaller airline. Many experts in the industry speculate that because there is little time for them to hire and train staff before the first flights, it would be a logical step for the rapidly growing company. In that scenario, the new chief's business contacts from his time leading two other aviation companies might come in handy in finding an ideal partner.

14. What do industry experts predict for Dalton Air?
(A) Some of its employees will be retrained.
(B) A plan will be unanimously approved.
(C) Additional offices will be opened.
∗ (D) The number of personnel will increase.

● Part 7：ちらばった情報を数珠つなぎ式にまとめる

　この問題は、設問中のキーワード、industry expertsを文書中に求め（第3段落のMany experts in the industry)、その周辺を読んでも、解答に必要な明確な根拠が得られません。しかし、第2段落から「Dalton Airは従業員数を増やすことを検討している」という情報を読み取れていれば、第3段落で述べられる「合併」が、社員獲得のための手段であることがすんなりと理解できるはずです。「Dalton Airの新CEO就任→機体の購入→ルート拡大→従業員も必要→新規雇用ではなく合併

でまかなう」のように**情報を数珠つなぎにしていき、相関関係を把握する**わけです。こういった読み方ができれば、ちらばった情報を統合して答える問題も、文書内を右往左往することなく即答できます。

　本番のテストでは、要約ができなくても、消去法等を駆使すれば9割程度の問題には正解できるでしょう。しかし、わずかながら出題されるBEYOND 990erとその他を分ける問題には、正解できないかもしれません。要約力を身につけるには、模試などでPart 6や7を解く際、いったん設問から離れて文書を通読し、要点把握をしてみることをお勧めします。また、次ページからの高地トレーニングも試してみてください。

POINT

- ☐ 長文読解はつながりとイメージの把握が上級へのレベルアップのカギ。
- ☐ Part 6の文脈型問題は要約力＋情報検索力で効率と精度を両立。
- ☐ Part 7の「ちらばった情報」は、「お互いに関連した情報」にすることで即答可能。

CHAPTER 3
要約力 SUMMARIZING

→ トレーニング

Menu 1

問題文を要約しながら読むトレーニングをしよう。

文書を読み、英語の要約文の空所を適切な語句（文書中にあるとは限らない）で埋めよう。先頭の1文字がヒントとして与えられている。**制限時間は5〜8分。**

1. レター　　　5分

Dear Mr. Peterson,

Thank you for interviewing for the senior accountant position at Drummond Engineering last week.

We were very impressed by your strong credentials and proven track record in accounting. We will be conducting several more interviews with other candidates over the coming two weeks, so please bear with us until we contact you regarding the next step.

In the meantime, could you double-check the phone number for your reference, Ms. Jane Adoyo, that you indicated on your application? We tried to reach her at the phone number you provided, only to receive an automated message saying it was no longer in use. If she is not available for us to contact, please nominate another person as your professional reference.

We are looking forward to hearing from you.

Sincerely,

Roberta Paris
Head of Human Resources
Drummond Engineering

要約 ▶ The human resources manager asks Mr. Peterson to (1. s------) by for instructions regarding the next course of action. She also requests (2. c------) of some (3. c------) information. Mr. Peterson may need to (4. n------) another person from his (5. p------) places of work.

2. 社内メモ

⏰ 5分

To: All employees
From: Kate Winehouse
Date: April 9
Subject: Welcome to Randy Davis

It is an honor to welcome Mr. Davis to the research department at FemChem Pharmaceuticals. We all enjoyed meeting with him in March when he came to discuss a study he was conducting at the University of Southern Maine (USM). He is taking over from Jenny Vasquez whom, coincidentally, he worked alongside as a junior researcher at USM more than 10 years ago. He will be bringing a vast amount of knowledge and expertise to the team, and I am sure you are all looking forward to working with him.

Aside from his work as a chemical researcher, he is a great person and an excellent manager. It goes without saying that he will be sorely missed at the university. Nevertheless, we are hoping that his appointment here will help strengthen our ties with the excellent researchers there and that we will continue to experience the mutual benefits of our collaborative work.

To formally welcome Mr. Davis to the team, the company is hosting a dinner party at the Sunshine Hotel on East Street. The date is set for April 15 from 7 P.M. If you are unable to attend, please inform my personal assistant, Jim Norris, by e-mail no later than Friday this week.

Sincerely,
Kate

要約 ▶ Mr. Davis is (1. r------) Ms. Vasquez, who was a (2. c------) of his at the University of Southern Maine. The company intends to (3. m------) its relationship with the university. A party will be held to celebrate his joining the team and people who will be (4. a------) are required to provide (5. n------).

3. 広告とメール

⏱ 8分

Andy's Car Rental
12 Quarry Street Newfarm Minnesota 56214
Top Quality Cars at Competitive Rates

To celebrate the opening of our new depot in Michigan, we are offering a special package. Rent a luxury sedan at the price of a budget hatchback car during July. This includes free satellite navigation and unlimited kilometers.

Additionally, you can pick up and drop off your car in different locations without paying a relocation fee. Check out some of our standard low rates:

Economy Car $45 per day   Large Wagon $60 per day
Mid-sized Sedan $55 per day   Luxury Sedan $80 per day

All of our cars are high-quality, dependable, late model vehicles. We can even deliver to your home or place of work for a modest fee. Another new depot is on its way to Missouri. Check us out on the Web at andyscarrental.com!

From: Jon Bay <jbay@andyscarrental.com>
To: Mohandas Singh <msingh@wonwebone.com>
Subject: Information
Date: 23 June

Dear Mr. Singh:

Thank you for renting from Andy's Car Rental. You are one of the first customers at our new depot and therefore qualify for our special offer. I've taken the liberty of applying the offer to your request, so I hope you are pleasantly surprised when you come to pick up the vehicle.

Please check the particulars below to ensure your booking is entirely accurate. If it is as you requested, please contact us by phone with your credit card details to finalize the reservation.

Mr. Mohandas Singh 45 Juliet Street Milwaukee WI 53217	**Pick up:** Michigan Depot
	Time: 7:00 A.M. July 7
	Return: NY APT
	Time: 10:00 A.M. July 9
Extras: Satellite Navigation	
Rate: $45 per day (Special Celebration Package)	

要約 ▶ Mr. Singh is going to pick up his rental car in (1. M------). He is offered an (2. u------) on his car as the rental company is running a (3. p------). He is asked to confirm the (4. d------) of his request and make a phone call regarding the (5. p------ m------).

4. 記事とメール

8分

The Mansfield Times

September 1 – Jason Cox from the band X-Fayed is to be honored for his contributions to charity this week. He encouraged a group of fellow musicians to join him in providing the charity concert, Bona Fide Ride to raise money for medical research. Five of the country's most popular bands, including the Surf Riders, agreed to take part in the concert and their combined fan base ensured sold-out shows across the country.

The goal was to raise a million dollars, but due to massive public support, they more than doubled that amount. The money was divided among three very promising research foundations.

The award is known as the DAP Award and is sponsored by the David Association to celebrate people making a difference through art. Mr. Cox says that he is very appreciative of the honor, but also took the time to mention each of the other bands that gave up their time and effort to make the events possible.

To: Jason Cox <jcox@xfayed.com>
From: Roland Turner <rturner@mrsax.com>
Subject: Thanks
Date: September 2

I'm just writing to let you know how happy we all are that you got the award. Your leadership is always an inspiration to all of us, and it was a real honor to be called upon to perform at such an important event.

Don't forget the barbeque at Dwayne Smith's house on Saturday. He has invited people involved in the event to get together, so it will be important to everyone that you are there.

Best,
Roland

要約 ▶ Mr. Cox organized a charity concert in support of a good (1. c------). The (2. p------) were donated to several institutions. Mr. Cox's work is to be (3. r------) with an award. He received an e-mail from Mr. Turner, who is a (4. m------). The e-mail was to (5. r------) him of an event scheduled for the weekend.

Menu 1 の解答・解説

文書中、要点として拾うべき情報は▢で示してある。**色数字**は空所の番号と対応している。

※問題文の訳文は紙面では省略（訳文の入手方法はp. 7をご覧ください）。

1. レター

> Dear Mr. Peterson,
>
> Thank you for interviewing for the senior accountant position at Drummond Engineering last week.
>
> We were very impressed by your strong credentials and proven track record in accounting. We will be conducting several more interviews with other candidates over the coming two weeks, so **¹please bear with us** until we contact you regarding the next step.
>
> In the meantime, **²could you double-check ³the phone number for your reference**, Ms. Jane Adoyo, that you indicated on your application? We tried to reach her at the phone number you provided, only to receive an automated message saying it was no longer in use. If she is not available for us to contact, **⁴please nominate ⁵another person as your professional reference**.
>
> We are looking forward to hearing from you.
>
> Sincerely,
>
> Roberta Paris
> Head of Human Resources
> Drummond Engineering

● senior accountant 上級会計士 ● credentials 資格 ● proven track record 実績

要約 ▶ The human resources manager asks Mr. Peterson to (1. stand) by for instructions regarding the next course of action. She also requests (2. confirmation) of some (3. contact) information. Mr. Peterson may need to (4. nominate / name) another person from his (5. previous / past) places of work.

解説 ▶ 冒頭部分は場面・状況・登場人物の関係などの基本的情報が述べられることが多いので、時間をかけてじっくり読もう。ここをあいまいな理解のまま通り過ぎると、かえって読解スピードが落ちる。この文書は、最初の1文で面接後のフォローアップのレターだとわかる。2文目のWe were very impressed by your ...のような表現は読み流していい社交辞令なので、「Peterson氏は会計の専門家」という人物に関する情報だけを拾う。一方、その後ろのplease bear with us ...や、第3段落のcould you double-check ...?のような依頼事項は注意を払うべきポイントだ。1はstand byで「待機する」の意を持つ句動詞で、後ろに[for＋名詞] や [to不定詞] を取ることができる。2は連絡先情報のconfirmation（確認）が入る。ここにclarification（意味を明らかにするための説明）は不適切。

104

2. 社内メモ

To: All employees
From: Kate Winehouse
Date: April 9
Subject: Welcome to Randy Davis

It is an honor to welcome Mr. Davis to the research department at FemChem Pharmaceuticals. We all enjoyed meeting with him in March when he came to discuss a study he was conducting at the University of Southern Maine (USM). [1]He is taking over from Jenny Vasquez whom, coincidentally, [2]he worked alongside as a junior researcher at USM more than 10 years ago. He will be bringing a vast amount of knowledge and expertise to the team, and I am sure you are all looking forward to working with him.

Aside from his work as a chemical researcher, he is a great person and an excellent manager. It goes without saying that he will be sorely missed at the university. Nevertheless, we are hoping that his appointment here will help [3]strengthen our ties with the excellent researchers there and that we will continue to experience the mutual benefits of our collaborative work.

To formally welcome Mr. Davis to the team, the company is hosting a dinner party at the Sunshine Hotel on East Street. The date is set for April 15 from 7 P.M. If you are [4]unable to attend, [5]please inform my personal assistant, Jim Norris, by e-mail no later than Friday this week.

Sincerely,
Kate

- take over from 〜 〜から引き継ぐ ● expertise 専門知識・技能 ● sorely ひどく、非常に

要約 Mr. Davis is (1. replacing) Ms. Vasquez, who was a (2. colleague / coworker) of his at the University of Southern Maine. The company intends to (3. maintain) its relationship with the university. A party will be held to celebrate his joining the team and people who will be (4. absent / away) are required to provide (5. notice / notification).

解説 件名や第1段落1文目から、Davis氏が新しく会社に加わることを知らせる社内通知だとわかる。同段落4〜5行目から、Davis氏の前任者であるVasquez氏は、Davis氏と大学で一緒に働いていたことがわかる。こういった登場人物の関係に関する情報は、高確率で設問に絡んでくる。第2段落ではDavis氏を褒めたたえる部分は読み流し、彼を引き抜いた後も大学との関係は継続したい、という意思表明をチェックしよう。第3段落は業務連絡。「欠席の場合は連絡が必要」ということが読み取れれば要約としては十分だ。本番のテストでは、設問に応じて、必要があれば詳細を拾いに戻ろう。

3. 広告とメール

Andy's Car Rental

12 Quarry Street Newfarm Minnesota 56214
Top Quality Cars at Competitive Rates

To celebrate the opening of [1]our new depot in Michigan, [2, 3]we are offering a special package. Rent a luxury sedan at the price of a budget hatchback car during July. This includes free satellite navigation and unlimited kilometers.

Additionally, you can pick up and drop off your car in different locations without paying a relocation fee. Check out some of our standard low rates:

[2]Economy Car $45 per day   Large Wagon $60 per day
Mid-sized Sedan $55 per day   [2]Luxury Sedan $80 per day

All of our cars are high-quality, dependable, late model vehicles. We can even deliver to your home or place of work for a modest fee. Another new depot is on its way to Missouri. Check us out on the Web at andyscarrental.com!

From: Jon Bay <jbay@andyscarrental.com>
To: Mohandas Singh <msingh@wonwebone.com>
Subject: Information
Date: 23 June

Dear Mr. Singh:

Thank you for renting from Andy's Car Rental. [1]You are one of the first customers at our new depot and therefore [2]qualify for our special offer. I've taken the liberty of [2]applying the offer to your request, so I hope you are pleasantly surprised when you come to pick up the vehicle.

[4]Please check the particulars below to ensure your booking is entirely accurate. If it is as you requested, [5]please contact us by phone with your credit card details to finalize the reservation.

Mr. Mohandas Singh 45 Juliet Street Milwaukee WI 53217	[1]**Pick up:** Michigan Depot
	Time: 7:00 A.M. July 7
	Return: NY APT
	Time: 10:00 A.M. July 9
Extras: Satellite Navigation	
[2]**Rate:** $45 per day (Special Celebration Package)	

［広告］● depot 車両基地、倉庫　● budget 予算に合った、手頃な　● hatchback car ハッチバック車
※車体後部に上に開く大きなドアがある自動車。　● relocation fee 移動費用
［メール］● take the liberty of ~ 失礼ながら~する　● particulars 詳細

要約 ▶ Mr. Singh is going to pick up his rental car in (1. Michigan). He is offered an (2. upgrade) on his car as the rental company is running a (3. promotion). He is asked to confirm the (4. details) of his request and make a phone call regarding the (5. payment method).

解説 ▶ 広告の場合は、当然ながら「どんな製品・サービス」が宣伝されているのかが最初の要点。各製品・サービスの違いや特別提供、利用条件なども、ひと通り確認しておきたい。客であるSingh氏がレンタカーをピックアップする場所や、利用できる特別提供の内容は、広告とメールの両文書を参照して導くべき情報。メール第2段落には、Singh氏への依頼事項が2つ述べられている。TOEICでもビジネス英語でも、中心となる情報は依頼事項や提案内容だ。関連する表現には自然と目が留まるよう、日頃から意識しておこう。2は、広告第1段落2行目に「低料金のハッチバックカーの価格で高級セダンをご利用ください」とあるので、「値引き」のような語句ではなくupgrade（アップグレードする、ランクを上げる）が正解。5は「クレジットカード情報」を抽象化したpayment method（支払い方法）が入る。

4. 記事とメール

The Mansfield Times

September 1 – [1, 3]Jason Cox from the band X-Fayed is to be honored for his contributions to charity this week. [4]He encouraged a group of fellow musicians to join him in providing the charity concert, Bona Fide Ride [1]to raise money for medical research. Five of the country's most popular bands, including the Surf Riders, agreed to take part in the concert and their combined fan base ensured sold-out shows across the country.

The goal was to raise a million dollars, but due to massive public support, they more than doubled that amount. [2]The money was divided among three very promising research foundations.

The award is known as the DAP Award and is sponsored by the David Association to celebrate people making a difference through art. Mr. Cox says that he is very appreciative of the honor, but also took the time to mention each of the other bands that gave up their time and effort to make the events possible.

To: Jason Cox <jcox@xfayed.com>
From: Roland Turner <rturner@mrsax.com>
Subject: Thanks
Date: September 2

I'm just writing to let you know how happy we all are that you got the award. Your leadership is always an inspiration to all of us, and [4]it was a real honor to be called upon to perform at such an important event.

[5]Don't forget the barbeque at Dwayne Smith's house on Saturday. He has invited people involved in the event to get together, so it will be important to everyone that you are there.

Best,
Roland

［記事］● fan base ファン層　● massive 圧倒的な　● promising 前途有望な　● appreciative of ~ ~に感謝している
［メール］● inspiration 刺激をくれる人、鼓舞する人

要約 ▶ Mr. Cox organized a charity concert in support of a good (1. cause). The (2. proceeds / profits) were donated to several institutions. Mr. Cox's work is to be (3. recognized / rewarded) with an award. He received an e-mail from Mr. Turner, who is a (4. musician). The e-mail was to (5. remind) him of an event scheduled for the weekend.

Menu 1 の解答・解説

解説 まとまった文書が2つ並ぶダブルパッセージでは、特に1つ目の文書の要約を記憶にとどめることが重要だ。解答に必要な情報が1つ目の文書にないという確信が持てれば、それは2つ目の文書にあると断定でき、2文書の間をさまようことがなくなるからだ。この問題の1つ目の文書である記事の要点は、Cox氏がチャリティーイベントを行い、それについて表彰されるということ。「医療研究のための資金を集めた」という部分が要約文の1文目では抽象化され、in support of a good cause（慈善目的のために）と言い換えられている。記事にはCox氏が「仲間の音楽家たち」にイベント参加を呼び掛けたとあり、Turner氏がCox氏に宛てたメールには「演奏することができて光栄だった」と書かれているので、4はmusicianだ。memberでは「何のメンバーか」がわからないので不適。

CHAPTER 3 要約力 SUMMARIZING

実践問題

仕上げに、本番形式の難問にチャレンジ。文書を要約しながら効率よく解答しよう。

Part 7

文書に関する設問の解答として、最も適切なものを1つずつ選ぼう。

（解答・解説はpp. 118～130）

Questions 1-4 refer to the following article.

● 4分

While Australia's Gold Coast is best known for its world-class beaches, many people are unaware of its emergence as one of the fastest growing economies in the country. On May 5, Geoff Gray will bring together these two aspects of the city by launching a business with ties to one of the Gold Coast's most popular pastimes, surfing.

Gray has named this new retail company Bunya, and it is a highly anticipated venture from the five-time Surfing World Masters champion and Gold Coast native. As an endorser of PureShore, a major Brisbane-based surf company, Gray had to remain silent about the project until the expiration of his contract. However, rumors about his start-up had been circulating for some time. Due to Gray's high profile as a visionary surfer, there is a lot of anticipation in the surfing community. On Saturday, the founder will talk to the crowd at the Elkhorn Hall and introduce the key concepts of his new venture, which will reportedly make use of recycled materials at a completely refurbished local factory.

This is not his first foray into the retail sector. At the peak of his fame as a professional surfer, he launched a line of sunglasses called Gray Specs. The business looked bound for success but did not go as well as expected. Most people attributed the outcome to the substandard quality of the products. The end of Gray Specs' short life was marked by the sale of its only store to PureShore, which was seeking to expand its retail operation. The premises have been used as an outlet by the market leader ever since.

The venue for Bunya's launch event is, in fact, adjacent to the old Gray Specs store. Some have expressed concern about whether this location will be large enough to cope with the expected gathering. Those who would like to attend should be aware that parking will be hard to find. There is one more caveat. Although the venue is a conference center, the dress code is explicitly surf wear.

1. What is suggested about Bunya?
   (A) Its name is derived from the founder's.
   (B) It has been acquired by PureShore.
   (C) It is a surfing goods retailer.
   (D) It has won several prizes.

   Ⓐ Ⓑ Ⓒ Ⓓ

2. According to the article, why was Gray Specs unsuccessful?
   (A) Its products were poorly made.
   (B) Advertising was inadequate.
   (C) The brand name was unpopular.
   (D) Its items were priced too high.

   Ⓐ Ⓑ Ⓒ Ⓓ

3. Where will Mr. Gray speak?
   (A) At a surf resort
   (B) In a production facility
   (C) At Bunya's main office
   (D) Near a PureShore store

   Ⓐ Ⓑ Ⓒ Ⓓ

4. What advice does the article offer for people who want to attend the launch?
   (A) Check a map beforehand
   (B) Avoid formal attire
   (C) Make a reservation
   (D) Monitor schedule changes

   Ⓐ Ⓑ Ⓒ Ⓓ

Questions 5-9 refer to the following letter and Web page. 6分

E-Mail Message

To: Monica Yang <myang@limyangfinancial.co.kr>
From: George McHarris <george.mcharris@mcharrisconsulting.com>
Date: 11 October
Subject: Re: Network Security

Dear Ms. Yang,

I am writing in reply to your letter seeking advice about what company to trust with your network upgrades. Since you are in the banking sector, security is of the highest importance. I would suggest that you employ the most dependable company and refrain from trying to save money on this part of your business. There are a few companies that currently handle this level of contract, but there is only one that I can advocate with complete confidence.

NetOne Technology is the most advanced corporate systems integration company in Seoul. It was founded 10 years ago by Tony Wales and Lee Jung Nam, two graduates of the Lo Yam Institute of Technology. Despite its short history, the company has already gained a reputation for integrity in the industry. Mr. Wales, the chief technology officer, manages a team of highly qualified system engineers installing networks at the offices of their very upmarket clientele.

I am happy to provide this level of advice free of charge. Should you require further consultations on any aspect of Lim Yang Financial, I hope you will depend on our firm.

Sincerely,

George McHarris
McHarris Consulting

---

http://www.limyangfinancial.co.kr

Lim Yang Financial

Welcome to Lim Yang Financial, a young company with a modern approach to capital investment management. Since our founding a decade ago, we have been leading the industry by introducing the latest investment techniques for corporate as well as individual clients in need of secure and reliable financial solutions.

Returns

We employ only the finest professionals, backed up by the latest knowledge of asset management models so that you are always making the best possible financial decisions. Over the last year our clients' return on investment has been 14 percent on average – one of the most impressive figures in the industry.

Risk Management

Balancing the need for safety with high returns is the cornerstone of this industry. Lim Yang Financial reduces risk by accurately estimating various financial scenarios. We constantly research and monitor market events in order to find ways of addressing risk while maintaining high returns.

Security

Our networking and corporate security is all handled by NetOne Technology, whose reputation for excellence is second to none.

5. Why is Mr. McHarris contacting Ms. Yang?
   (A) To advertise his services
   (B) To nominate an executive
   (C) To share some expertise
   (D) To recommend a network system

6. What does Mr. McHarris ask Ms. Yang to do?
   (A) Inspect her company's infrastructure
   (B) Consider his firm for an advisory role
   (C) Prioritize budget needs over performance
   (D) Provide further information on her organization

7. What is indicated about Lim Yang Financial?
   (A) It is partnered with McHarris Consulting.
   (B) It only employs certified financial experts.
   (C) It guarantees high interest rates to its clients.
   (D) It is as old as NetOne Technology.

8. On the Web page, the word "second" in paragraph 4, line 2, is closest in meaning to
   (A) alternative
   (B) inferior
   (C) succeeding
   (D) additional

9. What is suggested about Ms. Yang?
   (A) She took advice from an external specialist.
   (B) She has worked with consultants before.
   (C) Her company renewed a service agreement.
   (D) Her business dispatches on-site engineers.

Questions 10-14 refer to the following memo and e-mail.

MEMO

PixelHouse Animation Inc.

From: Ding Junhui
To: Animation Staff, Chicago Office
Subject: Schedule
Date: May 23

We have a very tight schedule over the second half of the year. I fear that we may have taken on work in excess of our capacity. Nevertheless, turning down contracts at this stage in our company's growth seems unwise. I understand that many of you will probably feel tired and overworked, but you will all be duly compensated at bonus time for any extra tasks you take on.

Before I continue, I should thank Melinda Rosen and Karl Huttenmeister, who have been doing voice acting work on the GD Pet Food advertisements and the engineering video respectively. Despite the heavy workload in the visual effects section, the two invested their time in taking voice acting lessons at a local college prior to making their first attempts in this field. Having qualified voice actors on the staff has made our workflow much more flexible. While we are extremely pleased with the work of our two new voice actors, we want more people to diversify their skills. Staff who are interested and not currently involved in urgent projects should contact Travis Young in Talent & Development. He will arrange an interview with you first and coordinate scheduling of training with your supervisor if you are successful.

The following is a list of our current animation jobs. Let me know immediately if you are interested in taking part in any of these in particular. Provisional assignments will be posted on the bulletin board on Wednesday morning and they should be finalized by the end of the month.

Client	Length	Genre	Due Date
Giordano Hair Care	20 seconds	Advertising	July 10
Mondrian Educational Videos	90 minutes	Engineering	August 19
Jackson Entertainment (Out of Luck, Chuck Ep1)	17 minutes	Children's Entertainment	September 30
Granite Software Company (Ding Bats)	12 minutes	Games	October 12
Globus Films (Marty the Fly)	25 minutes	Movie	November 13

E-Mail Message

From: Denny House <dhouse@pixelhouse.com>
To: Ding Junhui <djunhui@pixelhouse.com>
Date: May 25
Subject: The schedule

Good morning Ding,

I have seen your memo from Monday. I agree that we need more people with a variety of skills on the staff and commend your encouragement of that.

I have a concern about work allocation. The children's entertainment project is an extremely important contract for us. This is only a pilot episode, and the broadcasting company will decide whether or not to make more based on the success of this video. Please make sure people who have shown creativity and experience are assigned. Also, I would like to receive an update on the status of the engineering video. It is a long complicated job but we cannot let it fall behind schedule.

I am sure you have already considered these points but I wanted to mention them, just in case. I will be in the office on Thursday to discuss various other matters.

All the best,
Denny House

10. What concern does Mr. Junhui mention in the memo?
(A) Some clients might terminate contracts.
(B) The staff have been engaged in many projects.
(C) The workload is becoming overly demanding.
(D) Requests for additional funding may be turned down.   Ⓐ Ⓑ Ⓒ Ⓓ

11. What is suggested about Ms. Rosen and Mr. Huttenmeister?
(A) They have worked together on some projects.
(B) They are employed as full-time voice actors.
(C) They will receive extra financial rewards.
(D) They are to undergo additional training.   Ⓐ Ⓑ Ⓒ Ⓓ

12. Who most likely is Travis Young?
(A) A human resources manager
(B) A graphic design specialist
(C) A television program producer
(D) A voice acting instructor   Ⓐ Ⓑ Ⓒ Ⓓ

13. What is a purpose of the e-mail?
(A) To offer advice on staff assignment
(B) To ask for an updated timetable
(C) To emphasize the importance of teamwork
(D) To praise Mr. Junhui for obtaining new skills   Ⓐ Ⓑ Ⓒ Ⓓ

14. About which project does Mr. House request further information?
(A) Giordano Hair
(B) Mondrian Educational Videos
(C) Jackson Entertainment
(D) Globus Films   Ⓐ Ⓑ Ⓒ Ⓓ

Questions 15-19 refer to the following advertisement and e-mail.

Maine's most-circulated local newspaper, *The Kilgore Times*, is looking to hire a financial expert to cover business and economic concerns around the state. The newspaper is read by leaders in Maine's business sector as well as the general public, so it is important that stories have information relevant and interesting to both. We have been increasingly successful with our Web site in recent years and been expanding into online broadcasting, with some of our writing staff doubling as newsreaders and commentators for video content.

The successful applicant will be required to appear on such projects or, periodically, write abridged versions of articles suitable for broadcast. Applicants with a background in this more fruitful aspect of our business are preferred. As we have strong relationships with the local community, our writers are required to travel and report on local sporting and cultural events.

Because the position is currently unfilled, we are looking for a candidate who is able to start this month. The deadline for applications is February 14. Applications should be made directly to the editor by e-mail at editor@kilgoretimes.com and include all relevant documents as attachments. Otherwise, they may be mailed to the following address:

Attention: Dave Gilbey
Kilgore Times Newspaper
13 Donald Street, Kilgore, Maine 04434

E-Mail Message

To: editor@kilgoretimes.com
From: groche@prolight.com
Date: February 9
Subject: Financial writer position
Attachment: GRoche_Samples.doc

Dear Mr. Gilbey,

I am writing with regard to the position for a financial writer, which I saw advertised in *West Hill Post* on Thursday.

I work as a business writer at *The Stanton Sentinel* and was originally hired for a position very similar to the one you are trying to fill. Over the past 12 years that I have been at the company's online content division, it has received a number of awards for the articles and other digital content that my team and I have produced but, unfortunately, the company has decided to rely more heavily on outsourced content for its Web site. Therefore, I am looking for a position which will provide me with the broader set of responsibilities I am accustomed to.

My educational background also makes me an ideal candidate for the business-oriented yet creative position. I completed a business and economics degree at Glen Ridge University and later received a diploma from Stanton Vocational College after undertaking a video production course there. Subsequently, I did a two-year post graduate course in journalism at Brighton College. You should note that Stanton

Vocational College was merged with Brighton College three years ago and that my diploma reflects that change.

I am still living in Stanton and the earliest I could move to Maine would be March 12. Nevertheless, should my application be successful, I am prepared to organize temporary accommodation so that there will be no conflict with work assignments during the week. Although the advertisement in Stanton's local newspaper did not indicate whether relocation costs would be borne by the company, financial support would be highly appreciated.

Please find attached the required documents. I look forward to hearing from you.

Sincerely,
Gunter Roche

15. What is suggested about *The Kilgore Times*?
　(A) It concentrates on financial news.
　(B) Its writers are required to direct videos.
　(C) It generates more profits online than in print.
　(D) Its newspaper sales have been growing.

16. What is a requirement of the advertised position?
　(A) Willingness to travel abroad
　(B) The ability to cover diverse subjects
　(C) Experience in news reporting
　(D) Current residence in Maine

17. According to the e-mail, why is Mr. Roche applying for the position?
　(A) To produce digital content
　(B) To work for a larger company
　(C) To experience life in Kilgore
　(D) To have more opportunities for promotion

18. What is suggested about *West Hill Post*?
　(A) It provides digital content.
　(B) It sponsors events in Maine.
　(C) It is a weekly publication.
　(D) It is based in Stanton.

19. What is NOT indicated about Mr. Roche?
　(A) He is concerned about an allowance.
　(B) He has contributed online articles in the past.
　(C) He is available to start work by the required date.
　(D) He transferred between two schools.

実践問題の解答・解説

※問題文の訳文は紙面では省略（訳文の入手方法はp. 7をご覧ください）。

問題 1-4 は次の記事に関するものです。

While Australia's Gold Coast is best known for its world-class beaches, many people are unaware of its emergence as one of the fastest growing economies in the country. On May 5, [1] Geoff Gray will bring together these two aspects of the city by launching a business with ties to one of the Gold Coast's most popular pastimes, surfing.

[2] Gray has named this new retail company Bunya, and it is a highly anticipated venture from the five-time Surfing World Masters champion and Gold Coast native. As an endorser of PureShore, a major Brisbane-based surf company, Gray had to remain silent about the project until the expiration of his contract. However, rumors about his start-up had been circulating for some time. Due to Gray's high profile as a visionary surfer, there is a lot of anticipation in the surfing community. [3] On Saturday, the founder will talk to the crowd at the Elkhorn Hall and introduce the key concepts of his new venture, which will reportedly make use of recycled materials at a completely refurbished local factory.

This is not his first foray into the retail sector. At the peak of his fame as a professional surfer, [4] he launched a line of sunglasses called Gray Specs. The business looked bound for success but did not go as well as expected. Most people attributed the outcome to the substandard quality of the products. [5] The end of Gray Specs' short life was marked by the sale of its only store to PureShore, which was seeking to expand its retail operation. The premises have been used as an outlet by the market leader ever since.

[6] The venue for Bunya's launch event is, in fact, adjacent to the old Gray Specs store. Some have expressed concern about whether this location will be large enough to cope with the expected gathering. Those who would like to attend should be aware that parking will be hard to find. There is one more caveat. [7] Although the venue is a conference center, the dress code is explicitly surf wear.

- emergence 台頭、浮上 ● pastime 娯楽 ● endorser 広告塔、推奨する人 ● visionary 明確なビジョンを持った ● anticipation 期待 ● refurbished 改装した ● foray 進出 ● attribute A to B AをBのせいにする ● substandard 低水準の、基準を満たさない ● premises 店舗 ● adjacent to ~ ～に隣接した ● caveat 注意 ● explicitly はっきりと、明示的に

1. What is suggested about Bunya?
(A) Its name is derived from the founder's.
(B) It has been acquired by PureShore.
＊(C) It is a surfing goods retailer.
(D) It has won several prizes.

解説 下線部1から、Gray氏が創業しようとしているビジネスはサーフィンに関するものとわかる。2からは、それがBunyaという名の小売企業ということが読み取れる。これらの情報を要約すると、Bunyaについて述べられていることとしては、(C)「サーフィン用品の小売店である」が正解となる。

2. According to the article, why was Gray Specs unsuccessful?
＊(A) Its products were poorly made.
(B) Advertising was inadequate.
(C) The brand name was unpopular.
(D) Its items were priced too high.

解説 設問を解くために文書を読み直すのは最小限で済むようにしたい。第3段落、下線部4から、Gray SpecsとはGray氏が以前所有していたサングラスのブランド／会社だとわかる。この事業が失敗した原因として述べられているsubstandard quality（低水準の品質）をpoorly madeで言い換えた、(A)「製品の作りが悪かった」が正解。

3. Where will Mr. Gray speak?
(A) At a surf resort
(B) In a production facility
(C) At Bunya's main office
＊(D) Near a PureShore store

解説 下線部3と6から、Gray氏が新事業の発表イベントを行うElkhorn Hallは、Gray Specsのかつての店舗に隣接しているとわかる。5によると、Gray Specsの唯一の店舗はPureShoreに売却されている。従って、(D)「PureShoreの店の近く」が正解。このように3カ所の情報を参照させる問題も公開テストで出題されることがある。

4. What advice does the article offer for people who want to attend the launch?
(A) Check a map beforehand　　＊(B) Avoid formal attire
(C) Make a reservation　　(D) Monitor schedule changes

解説 新規事業発表会に興味を持った人たちへの情報は最終段落にある。第3段落の7で「ドレスコードはサーフウエア」であると参加者へ注意を喚起している。会場がフォーマルな服装の人たちが集まることが多いカンファレンスセンターであるにもかかわらず、サーフウエアという異例のドレスコードであることを言い換えた、(B)「フォーマルな服装をしない」が正解。他の選択肢はどれもアドバイスとしては良いものだが、実際には述べられていない。

問題 5-9 は次のメールとウェブページに関するものです。

```
====================== E-Mail Message ======================
To:       Monica Yang <myang@limyangfinancial.co.kr>
From:     George McHarris <george.mcharris@mcharrisconsulting.com>
Date:     11 October
Subject:  Re: Network Security
```

Dear Ms. Yang,

[1]I am writing in reply to your letter seeking advice about what company to trust with your network upgrades. Since you are in the banking sector, security is of the highest importance. I would suggest that you employ the most dependable company and refrain from trying to save money on this part of your business. There are a few companies that currently handle this level of contract, but there is only one that I can advocate with complete confidence.

NetOne Technology is the most advanced corporate systems integration company in Seoul. [2]It was founded 10 years ago by Tony Wales and Lee Jung Nam, two graduates of the Lo Yam Institute of Technology. Despite its short history, the company has already gained a reputation for integrity in the industry. Mr. Wales, the chief technology officer, manages a team of highly qualified system engineers installing networks at the offices of their very upmarket clientele.

[3]I am happy to provide this level of advice free of charge. [4]Should you require further consultations on any aspect of Lim Yang Financial, I hope you will depend on our firm.

Sincerely,

George McHarris
McHarris Consulting

---

http://www.limyangfinancial.co.kr

Lim Yang Financial

Welcome to Lim Yang Financial, a young company with a modern approach to capital investment management. [5]Since our founding a decade ago, we have been leading the industry by introducing the latest investment techniques for corporate as well as individual clients in need of secure and reliable financial solutions.

Returns

We employ only the finest professionals, backed up by the latest knowledge of asset management models so that you are always making the best possible financial decisions. Over the last year our clients' return on investment has been 14 percent on average – one of the most impressive figures in the industry.

Risk Management

Balancing the need for safety with high returns is the cornerstone of this industry. Lim Yang Financial reduces risk by accurately estimating various financial scenarios. We constantly research and monitor market events in order to find ways of addressing risk while maintaining high returns.

Security

⁶Our networking and corporate security is all handled by NetOne Technology, whose reputation for excellence is second to none. ▼

[メール] ● refrain 差し控える ● advocate 〜を推薦する ● corporate systems integration company 企業システム総合会社 ● integrity（職業的）規範 ● upmarket 高級志向の ● clientele 顧客（集合的に）
[ウェブページ] ● capital investment management 資本投資管理 ● return 利益 ● asset management 資産管理 ● cornerstone 基礎

5. Why is Mr. McHarris contacting Ms. Yang?
   (A) To advertise his services
   (B) To nominate an executive
   ＊(C) To share some expertise
   (D) To recommend a network system

解説 メールの下線部1に「ネットワークシステムのアップグレードをどの会社に任せるべきかについて助言がほしい、というお手紙にご返答いたします」とあり、第2段落冒頭でNetOne Technologyという会社を紹介しているので、正解は(C)「専門知識を伝えるため」だ。推薦しているのは会社であって「システム」ではないので、(D)は間違い。第3段落からはサービスを売り込む意図も見えるので、(A)「自社のサービスを宣伝するため」も魅力的だが、advertise（宣伝する）という語は主に「メディアなどを通して宣伝を行う」という意味なので不適。

6. What does Mr. McHarris ask Ms. Yang to do?
   (A) Inspect her company's infrastructure
   ＊(B) Consider his firm for an advisory role
   (C) Prioritize budget needs over performance
   (D) Provide further information on her organization

解説 メールには直接的な依頼表現はないが、下線部4の「Lim Yang Financial社のいかなる業務分野に関することでも、ご相談が必要であれば、わが社を頼ってくださるよう望みます」という表現が遠回しな依頼になる。これを「彼の会社を顧問役として検討する」と言い換えた(B)が正解。I hope you will ... も依頼表現の一種だ。

7. What is indicated about Lim Yang Financial?
   (A) It is partnered with McHarris Consulting.
   (B) It only employs certified financial experts.
   (C) It guarantees high interest rates to its clients.
   ＊(D) It is as old as NetOne Technology.

解説 メールの2とウェブページの5に、NetOne TechnologyとLim Yang Financialがそれぞれ創立10年だという記述があるので、(D)が正解。Yang氏はMcHarris氏の助言は取り入れているが、彼の会社と「提携」をした根拠がないので(A)は不適切だ。ウェブページのReturnsの項でthe finest professionals（一流の専門家）を雇っているとあるが、certified（有資格者である）とは言っていないので(B)も不適。ReturnsやRisk Managementの項で、運用実績とリスク低減の取り組みに触れているが、「高利率を保証」してはいないので(C)も誤り。文書の本筋にとって重要ではない情報が絡むので、要約力に加え情報検索力も問われる問題だ。

8. On the Web page, the word "second" in paragraph 4, line 2, is closest in meaning to
   (A) alternative
   ＊(B) inferior
   (C) succeeding
   (D) additional

解説 選択肢の語はどれもsecondの同義語なので、文脈から判断しよう。be second to noneは「何者に対しても2番にならない＝何者にも劣らない」、つまり「一番だ」という意味の定型句。よって、「劣る」という意味を持つ(B) inferiorが正解。

9. What is suggested about Ms. Yang?
   ＊(A) She took advice from an external specialist.
   (B) She has worked with consultants before.
   (C) Her company renewed a service agreement.
   (D) Her business dispatches on-site engineers.

解説 解答のヒントが両文書のあちこちに分散している。メールの全文を読み、その内容を要約できていれば、選択肢の中で即除外できるもの、ウェブページ内に情報を求めるべきものの判断がしやすい。(B)はメールの中で述べられておらず、(D)はYang氏の会社、Lim Yang Financialの業務内容と矛盾する。(C)の契約「更新」の話はメールにはないし、ウェブページでも述べられていない。ウェブページの最下部6、セキュリティーの項目を見ると、Yang氏は、McHarris氏が推薦したNetOne Technology社にネットワーク業務を委託していることがわかる。よって、(A)「外部専門家の助言を採用した」が正解。

Ted流 TOEICの泳ぎ方　　………長続きする英語自己学習法………

続かない原因その2　Overdoing it
　プールに通い始めてまだ日が浅いのに、ものすごい長距離を泳いでぐったりしてしまう人がいます。こういう人もたいてい挫折します。1回1回の負荷が大きすぎると、次に来るのがおっくうになってしまうからです。調子がいいときでも、焦る気持ちを抑え、「もう少しいける」と思える程度で止めておきましょう。短期集中講座などの特別な機会は別ですが、日々の練習の量と強度は現実的なラインを考えて決め、徐々に負荷を上げていくべきです。

問題 10-14 は次の社内メモとメールに関するものです。

> **MEMO**
>
> **PixelHouse Animation Inc.**
>
> From: Ding Junhui
> To: Animation Staff, Chicago Office
> Subject: Schedule
> Date: May 23
>
> [1]We have a very tight schedule over the second half of the year. I fear that we may have taken on work in excess of our capacity. Nevertheless, turning down contracts at this stage in our company's growth seems unwise. I understand that many of you will probably feel tired and overworked, but [2]you will all be duly compensated at bonus time for any extra tasks you take on.
>
> Before I continue, I should thank [3]Melinda Rosen and Karl Huttenmeister, who have been doing voice acting work on the GD Pet Food advertisements and the engineering video respectively. [4]Despite the heavy workload in the visual effects section, the two invested their time in taking voice acting lessons at a local college prior to making their first attempts in this field. Having qualified voice actors on the staff has made our workflow much more flexible. While we are extremely pleased with the work of our two new voice actors, we want more people to diversify their skills. Staff who are interested and not currently involved in urgent projects should contact [5]Travis Young in Talent & Development. [6]He will arrange an interview with you first and coordinate scheduling of training with your supervisor if you are successful.
>
> The following is a list of our current animation jobs. Let me know immediately if you are interested in taking part in any of these in particular. Provisional assignments will be posted on the bulletin board on Wednesday morning and they should be finalized by the end of the month.
>
> | Client | Length | Genre | Due Date |
> | --- | --- | --- | --- |
> | Giordano Hair Care | 20 seconds | Advertising | July 10 |
> | Mondrian Educational Videos | 90 minutes | Engineering | August 19 |
> | Jackson Entertainment (Out of Luck, Chuck Ep1) | 17 minutes | Children's Entertainment | September 30 |
> | Granite Software Company (Ding Bats) | 12 minutes | Games | October 12 |
> | Globus Films (Marty the Fly) | 25 minutes | Movie | November 13 |

> **E-Mail Message**
>
> From: Denny House <dhouse@pixelhouse.com>
> To: Ding Junhui <djunhui@pixelhouse.com>
> Date: May 25
> Subject: The schedule
>
> Good morning Ding,
>
> I have seen your memo from Monday. I agree that we need more people with a variety of skills on the staff and commend your encouragement of that.
>
> [7]I have a concern about work allocation. The children's entertainment project is an

extremely important contract for us. This is only a pilot episode, and the broadcasting company will decide whether or not to make more based on the success of this video. Please make sure people who have shown creativity and experience are assigned. [8]Also, I would like to receive an update on the status of the engineering video. It is a long complicated job but we cannot let it fall behind schedule.

I am sure you have already considered these points but I wanted to mention them, just in case. I will be in the office on Thursday to discuss various other matters.

All the best,
Denny House

[メモ] ● fear 〜を心配する ● take on work 仕事を引き受ける ● in excess of 〜 〜を上回って ● unwise 軽率な ● duly 十分に ● compensate 〜に報酬を支払う ● prior to 〜に先立って ● workflow 作業の流れ ● provisional assignment 仮の割り当て ● bulletin board 掲示版
[メール] ● commend 〜を称賛する ● allocation 配分 ● pilot episode 見本作

10. What concern does Mr. Junhui mention in the memo?
(A) Some clients might terminate contracts.
(B) The staff have been engaged in many projects.
＊(C) The workload is becoming overly demanding.
(D) Requests for additional funding may be turned down.

解説 Junhui氏はメモの冒頭1に「今年の下半期はスケジュールが非常に厳しい。自分たちの処理能力を超える仕事を引き受けてしまったかもしれない」と書いている。よって、(C)が正解。スタッフが数多くのプロジェクトに従事してきたことは推測できるが、懸念としては述べられていないので、(B)は不正解。

11. What is suggested about Ms. Rosen and Mr. Huttenmeister?
(A) They have worked together on some projects.
(B) They are employed as full-time voice actors.
＊(C) They will receive extra financial rewards.
(D) They are to undergo additional training.

解説 (C)のextra financial rewards(追加の金銭報酬)については、第1段落2に「通常業務とは別に引き受けた仕事については、ボーナス時に十分な報酬で報いられる」とある。本来の業務以外に声優もこなしている2人も当然、ボーナスを受け取ると推測できるので、(C)が正解だ。2人の名はメモの第2段落3に登場している。この文では、2人はそれぞれ(respectively)別のプロジェクトで声の仕事をしたとしか書かれていないので、(A)は誤り。(B)は続く4の「視覚効果部門の仕事で忙しいにもかかわらず」に矛盾する。(D)は述べられていない。

12. Who most likely is Travis Young?
　＊(A) A human resources manager
　(B) A graphic design specialist
　(C) A television program producer
　(D) A voice acting instructor

解説 メモの5から、Travis YoungはTalent & Development（人材開発部門）で働いているとわかる。Young氏は、声優に興味を持った人に面接し、希望者の上長とトレーニングの予定を調整する役割を担っているので、(A)「人事マネージャー」であると考えるのが妥当だ。

---

13. What is a purpose of the e-mail?
　＊(A) To offer advice on staff assignment
　(B) To ask for an updated timetable
　(C) To emphasize the importance of teamwork
　(D) To praise Mr. Junhui for obtaining new skills

解説 House氏はメールの7で「仕事の配分について心配がある」と書き、子ども向けエンターテインメントのプロジェクトにどんな人材が適しているか、意見を述べている。従って、(A)「スタッフの割り振りについて助言するため」が正解。メールの目的は第1段落で述べられることが多いが、必ずしもそうとは限らない。

---

14. About which project does Mr. House request further information?
　(A) Giordano Hair
　＊(B) Mondrian Educational Videos
　(C) Jackson Entertainment
　(D) Globus Films

解説 メールの8に「engineering videoについて最新の進捗状況を知りたい」とあるので、メモの中の表を見ると、Engineeringというジャンルは2行目にあり、そのプロジェクトはMondrian Educational Videosのものだとわかる。よって、(B)が正解。

Ted流 TOEICの泳ぎ方　　………長続きする英語自己学習法………

続かない原因その3　Stuck with only one style
　挫折する人は、平泳ぎやクロールなど、1つの泳ぎ方だけを延々と続ける傾向があります。他の泳ぎ方を覚えるのは時間がかかるし、遠回りのような気がするからだと思います。しかし、バラエティーのない練習では飽きてしまいますし、体をバランス良く鍛えることもできません。TOEIC対策においても、問題演習だけをひたすら続けるのではなく、音読やサマライジング（要約）など、他のメニューも取り入れてみると、かえって効果が上がる場合があります。

問題 15-19 は次の広告とメールに関するものです。

Maine's most-circulated local newspaper, *The Kilgore Times*, is looking to hire a financial expert to cover business and economic concerns around the state. [1]The newspaper is read by leaders in Maine's business sector as well as the general public, so it is important that stories have information relevant and interesting to both. We have been increasingly successful with our Web site in recent years and been expanding into online broadcasting, with some of our writing staff doubling as newsreaders and commentators for video content.

[2]The successful applicant will be required to appear on such projects or, periodically, write abridged versions of articles suitable for broadcast. Applicants with a background in [3]this more fruitful aspect of our business are preferred. [4]As we have strong relationships with the local community, our writers are required to travel and report on local sporting and cultural events.

Because the position is currently unfilled, we are looking for a candidate who is able to start this month. The deadline for applications is February 14. Applications should be made directly to the editor by e-mail at editor@kilgoretimes.com and include all relevant documents as attachments. Otherwise, they may be mailed to the following address:

Attention: Dave Gilbey
Kilgore Times Newspaper
13 Donald Street, Kilgore, Maine 04434

E-Mail Message

To: editor@kilgoretimes.com
From: groche@prolight.com
Date: February 9
Subject: Financial writer position
Attachment: GRoche_Samples.doc

Dear Mr. Gilbey,

I am writing with regard to the position for a financial writer, which I saw advertised in *West Hill Post* on Thursday.

I work as a business writer at *The Stanton Sentinel* and was originally hired for a position very similar to the one you are trying to fill. Over the past 12 years that I have been at the company's online content division, it has received a number of awards for the articles and other digital content that my team and I have produced but, unfortunately, the company has decided to rely more heavily on outsourced content for its Web site. Therefore, [5]I am looking for a position which will provide me with the broader set of responsibilities I am accustomed to.

My educational background also makes me an ideal candidate for the business-oriented yet creative position. I completed a business and economics degree at Glen Ridge University and later received a diploma from Stanton Vocational College after undertaking a video production course there. Subsequently, I did a two-year post graduate course in journalism at Brighton College. You should note that Stanton Vocational College was merged with Brighton College three years ago and that my diploma reflects that change.

I am still living in Stanton and the earliest I could move to Maine would be March 12. Nevertheless, should my application be successful, I am prepared to organize temporary accommodation so that ⁶there will be no conflict with work assignments during the week. ⁷Although the advertisement in Stanton's local newspaper did not indicate whether relocation costs would be borne by the company, financial support would be highly appreciated.

Please find attached the required documents. I look forward to hearing from you.

Sincerely,
Gunter Roche

[広告] ● circulated 配布されている ● relevant 関連のある ● double 兼ねる ● periodically 定期的に ● abridged 要約した ● suitable for ～に適している ● fruitful 収益の多い ● unfilled 空いている
[メール] ● with regard to ～に関して ● outsourced content 外部から調達した内容 ● accustomed 慣れた ● no conflict with ～ ～と相いれないことは生じない ● bear（費用を）負担する

15. What is suggested about *The Kilgore Times*?
　　(A) It concentrates on financial news.
　　(B) Its writers are required to direct videos.
　＊(C) It generates more profits online than in print.
　　(D) Its newspaper sales have been growing.

解説 第1段落で近年成長中であると述べられているオンライン事業について、第2段落3ではthis more fruitful aspect of our business（より利益をもたらすこの部門）という説明が追加されている。つまり、オンライン事業の方が新聞社のその他の事業、つまり紙の新聞販売より収益が多いと推測できる。よって(C)が正解。

16. What is a requirement of the advertised position?
　　(A) Willingness to travel abroad　　＊(B) The ability to cover diverse subjects
　　(C) Experience in news reporting　　(D) Current residence in Maine

解説 新聞社の特徴や応募条件として明記されていることを組み合わせたり、そこから推測したりして正解を選ぶ必要がある。募集されているのは経済記者だが、4に「地元で行われるスポーツや文化イベントの取材にも行く」とある。つまり、一般記事も書ける記者を必要としているので、(B)「さまざまなテーマを扱える能力」が正解だ。海外取材については触れられていないので(A)は除外。(C)の「ニュース報道の経験」は条件ではない。(D)「メーン州に住んでいること」は求められていない。

17. According to the e-mail, why is Mr. Roche applying for the position?
   ∗ (A) To produce digital content
   (B) To work for a larger company
   (C) To experience life in Kilgore
   (D) To have more opportunities for promotion

解説 ▶ メールの第2段落の5、職歴の説明の最後の部分に「慣れ親しんできた幅広い責任のある職を探している」とある。「慣れ親しんだ職」の内容については、この手前の文で「オンラインコンテンツを作る部署で記事やデジタルコンテンツを作っていた」と述べられている。よって(A)「デジタルコンテンツを制作するため」が正解だ。

---

18. What is suggested about *West Hill Post*?
   (A) It provides digital content.
   (B) It sponsors events in Maine.
   (C) It is a weekly publication.
   ∗ (D) It is based in Stanton.

解説 ▶ メールの冒頭から、*West Hill Post*紙はRoche氏が求人情報を見つけた新聞だとわかる。7にthe advertisement in Stanton's local newspaper (Stantonの地元紙にあった広告)とあるので、*West Hill Post*紙はStantonの新聞だとわかる。ここから同紙は「Stantonに拠点がある」と推測できるので、(D)が正解だ。

---

19. What is NOT indicated about Mr. Roche?
   (A) He is concerned about an allowance.
   (B) He has contributed online articles in the past.
   (C) He is available to start work by the required date.
   ∗ (D) He transferred between two schools.

解説 ▶ ヒントはすべてメールの中にある。要点をつなぎ合わせながら読んでいれば、設問と選択肢を読むだけで解答できる。少なくとも、文書のどこを確認すればいいかがわかる程度にはしておきたい。下線7の部分で「引っ越し費用を負担してもらえるか」を問うているので(A)は文書の内容に合致。(B)は第2段落の職歴にある内容。6に、「仕事を問題なく期日までに始められる」とあるので(C)もOKだ。第3段落の学歴の説明には数多くの学校名が出てくるが、transferred (転校した)とは述べられていないので、文書の内容と一致していないのは(D)だ。

Ted's Talks ❸
BEYOND対談 ── TOEIC講師　ヒロ前田

> **TOEIC以外の英語との接触が難問対応のカギ**

Ted ： 最近の公開テストは難化しているという見方をする人が多いようですが、前田さんはどう思われますか。

前田 ： わざわざ難化と呼ぶに値するような現象は起きていないと思います。最低でも1年くらい連続で難しい回が続き、それがその後も続いて初めて難化したと言えるのではないでしょうか。ただ、出題傾向にはやや変化が起きていますね。この3年くらいで、Part 6の文脈依存型問題の比率が高くなりました。12問のうち6問、出題されることも珍しくありません。

Ted ： 全体としては難化していなくても、難問が増えているという可能性はないでしょうか。例えば、becauseが正解の問題とinasmuch asが正解の問題では、後者の方が一般的に難度は高いですよね。そういう問題は増えてきていると思いますか。

前田 ： 多くの人にとってなじみがない語句が正解になる問題は確かに出ますが、それは昔からあったことです。TOEICでは、おそらく過去の出題時の正答率などを基に、さまざまなレベルの問題が一定比率で出題されています。495点を取る集団と、490点以下の集団を区別するための問題もいくつか入っているでしょう。そういう問題の数が増えたとは思いませんが、超易問が出題される頻度が落ちたとは言えそうです。

Ted ： BEYOND 990erになるためには、リーディングセクションは安定的に、ほぼノーミスでクリアする必要があります。でも、公開テストでは、過去のテストや問題集では遭遇したことがないような難しい語句や、新しいパターンを利用した問題が出ることもあります。どう対処すべきでしょう。

前田 ： そういう問題に違和感を覚えないくらい、普段から幅広く英語に接するべきでしょう。例えば、TOEICに出題されることもあるadhereという動詞の使い方をボクが学んだのは、問題集ではなく、大学のディベートにおいてです。確か「企業と政府が癒着する」という文脈でした。TOEICとは無

Ted's Talks ❸

　　　　関係な場所で出会う英語にも丁寧に接していくことが大切でしょう。

Ted ： 確かにBEYOND 990erには、テスト対策以外で何かしら英語に触れた経験がある人が多いですね。TOEICでは英語力はもちろん要求されますが、それ以外の要素もあるような気がしています。

前田 ： 英語力だけが問われているわけではないのは確実です。「不正解を思わず選んでしまった」背景には「正解が正解であることに気づかなかった」という事実もあります。TOEICは正解が1つしかないマークシートテストなので、ミスをする理由は1つではなく2つ以上あります。よって、注意深く選択肢を検討する姿勢も問われるでしょう。

Ted ： 例えば、「Aさんは小売企業に勤務していた」という記述を見て「Aさんはセールスの経験がある」と解釈してしまうようなミスは、英語力というよりも論理力の問題ですよね。

前田 ： ワラント（証明するもの）が足りないですね。「小売企業の従業員は全員がセールスをする」という情報が、誰にとっても当たり前とは言えませんから。

Ted ： 本書の「裏取り力」の章には、論理力を鍛えるためのトレーニングに加え、不正解を排除するトレーニングとして選択肢の一部を黒塗りにしたPart 5問題を収録しました。英語力先行タイプの受験者の中には、その辺りが原因で失点している人がいるのではないかと思ったからです。

前田 ： 実は、論理力を鍛えた者として言うと、TOEICには論理的に根拠が不十分な正解も存在します。例えば、What is suggested ...?という問題では、「必ずしもそうとは言えない」ことも正解になり得ます。でも、他の選択肢が明らかに不正解であれば、残る1つを正解と考えざるを得ません。消去法が絶対に必要な問題が存在するのです。そういう意味で、この本が取り上げる「裏取り力」は、Beyond 990erにとって最も重要なスキルの1つと言えると思います。

CHAPTER 4

裏取り力
CORROBORATING

このスキルが足りない人は…

- [ ] 二択にまでは絞り込めるが、そこから迷うことが多い
- [ ] うっかりミスをよくしてしまう
- [ ] 知らない語句が選択肢にあるとうろたえる

CHAPTER 4
裏取り力
CORROBORATING

➡ **根拠を持って正解・不正解を証明できる力**

必要になるパート：Part 5／6／7

　「裏取り力」とは、**正解が正解であることを証明する力**と、**不正解が不正解であることを証明する力**を指します。これは第1～3章で取り上げた基本的な読解力をベースにした発展的スキルです。正解・不正解の根拠を問題文・文書から探し出して積み上げていく、論理的思考力も必要とします。

　解答に時間がかかってしまう原因の1つが、裏取り不足です。**解答に必要な手掛かりが十分にそろっていないことに気づかず、選択肢の解釈でなんとかしようとして、タイムロスしてしまう**のです。裏取りがしっかりできれば、無理な解釈や推測に走ることなく、根拠と自信を持って解答できるようになります。また、正解候補を選んだ後、残りの選択肢がなぜ不正解なのかを裏取りすることで、うっかりミスを防ぐこともできます。

　皆さんは、自分がなぜその不正解選択肢を選んでしまったのかは説明できても、正解選択肢を選ばなかった理由ははっきり説明できない、ということはないでしょうか。そのような状態を脱却し、正解も不正解も常に根拠をもって判定できるようになることが満点への必須条件です。診断テストの設問を例にとって、「裏取り力」を発揮すべきパターンを見ていきましょう。

【Part 5】 p. 9, 4（色字の選択肢が正解）

4. It took technicians at the manufacturing facility several days to ------- the cause of a malfunction that had halted production.
 ＊(A) establish 動 〜を立証する、証明する
  (B) attribute 動 〜に帰する
  (C) arrive 動 到着する
  (D) search 動 探す

　Part 5や6には、受験者が正解選択肢をストレートに選べると出題者が想定していない（であろう）問題が含まれています。**4**の正解の(A) establishという語には、「〜を立証する、証明する」という意味がありますが、この問題はこの語義の知識を問うものではありません。attribute A to B、arrive＋前置詞、search forという語法の知識により、(A) establish以外の選択肢をすべて排除できるかどうかを問うているのです。

　このように積極的に消去法を使うことが求められる問題に対応するためには、**日頃から文法・語法の正確な知識を蓄積しておき、各選択肢の正誤判断で裏取りをする**必要があります。

　ちなみに、この問題の不正解選択肢の単語を使って正しい文を作るとすれば、以下のような例が考えられます。この機会に語法を覚えておくといいでしょう。

- It took technicians several days to attribute the cause of the malfunction to overheating of equipment.
- It took technicians several days to arrive at a solution for the malfunction.
- It took technicians several days to search for the cause of the malfunction.

Part 5で「裏取り力」が必要なパターンをもう1つ見てみましょう。

【Part 5】 p. 10, 5

5. McClymont Books sells its publications more cheaply in Canada, ------- the fact that they are based in the United States results in significant additional costs.
   (A) despite　　前 〜にもかかわらず
   (B) due to　　　〜が原因で
   (C) besides　　前 〜の他にも
   ＊(D) although 接 〜とはいえ

　despite the fact thatというコロケーションを知っていると、つい(A)を選びたくなるでしょう。TOEICの問題の9割方は、コロケーションや定番フレーズの知識で正解できるようになっているので、そういった感覚はむしろ利用すべきです。しかし、いったん選んでみた選択肢をどれだけ客観的に「確かに正解である」と証明できるかが、パーフェクトスコア達成には重要です。**正解の候補を空所に当てはめ、文の構造と意味の両面で不具合がないかどうかを確認**しましょう。この裏取りの作業をしていれば、この問題ではthe factがalthoughの導く節の主語でなければならないということに気づき、正解を選び直せるはずです。

　続いてPart 7における「裏取り力」の必要性を見てみましょう。

【Part 7】 p. 12, 12（抜粋）

Dalton Air Finds New Direction

Sydney (August 10)—Since the leadership change in mid-May, there has been much speculation about how David Panetta, the new CEO, will make his mark on Australia's largest international airline.

The first hint of what the future holds came this week, when Dalton Air purchased 14 additional aircraft, albeit used, from Borden Aerospace. The company released a statement on Thursday saying that it would add eight destinations in Asia and Europe by next spring and is considering expanding the workforce accordingly. However, public relations manager, Joe Walker, acknowledged in an interview with the press that the latter piece of news would still require approval at the general meeting of shareholders next month. (後略)

12. What is NOT indicated about Dalton Air?
　(A) It has new management.
　＊(B) It is partnered with Borden Aerospace.
　(C) It is expanding its service.
　(D) It operates in foreign countries.

　　設問文にindicatedやsuggestedを伴う選択肢照合型問題やNOT型問題は、裏取り・消去力が求められる問題の典型です。上の問題は、文書で「述べられていないこと」はどれかを選ぶNOT問題ですから、各選択肢の内容に合致する記述を文書中に探し、あれば消去していきます。
　　ただし、選択肢と文書の間でギャップのある言い換えが行われていて、内容が合致しているか否かを見抜くのが難しいこともあります。私たちが持つ語感とズレがある言い換えも用いられます。例えば、grocery store（食料雑貨店）とsupermarketはTOEICでは同じものとして扱われますが、一般的にはsupermarketはgrocery storeよりも規模が大きいので、違和感を覚える人もいるでしょう。
　　この問題でも、(A)のnew management（新しい経営者）は、文書中のthe leadership change（指揮者の交代）やthe new CEO（新しいCEO）と合致します。(C)のis expanding its service（サービスを拡大しようとしている）はadd

eight destinations（8つの目的地を加える）の言い換えです。(D)のoperates in foreign countries（外国で営業している）はinternational airline（国際線航空会社）と合致します。

　しかし、(B)のis partnered with Borden Aerospace（Borden Aerospaceと提携している）についても、purchased 14 additional aircraft（追加の航空機を14機購入した）の言い換えではないかと迷って、正解候補から排除しきれない人もいるでしょう。こういう場合は、**消去法と正解候補の裏取りをうまく併用**しましょう。前述のとおり、(A)(C)(D)が(B)より確実に消去できそうなことと、(B) Dalton AirがBorden Aerospaceから航空機を購入したことをもって「提携している」とは言えないという論理の両面から、(B)を正解と判断できます。

● POINT

- ☐ うっかりミスは、選択肢を「選ぶ理由」に加え、「選ばない理由」を意識することで解消。
- ☐ 感覚やコロケーション知識からの選択は有効だが、それに頼りきるのは禁物。
- ☐ 言い換え表現がピンとこなければ、正解候補の裏取りと消去法の併用でベストな判断を。

CHAPTER 4
裏取り力 CORROBORATING

→ トレーニング

Menu 1

　正解は確信を持って選び、不正解は自信を持って排除できなければならない。例えば、ある選択肢が未知語であっても、残り3つの選択肢が不正解だとわかれば、その選択肢が正解だと判断できる。ここでは選択肢に未知語がある状況を強制的に作り、消去力をチェックする。

　Part 5形式の問題だが、選択肢(A)~(D)のうち1つが黒塗りになっている。残りの選択肢の正誤を判断し、空所に入るべきものがどれかを選ぼう。**制限時間は1問30秒**。黒塗りの選択肢が正解だった場合は、解答・解説で正解例の語が示されている。

【 例　題 】

Varios is the ------- of one of the most innovative software design teams in the world.
(A) producer　(B) produce　(C) production　(D) ■■■■■■

正解 (D)。「世界で最も革新的なソフトウエアデザインチームの1つによる〜」という文意なので、空所には(A) producer(製作者)、(B) produce(農産物)、(C) production(制作)のいずれも不適切。よって、消去法で正解は(D)と確定できる。product(製品)などが入ると予測できるとなお良い。

🕐　●各30秒

1. The rules regarding the use of SugarApp are ------- in the user agreement and on the help section of the Web site.
    (A) accounted
    (B) referred
    (C) outlined
    (D) ■■■■■■

2. Dobster Supplies has ------- its shipping process so much that it can now offer same-day delivery services to neighboring areas.
   (A) ■■■■
   (B) performed
   (C) invented
   (D) streamlined

3. Mr. Timms asked that delivery of building materials to the worksite be ------- as construction was already behind schedule.
   (A) issued
   (B) dedicated
   (C) ■■■■
   (D) reproduced

4. Millway Meats will resume its home delivery service as soon as ------- permit.
   (A) attitudes
   (B) expending
   (C) incentives
   (D) ■■■■

5. GH Technologies has decided to invest less in advertising and more in design, relying on consumers' ability to make ------- decisions.
   (A) informing
   (B) informative
   (C) information
   (D) ■■■■

6. It has been increasingly hard for Smither's Manufacturing to ------- its factory as the declining local population has left it in isolation.
   (A) staff
   (B) regard
   (C) ■■■■
   (D) locate

7. Topics covered in the employee training manual include team building and office -------.
   (A) administrative
   (B) ■■■■■
   (C) administrate
   (D) administrator

8. Although new additions to the Spargo's menu are tried -------, the main dishes have been unchanged for over 30 years.
   (A) temporarily
   (B) periodically
   (C) formerly
   (D) ■■■■■

Menu 1の解答・解説

※正解選択肢は色字。黒塗りの選択肢が正解となる場合は ■■■ に正解候補を示してある。問題文の訳文は紙面では省略（訳文の入手方法はp.7をご覧ください）。

1. The rules regarding the use of SugarApp are ------- in the user agreement and on the help section of the Web site.
   (A) accounted
   (B) referred
   ＊(C) outlined
   (D) ■■■■■

   解説 ▶ 規則はユーザー同意書で「説明されている」という文意を作る(C) outlinedが正解。「～の概要を説明する」という意味は、「～の輪郭を描く」という元の意味と関連付けて覚えよう。(A)はaccounted for（説明された）、(B)はreferred to（示された）と、後ろに前置詞が必要。(C)の単語の知識に加え、(A)と(B)の用法を覚えているかが問われる問題だ。

2. Dobster Supplies has ------- its shipping process so much that it can now offer same-day delivery services to neighboring areas.
   (A) ~~(redacted)~~
   (B) performed
   (C) invented
   ＊(D) streamlined

   解説　「同日配送サービスが提供できる」ようになるという結果を導く節がso ～ that ...（とても～なので…する）の前に必要だ。出荷のプロセスを「合理化した」が適切なので、正解は(D) streamlined。「～を流線形にする」というこの単語の元の意味をイメージすると覚えやすい。(C) invented（～を発明した）はmuch（非常に）で強調することができないので不可。

3. Mr. Timms asked that delivery of building materials to the worksite be ------- as construction was already behind schedule.
   (A) issued
   (B) dedicated
   ＊(C) expedited
   (D) reproduced

   解説　(A) issued（支給される）や(D) reproduced（複製される）は、delivery（搬入）を意味上の目的語（受動態の場合の主語）に取れない。(B) dedicated（ささげられる）は「何に」という部分がないので意味を成さない。よって、消去法により正解は黒塗りの(C)。正解としては、process（過程）とも相性が良い動詞、expedited（～を早めた）などが適切。

4. Millway Meats will resume its home delivery service as soon as ------- permit.
   (A) attitudes
   (B) expending
   (C) incentives
   ＊(D) circumstances

   解説　「何が」許せば宅配サービスを再開できるかを考える。(A) attitudes（態度）はconsumer attitude（消費者動向）のように用いられるが、ここでは不適。(B) expending（支出すること）は単数扱いなので動詞permitに合わない。(C) incentives（動機、報奨金）は宅配ができないという事態と関連がない。よって、消去法により黒塗りの(D)が正解。circumstances（状況）などが適切。

5. GH Technologies has decided to invest less in advertising and more in design, relying on consumers' ability to make ------- decisions.
   (A) informing
   (B) informative
   (C) information
   ＊(D) informed

解説 decisions（決断）にかかる語が空所に入る。(A) informing は現在分詞なので、decisions が「情報提供する」という意味になり不適。(B) informative は形容詞だが、「情報に富んだ決断」とは言わない。(C) information は decisions との複合名詞と解しても意味を成さない。よって、消去法で正解は黒塗りの (D)。informed decisions は「よく理解した上での決断」。

---

6. It has been increasingly hard for Smither's Manufacturing to ------- its factory as the declining local population has left it in isolation.
   * (A) staff
   (B) regard
   (C) ■■■■■■
   (D) locate

解説 「地元の人口減少で孤立した状態になっている」ために、何をすることが困難になっているかという文脈で考える。正解は「〜に人員を配置する」という意味の (A) staff。名詞用法の staff（職員、従業員）は誰もが知っているが、動詞用法はあまり知られていない。一見平易な語句の別用法や第一義以外の意味は、TOEIC出題ポイントの1つ。(B) は regard A as B（A を B とみなす）との混同を狙った不正解選択肢だ。

---

7. Topics covered in the employee training manual include team building and office -------.
   (A) administrative
   * (B) administration
   (C) administrate
   (D) administrator

解説 空所は team building という名詞句と and で並列につながれている句の一部だ。office は冠詞がなく複数形でもないことから、形容詞的に使われているとわかる。よって、空所には複合名詞の核となる名詞が入る。(A) administrative は形容詞、(C) administrate は動詞の原形なので、いずれも不適。(D) administrator（管理者）は名詞だが、人なので文意に合わない。よって、黒塗りの (B) が正解。office administration は「業務管理」の意。

---

8. Although new additions to the Spargo's menu are tried -------, the main dishes have been unchanged for over 30 years.
   (A) temporarily
   * (B) periodically
   (C) formerly
   (D) ■■■■■■

解説 新メニューアイテムの追加が「どのように」試されるかを表すのが、空所に入る副詞の役割。正解は (B) periodically（定期的に）。(A) temporarily（一時的に）は、try（試す）という行為自体に一時性が含まれるので、意味的に重複し不適切。(C) formerly（以前は）が修飾する動詞は過去形でないといけない。

Menu 2

問題文書中にどんな情報があれば、その選択肢を正解と判断できるか。Part 7では、正解に必要な根拠がすべてそろっているかを冷静に裏取りする力が求められる。

1～6の文は、ある1つの文書からの抜粋だ。続く(A)～(D)がそれぞれ真であると証明するには、1～6のうち、最低限どの情報が必要であるか、解答欄にその番号を記入しよう。[　]内は必要な情報の数だ。**制限時間は各10分**。

【 例 題 】
1 ハナコはタロウとアパートの同じ部屋に住んでいます。
2 タロウはハナコが飼っている犬の名前です。
3 ハナコが飼っている犬は秋田犬です。
4 ハナコは秋田犬が大好きです。
5 ハナコは家が小さいという理由でたくさんの犬は飼えないので、1頭しか飼っていません。
6 大好きな犬種の犬をたくさん飼える家に引っ越したいとハナコは思っています。

(A) タロウは秋田犬だ。[2]　_____
(B) ハナコは秋田犬を部屋の中で飼っている。[3]　_____
(C) ハナコはたくさんの秋田犬に囲まれて生活したいと思っている。[2]　_____
(D) ハナコは大きい家に引っ越したいと思っている。[2]　_____

正解：(A) 2, 3　(B) 1, 2, 3　(C) 4, 6　(D) 5, 6

各10分

1.
1　Shipping Notification Date: July 21
2　Dear Mr. Bonhoff, thank you for purchasing from Music Control for your purchase. Please find the status of your order below. Our contracted agent will deliver your order and conduct on-site services if required.
3　Shipped to: Pauna Truong
4　Dispatch Date: July 20 Estimated Arrival Date: July 23

5 Item: HDP-600 Quantity: 1 Assembly service (for digital pianos): YES
6 Other service requirements: Collect the packaging after the recipient has inspected the instrument.

....

(A) Mr. Bonhoff has bought a piano. [2] _____
(B) The shipment is currently in transit. [2] _____
(C) A contractor will set up an instrument at Ms. Truong's location. [3] _____
(D) Ms. Truong will examine an item. [2] _____

2.

1 Textron, Inc., an acclaimed fabric manufacturer, is headquartered in Berlin.
2 Martina Schmidt was transferred from the Munich plant, where she had started her career at Textron, to the Scheffler Center.
3 The Scheffler Center, which is located in the west wing of the Textron headquarters, is responsible for the company's entire new product development process.
4 The Scheffler Center will soon hand over Flexilk, the latest product from Textron, to engineers who will implement the production process in their factory.
5 Ms. Schmidt will return to her former location for a short period in order to meet with the engineers and discuss Flexilk's processing.
6 Ms. Schmidt is expected to continue her excellent work leading a team at the Scheffler Center.

....

(A) Ms. Schmidt is currently based in Berlin. [3] _____
(B) Ms. Schmidt leads product development. [2] _____
(C) Flexilk will be produced in Munich. [3] _____
(D) Flexilk is a new type of fabric. [2] _____

3.

1 All crane operators who apply to renew their licenses are required to present a Safety Accreditation for Crane Operators (SACO) certificate.
2 The administration fee will not be charged for the renewal of a crane operator's license for the first three years. A fee of $25 will be applied to every renewal application thereafter.
3 Applicants are required to attend a training workshop and obtain the SACO certificate from one of the designated training centers.
4 Participating in a SACO workshop costs $45, but the fee will be waived if you are a member of the Orange County Transport Association (OCTA) and attend a members-only workshop.
5 Rockton Training Center offers SACO workshops exclusively for OCTA members in the afternoon. Open-to-the-public workshops are available in the evening at Lifelong Learning Hub.
6 The workshops at Rockton Training Center do not require reservations whereas you must book your seat if you wish to attend a workshop at Lifelong Learning Hub.

(A) Crane operators need to attend a class to renew their license. [2] _____
(B) Some OCTA members may be able to renew their crane operator's license free of charge. [4] _____
(C) Those who take a SACO workshop in the evening will need a reservation. [2] _____
(D) OCTA members can take a SACO workshop free in the afternoon. [2] _____

Menu 2の解答・解説

1.

1 Shipping Notification Date: July 21
2 Dear Mr. Bonhoff, thank you for purchasing from Music Control for your purchase. Please find the status of your order below. Our contracted agent will deliver your order and conduct on-site services if required.
3 Shipped to: Pauna Truong
4 Dispatch Date: July 20 Estimated Arrival Date: July 23
5 Item: HDP-600 Quantity: 1 Assembly service (for digital pianos): YES
6 Other service requirements: Collect the packaging after the recipient has inspected the instrument.

- on-site service 現地（組み立て）サービス、出張サービス ● assembly 組み立て

(A) Mr. Bonhoff has bought a piano. 2, 5
購入者はBonhoff氏（2）で、電子ピアノ向けの組み立てサービスにYES（有）と記されている（5）ので、購入品はピアノ。

(B) The shipment is currently in transit. 1, 4
この発送通知の日付は7月21日（1）。商品が発送されたのは20日で、到着予定日は23日（4）。よって、商品は現在輸送中。

(C) A contractor will set up an instrument at Ms. Truong's location. 2, 3, 5
現場でのサービスを行うのは請負業者（2）。Truong氏宛てに配送される（3）ピアノについて、組み立てサービスが依頼されている（5）。よって、請負業者はTruong氏宅で楽器を組み立てると言える。

(D) Ms. Truong will examine an item. 3, 6
発送はTruong氏宛て（3）で、受取人は楽器を確認する（6）とあるので、Truong氏は品物を検査するはずだ。

2.

1 Textron, Inc., an acclaimed fabric manufacturer, is headquartered in Berlin.
2 Martina Schmidt was transferred from the Munich plant, where she had started her career at Textron, to the Scheffler Center.
3 The Scheffler Center, which is located in the west wing of the Textron headquarters, is responsible for the company's entire new product development process.
4 The Scheffler Center will soon hand over Flexilk, the latest product from Textron, to engineers who will implement the production process in their factory.
5 Ms. Schmidt will return to her former location for a short period in order to meet with the engineers and discuss Flexilk's processing.
6 Ms. Schmidt is expected to continue her excellent work leading a team at the Scheffler Center.

- acclaimed 評判の高い

(A) Ms. Schmidt is currently based in Berlin. 1, 3, 6
Textronの本社はベルリンで(1)、Scheffler Centerはその本社内にある(3)。Schmidt氏が今後もScheffler Centerでチームを率いることが期待されている(6)ということは、彼女の拠点はベルリンだ。2はwas transferred(異動した)と過去形で書かれているので、Schmidt氏の現在の勤務地とは無関係な情報。

(B) Ms. Schmidt leads product development. 3, 6
Scheffler Centerは新製品開発を担っており(3)、そのチームをSchmidt氏が率いている(6)。よって、Schmidt氏は製品開発を指揮している。

(C) Flexilk will be produced in Munich. 2, 4, 5
Schmidt氏はミュンヘン(Munich)工場に勤務していた(2)。Flexilkはエンジニアたちのいる工場で生産される(4)。Schmidt氏はFlexilkの加工についてエンジニアたちと話し合うために以前の職場に戻る(5)。よって、FlexilkはSchmidt氏が以前働いていたミュンヘンで生産される。

(D) Flexilk is a new type of fabric. 1, 4
Textron社は繊維製造業者で(1)、Flexilkは同社の最新の製品(4)。よって、Flexilkは新しい繊維製品であるという推論が成り立つ。厳密にはFlexilkについてさらに情報が必要だが、TOEICにおいてはこれで十分だ。

3.

1　All crane operators who apply to renew their licenses are required to present a Safety Accreditation for Crane Operators (SACO) certificate.
2　The administration fee will not be charged for the renewal of a crane operator's license for the first three years. A fee of $25 will be applied to every renewal application thereafter.
3　Applicants are required to attend a training workshop and obtain the SACO certificate from one of the designated training centers.
4　Participating in a SACO workshop costs $45, but the fee will be waived if you are a member of the Orange County Transport Association (OCTA) and attend a members-only workshop.
5　Rockton Training Center offers SACO workshops exclusively for OCTA members in the afternoon. Open-to-the-public workshops are available in the evening at Lifelong Learning Hub.
6　The workshops at Rockton Training Center do not require reservations whereas you must book your seat if you wish to attend a workshop at Lifelong Learning Hub.

● accreditation 認定　● thereafter その後　● waive 無料にする

(A) Crane operators need to attend a class to renew their license. 1, 3
クレーン運転免許証を更新するためにはSACO証明書が必要（1）。SACO証明書を取得するためには研修会に出席しなければならない（3）。よって、クレーン運転手は研修会に出席する必要がある。

(B) Some OCTA members may be able to renew their crane operator's license free of charge. 1, 2, 3, 4
(A)で述べられたこと（1,3）に加え、クレーン運転手は免許取得後最初の3年間は更新料無料（2）で、OCTA会員であれば会員限定の研修会の参加費は免除（4）との記述がある。よって、免許取得3年以内という条件に該当する「何人かのOCTA会員」は、無料で免許が更新できる。

(C) Those who take a SACO workshop in the evening will need a reservation. 5, 6
Lifelong Learning Hubで行われるSACO研修は夕方に行われ（5）、それに参加するためには予約が必要（6）。

(D) OCTA members can take a SACO workshop free in the afternoon. 4, 5
OCTA会員は、会員限定の研修会に出席すればSACO研修の参加費は免除される（4）。その研修会は午後に行われる（5）。よって、午後であれば参加無料だ。

CHAPTER 4 裏取り力 CORROBORATING

実践問題

仕上げに、本番形式の難問にチャレンジ。消去法と裏取りの両面から攻めてみよう。

Part 5

空所に入る語句として、最も適切なものを1つ選ぼう。(解答・解説はpp. 158〜160)

● 3分20秒

1. The landscaping around the new office building includes a ------- area for outdoor dining in the central courtyard.
   (A) diverted
   (B) confronted
   (C) raised
   (D) presented

2. Management is normally not in favor of ------- suggestion that could lead to a decrease in sales, regardless of other possible benefits.
   (A) such
   (B) any
   (C) much
   (D) most

3. ------- the weather will be favorable for the next few months, it is unlikely that milk prices will vary greatly.
   (A) Supposing that
   (B) Soon after
   (C) Resulting from
   (D) The fact that

4. If customers should wish to cancel their purchases, Revo Music Store will ------- the amount to their credit card within 14 days.
   (A) settle
   (B) recharge
   (C) adjust
   (D) restore

5. Purchasers of GH automobiles are reminded that ------- unlikely the chances are of a breakdown, they are covered by a five-year guarantee.
   (A) unless
   (B) however
   (C) quite
   (D) although

6. With many people predicting growth in the popularity of computerized watches, Cleminson Technology has decided to ------- that market.
   (A) pursue
   (B) acquire
   (C) strengthen
   (D) expand

7. At the tenant meeting, some questions on the renovation project were ------- to the owner of Kralingse Building.
   (A) remarked
   (B) inquired
   (C) fielded
   (D) directed

8. For readers wishing to ------- further into the subject of personal investment, Richmond Publications has a more advanced book to be released in September.
   (A) solicit
   (B) analyze
   (C) delve
   (D) follow

9. As the new identification badges have now been delivered, ------- holding the previous type is required to exchange it by Friday this week.
   (A) those
   (B) whoever
   (C) anyone
   (D) the one

10. Fielding Automotive has been ------- since it was founded 25 years ago and shows no sign of decline in its profitability.
    (A) institutional
    (B) prosperous
    (C) practical
    (D) comparable

Part 6

空所に入る語句として、最も適切なものを1つずつ選ぼう。(解答・解説はpp. 162〜163)

Questions 11-13 refer to the following announcement. 1分30秒

Last Thursday, it was reported that water had been leaking from the roof into the storage locker on the third floor. A building inspector was called to investigate the problem, and she found that over the years, the tiling on the roof had ------- to the point that leaks were starting to occur in various

11. (A) deteriorated
(B) overseen
(C) resolved
(D) advanced Ⓐ Ⓑ Ⓒ Ⓓ

locations.

Rather than fix these issues as they -------, it has been decided that we

12. (A) yield
(B) surface
(C) incur
(D) raise Ⓐ Ⓑ Ⓒ Ⓓ

should replace the entire roof at the earliest opportunity. A local construction company has assured us that the whole project can be completed in as few as three days.

Due to the inevitable disruption to the entire building, all employees ------- time off work from November 16 to November 18. Please notify all

13. (A) were given
(B) are giving
(C) are being given
(D) will have given Ⓐ Ⓑ Ⓒ Ⓓ

clients of the situation and apologize for any inconvenience.

Part 7

文書に関する設問の解答として、最も適切なものを1つずつ選ぼう。

(解答・解説はpp. 164〜168)

Questions 14-16 refer to the following article.

3分

Tokyo, May 6–Evergrow Corporation yesterday revealed its intention to appoint Carly Nguyen as its new president, taking over from Masahiro Masunaga, the firm's longtime leader. She is expected to help the Japanese retailer recover from the slump it has been experiencing for the last five years as a result of the increased competition from foreign entrants to the market.

Nguyen is no stranger to the industry or to helping struggling companies succeed. For the last eight years, she has been working as chief executive officer for VMD in Britain, an electronics and appliances retailer which has gone from No. 4 in the country to become the market leader during her term. Before that, she was one of the co-founders of Macrodine, a computer manufacturer in China that started as a venture 20 years ago and now has a 25 percent share of its market segment worldwide.

There was a heated contest for the position at Evergrow which, despite the downturn in sales, is still Japan's foremost department store chain. When making the decision, the board of Evergrow, as well as the president, acknowledged that Nguyen's ability to overcome adversities was what made them choose her over a list of other very qualified candidates. She has a month to get ready for her new position. She will familiarize herself with both corporate and local cultures with the help of her predecessor, who will continue to serve as a board member.

14. What is Ms. Nguyen known for?
   (A) Her work in Japan
   (B) Her managerial competence
   (C) Designing computer products
   (D) Founding an appliance store   Ⓐ Ⓑ Ⓒ Ⓓ

15. What is suggested about Masahiro Masunaga?
   (A) He deliberated on a decision.
   (B) He intends to retire from business.
   (C) He has worked in other industries.
   (D) He convinced the board of directors.   Ⓐ Ⓑ Ⓒ Ⓓ

16. What is indicated about Evergrow Corporation?
   (A) It has withdrawn from some markets.
   (B) It handles a range of items.
   (C) It has offices in other countries.
   (D) It is a family-owned company.   Ⓐ Ⓑ Ⓒ Ⓓ

Questions 17-21 refer to the following e-mails.

E-Mail Message

To: Mira Khan <mira.khan@firemark.com>
From: Toby Kline <tkline@goldwingair.com>
Date: December 2
Subject: Your Flight with Goldwing Air

Dear Ms. Khan,

Thank you for flying with Goldwing Air. We look forward to serving you on your journey. We would like to inform you that, as a customer of Goldwing Air, you are entitled to a number of privileges.

We have a partnership with Beaumont Hotels which provides some attractive perks you might be interested in making the most of. If you make an online reservation at one of the Beaumont Hotels, please be sure to input your ticket booking number. You will automatically be upgraded to a business suite at the standard room rate. The half-hourly shuttle service between the airport and the nearest Beaumont Hotel in each capital city is free when you show the driver your ticket stub.

We also urge you to take advantage of some of Goldwing Air's own features. We have private passenger lounges at most major airports in the country, where you will be served complimentary drinks and light meals. These lounges are connected to wireless Internet and also have special facilities for people traveling on business, which include mobile phone charging stations, private booths with desks, as well as fax and printing facilities. There is even a meeting room available for bookings at a small additional charge. When you reach your destination, you should find your luggage waiting for you as all business class suitcases are given preference when unloading.

You can learn more about our services by visiting the Web site at www.goldwingair.com or by contacting me or other members of our customer service team by phone at 555-0930.

Enjoy your flight!

Toby Kline
Goldwing Air

E-Mail Message

To: Toby Kline <tkline@goldwingair.com>
From: Mira Khan <mira.khan@firemark.com>
Date: December 4
Subject: Re: Your Flight with Goldwing Air

Dear Mr. Kline,

I am sorry to inform you that my experience on a recent trip was quite different from what was promised in your e-mail. I faced a number of delays before reaching my hotel.

The first of which was at the baggage collection area, where my suitcase was not waiting for me. Instead, I had to wait for around 30 minutes. The shuttle bus was also delayed, so I was forced to take a taxi at an exorbitant price. When I finally got settled in, it was after 10 P.M.

I did like the passenger lounge, although I should say that it could use some more seating. I had nowhere to sit when I entered, and one of the kind staff explained that if I waited a few minutes, a personal desk would become available. I ended up waiting 20. So, all in all, I would have been just as content sitting in the waiting area by the departure gate. I had wanted to make use of the other facilities, especially the mobile phone charger, but they too were overcrowded.

On the positive side, the dinner I was served in the hotel restaurant was excellent and the room was certainly more luxurious and relaxing than what we can usually expect for such a price.

Sincerely,
Mira Khan

17. What is the purpose of the first e-mail?
    (A) To explain the conditions of air tickets
    (B) To detail an upcoming itinerary
    (C) To request feedback on a service
    (D) To notify customers of benefits

18. Who most likely is Mr. Kline?
    (A) A hotel manager
    (B) A client liaison officer
    (C) A travel agent
    (D) A survey administrator

19. What benefit of the airline described in the first e-mail did Ms. Khan enjoy?
    (A) A shuttle bus service
    (B) A complimentary dinner
    (C) A mobile phone charger
    (D) A private booth

20. In the second e-mail, the word "content" in paragraph 2, line 4, is closest in meaning to
    (A) plentiful
    (B) keen
    (C) satisfied
    (D) calm

21. What is indicated about Ms. Khan?
    (A) She managed to retrieve her lost baggage.
    (B) She arrived too late to eat at the hotel.
    (C) She did not plan to fly business class.
    (D) She booked her hotel room online.

実践問題の解答・解説

※問題文の訳文は紙面では省略（訳文の入手方法はp. 7をご覧ください）。

Part 5

1. The landscaping around the new office building includes a ------- area for outdoor dining in the central courtyard.

   (A) diverted　動 転換された
   (B) confronted　動 直面した
   ＊(C) raised　動 高くした
   (D) presented　動 提示された

   ● landscaping 景観、景色

   解説 選択肢はすべて動詞の過去分詞で、空所直後の名詞area（場所）にかかる。(A) divertedは、「転換された」という意味では空所に入れることができそうだが、その場合はfrom ~（~から）を述べる必要があるので不適切。(B) confronted（直面した）も「何に」を伴わないと意味を成さない。(D) presented（提示された）は意味自体が空所に合わない。よって、残った(C) raised（高くした）が正解。

2. Management is normally not in favor of ------- suggestion that could lead to a decrease in sales, regardless of other possible benefits.

   (A) such　形 そのような
   ＊(B) any　形 いかなる
   (C) much　形 多くの
   (D) most　形 たいていの

   解説 空所直後のsuggestion（提案）という可算単数名詞を修飾できる(B) any（いかなる）が正解。(A) such（そのような）は後ろの可算単数名詞にa/anが必要。(C) much（多くの）は不可算名詞を修飾する。(D) most（たいていの）は可算・不可算両方の名詞を修飾できるが、可算名詞の場合は複数形でなければならない。

3. ------- the weather will be favorable for the next few months, it is unlikely that milk prices will vary greatly.

   ＊(A) Supposing that　~と仮定して
   (B) Soon after　~の後すぐに
   (C) Resulting from　~の結果として
   (D) The fact that　~という事実

   解説 空所後は主語the weatherと動詞will beが節を作っているので、節を後ろに取れない(C) Resulting from ~（~の結果として）は不適切。(B) Soon after ...（...のすぐ後に）が時を表す副詞節を作る場合、未来のことは現在形で表すべきだが、動詞はwill beなので誤り。(D) The fact that（~という事実）は名詞節を作るが、カンマの前後の節が文法的につながらなくなるので不適切。よって、答えは(A) Supposing that（~と仮定して）。

158

4. If customers should wish to cancel their purchases, Revo Music Store will ------- the amount to their credit card within 14 days.

(A) settle　動（勘定）を済ませる
(B) recharge　動 ～に入金する、～を再充電する
(C) adjust　動 ～を調整する
＊(D) restore　動 ～を戻す、返す

解説▶ (A) settle（～を済ませる）は settle a bill（勘定を済ませる）のように使い、目的語に the amount（金額）は取らない。(B) recharge には「～を再充電する、～に（電子マネーなどを）入金する」という意味があるが、「入金する」の意味と取るとしても、目的語は「金額」ではなく「カード」のような語なので誤り。(C) adjust（～を調整する）は adjust A to B で「A を B に合うよう調整する」となるが、ここでは文意が通らない。よって、答えは (D) restore。restore A to B で「A を B に戻す」という意味になる。

5. Purchasers of GH automobiles are reminded that ------- unlikely the chances are of a breakdown, they are covered by a five-year guarantee.
● breakdown 故障

(A) unless　接 ～でない限り
＊(B) however　副 どんなに～しても
(C) quite　副 完全には～でない
(D) although　接 ～だけれども

解説▶ 空所の後ろは「形容詞＋SV」になっている。このかたまりをカンマ以下の節とつなぐ、接続詞的な用法を持つ副詞の (B) however（どんなに～しても）が正解。この用法は no matter how unlikely the chances are と言い換えができ、「どんなに故障の見込みがなくても」という「譲歩」を表す。

6. With many people predicting growth in the popularity of computerized watches, Cleminson Technology has decided to ------- that market.

＊(A) pursue　動 ～を追い求める
(B) acquire　動 ～を獲得する、買収する
(C) strengthen　動 ～を強化する
(D) expand　動 ～を拡大させる

解説▶ 空所に入る動詞の目的語 that market とは、カンマ前の内容から、computerized watches（コンピューター搭載時計）の市場を指すとわかる。企業が市場の「シェア」を獲得したり拡大したりすることはできても、「市場そのもの」を獲得、拡大することはできないため、(B) acquire と (D) expand は不適切。(C) strengthen も「強化する」べきなのは製品やマーケティングで、市場ではないので意味を成さない。市場を「追い求める、狙う」という意味の (A) pursue が正解。

CHAPTER 4

159

7. At the tenant meeting, some questions on the renovation project were ------- to the owner of Kralingse Building.
   (A) remarked 動 言われた
   (B) inquired 動 (〜を) 聞かれた
   (C) fielded 動 (〜を) 上手に処理された
   ＊(D) directed 動 向けられた

   解説 空所後にto＋〈人〉を取れる(D) directedが正解。were directed to the ownerで「(いくつかの質問が) オーナーに向けられた」という意味。(B) のinquireは、inquire〈物・事〉of〈人〉、またはinquire of/about 〜の形で用いる。(C)のfieldは、field questionsで「質問にうまく対応する」という意味になる。

8. For readers wishing to ------- further into the subject of personal investment, Richmond Publications has a more advanced book to be released in September.
   (A) solicit 動 (〜を) 強く求める
   (B) analyze 動 〜を分析する
   ＊(C) delve 動 掘り下げて研究する
   (D) follow 動 (〜を) 追う

   解説 前置詞into＋名詞subject (テーマ・話題) を伴って意味が通る動詞を選ぶ。(A) solicit ([〜を] 強く求める) は意味が合わず、また自動詞の場合はintoではなくforを取る。(B) analyze (〜を分析する) と(D) follow (〜を追う) は前置詞intoを必要としないので誤り。よって、正解は(C) delve。delve into 〜 で「〜 (資料・情報など) を掘り下げて研究する」という意味。

9. As the new identification badges have now been delivered, ------- holding the previous type is required to exchange it by Friday this week.
   (A) those 代 それらの人々
   (B) whoever 関代 〜するのは誰でも
   ＊(C) anyone 代 誰でも
   (D) the one それ、その人

   解説 空所には主語が入り、それに呼応する動詞はisなので、まず複数扱いの(A) thoseを消去。(B) whoeverは関係代名詞で、後ろにはholdingのような分詞ではなく述語動詞が続くべきなので不適切。(D) the oneは既出の名詞の言い換えとして使うが、空所にthe identification badgeを入れても文意が通じない。よって、分詞を後ろに伴うことができ、「以前のタイプの身分証明書を持っている人なら誰でも」という意味になる代名詞(C) anyoneが正解。

10. Fielding Automotive has been ------- since it was founded 25 years ago and shows no sign of decline in its profitability.
    (A) institutional 形 制度上の
    ＊(B) prosperous 形 経済的に成功した
    (C) practical 形 実践的な
    (D) comparable 形 比較できて

    解説 主語であるFielding Automotive社が、25年前の設立以来どのような状態であるかを形容する単語を空所に入れる。文末にshows no sign of decline in its profitability (利益が減る兆候がない) とあるので、(B) prosperous (経済的に成功した) を入れると文意が通る。

CHAPTER 4

Ted流 TOEICの泳ぎ方　　　　……長続きする英語自己学習法……

続かない原因その4　Neglecting the basics (awkward forms)
　挫折する人は泳ぐフォームが悪い傾向があります。フォームが悪いと、泳いでいても爽快感が得られず、体幹もうまく鍛えられません。英語学習におけるフォームとは何でしょうか。発音や、英語を英語の語順通りに理解することなどと並んで、文字通り「姿勢」も大事だと私は思います。学生が机に突っ伏すような体勢で勉強しているのをよく見掛けますが、あれでは広い視野をもって素早く文書が読めません。

Part 6

問題 11-13 は次の告知に関するものです。

Last Thursday, it was reported that water had been leaking from the roof into the storage locker on the third floor. A building inspector was called to investigate the problem, and she found that over the years, the tiling on the roof had ------- to the point that leaks were starting to occur in various

11. (A) deteriorated
　　(B) overseen
　　(C) resolved
　　(D) advanced

locations.

Rather than fix these issues as they -------, it has been decided that we

12. (A) yield
　　(B) surface
　　(C) incur
　　(D) raise

should replace the entire roof at the earliest opportunity. A local construction company has assured us that the whole project can be completed in as few as three days.

Due to the inevitable disruption to the entire building, all employees ------- time off work from November 16 to November 18. Please notify all

13. (A) were given
　　(B) are giving
　　(C) are being given
　　(D) will have given

clients of the situation and apologize for any inconvenience.

- leak 漏れる ● storage locker 保管庫 ● inspector 調査員 ● investigate 〜を調査する ● tiling タイル
- assure 〜を保証する ● inevitable 避けられない ● disruption 中断

11. ＊(A) deteriorated　動 劣化した
　　(B) overseen　動 ～を監督した
　　(C) resolved　動 決心した
　　(D) advanced　動 進行した

解説　「さまざまなところで水漏れが起こり始める」状態になったのは、社屋の屋根がどうなったからか、という文意で考える。正解は(A) deteriorated（劣化した）。(B) overseenは「～を監督した」という意味の他動詞なので、通常、後ろに目的語が必要。(C) resolvedも「～（問題など）を解決した」という意味では同じく他動詞。(D) advancedには「発展した、進行した」という意味があり、主語が、例えば、the flaw in the tiling（タイルの欠陥）などであれば、動詞として適切だ。

12. (A) yield　動 ～（利益など）を生む、～に報酬をもたらす
　　＊(B) surface　動（問題などが）表面化する
　　(C) incur　動 ～（負債など）を負う
　　(D) raise　動 ～（問題）を提起する

解説　空所直前のtheyは、these issues（これらの問題）を指していて、空所はそれを主語に取る動詞が入る。正解は「表面化する」という意味の(B) surface。(A) yieldは自動詞では「負ける、道を譲る」という意味なので、文意に合わない。(C) incur（～を負う、～をこうむる）は他動詞で、負債や損害などを意味する語句を目的語に取る。(D) raiseには「～（問題など）を提起する」という意味があるが、「問題」は主語ではなく目的語であるべきだ。

13. (A) were given
　　(B) are giving
　　＊(C) are being given
　　(D) will have given

解説　選択肢には異なる時制・態の動詞が並んでいる。まず主語であるall employees（全従業員）は休みを「与えてもらう」立場なので、空所には受け身形が入る。これがわかった時点で、(A) were givenか、(C) are being givenの2択になる。さらに、休みは今後、建物の改修工事が行われる際に与えられるので、未来時制でないといけない。よって、近い未来を表す現在進行形の(C) are being givenが正解となる。

Part 7

問題 14-16 は次の記事に関するものです。

Tokyo, May 6–Evergrow Corporation yesterday revealed its intention to appoint Carly Nguyen as its new president, taking over from Masahiro Masunaga, the firm's longtime leader. She is expected to help the Japanese retailer recover from the slump it has been experiencing for the last five years as a result of the increased competition from foreign entrants to the market.

[1] Nguyen is no stranger to the industry or to helping struggling companies succeed. For the last eight years, she has been working as chief executive officer for VMD in Britain, an electronics and appliances retailer which has gone from No. 4 in the country to become the market leader during her term. Before that, she was one of the co-founders of Macrodine, a computer manufacturer in China that started as a venture 20 years ago and now has a 25 percent share of its market segment worldwide.

There was a heated contest for the position at Evergrow which, despite the downturn in sales, is still [2] Japan's foremost department store chain. [3] When making the decision, the board of Evergrow, as well as the president, acknowledged that Nguyen's ability to overcome adversities was what made them choose her over a list of other very qualified candidates. She has a month to get ready for her new position. She will familiarize herself with both corporate and local cultures with the help of her predecessor, who will continue to serve as a board member.

- reveal 〜を明らかにする ● appoint 〜を任命する ● take over from 〜 〜から引き継ぐ ● entrant 新規参入者 ● term 在任期間 ● co-founder 共同設立者 ● market segment 市場区分 ● downturn 下落 ● foremost 主要な ● acknowledge 〜を認める ● predecessor 前任者

14. What is Ms. Nguyen known for?
  (A) Her work in Japan
  ∗ (B) Her managerial competence
  (C) Designing computer products
  (D) Founding an appliance store

  ● managerial 経営の、管理職の

解説 ▶ Evergrow社の次期社長候補、Nguyen氏に関する記事。彼女の経歴は2段落目に書かれている。下線部1に「低迷する企業を救済することに精通している」とあり、これ以降で彼女のCEOや会社創業者としての業績が挙げられている。これはHer managerial competence（彼女の経営能力）と言い換えることができる内容なので、(B)が正解。(A)「日本での実績」、(C)「コンピューター製品のデザイン」、(D)「家電量販店の創業」については述べられていない。

15. What is suggested about Masahiro Masunaga?
  ∗ (A) He deliberated on a decision.
  (B) He intends to retire from business.
  (C) He has worked in other industries.
  (D) He convinced the board of directors.

  ● deliberate on ~ ~を熟考する、慎重に審議する

解説 ▶ 第1段落冒頭の1文から、Masunaga氏は現在の社長であることがわかる。3段落目3に、取締役会と社長が次期社長候補を決定した際の状況が述べられている。「非常に有力な候補者たちの中から（Nguyen氏を）選んだ」とあるので、(A)「決定について熟考した」が正解。残りの選択肢に関する記述はないので、deliberate onの意味がわからなくても、時間をかければ消去法で解ける問題。

16. What is indicated about Evergrow Corporation?
  (A) It has withdrawn from some markets.
  ∗ (B) It handles a range of items.
  (C) It has offices in other countries.
  (D) It is a family-owned company.

解説 ▶ Evergrow社に関する情報を問う問題。第3段落2から同社が百貨店チェーン（department store chain）であることがわかる。百貨店は通常さまざまな品物を置いてあるので、その言い換えとなる(B)「さまざまな商品を取り扱っている」が正解。(A)は、最初の段落に業績不振に関する内容はあるが、「いくつかの市場から撤退した」とは述べられていないので不正解。(C)「他の国に事務所がある」や(D)「家族経営である」も、記述がないため誤り。

問題 17-21 は次のメールに関するものです。

E-Mail Message

To: Mira Khan <mira.khan@firemark.com>
From: Toby Kline <tkline@goldwingair.com>
Date: December 2
Subject: Your Flight with Goldwing Air

Dear Ms. Khan,

Thank you for flying with Goldwing Air. We look forward to serving you on your journey. [1]We would like to inform you that, as a customer of Goldwing Air, you are entitled to a number of privileges.

We have a partnership with Beaumont Hotels which provides some attractive perks you might be interested in making the most of. [2]If you make an online reservation at one of the Beaumont Hotels, please be sure to input your ticket booking number. You will automatically be upgraded to a business suite at the standard room rate. The half-hourly shuttle service between the airport and the nearest Beaumont Hotel in each capital city is free when you show the driver your ticket stub.

We also urge you to take advantage of some of Goldwing Air's own features. We have private passenger lounges at most major airports in the country, where you will be served complimentary drinks and light meals. These lounges are connected to wireless Internet and also have special facilities for people traveling on business, which include mobile phone charging stations, [3]private booths with desks, as well as fax and printing facilities. There is even a meeting room available for bookings at a small additional charge. When you reach your destination, you should find your luggage waiting for you as all business class suitcases are given preference when unloading.

You can learn more about our services by visiting the Web site at www.goldwingair.com or [4]by contacting me or other member of our customer service team by phone at 555-0930.

Enjoy your flight!

Toby Kline
[5]Goldwing Air

E-Mail Message

To: Toby Kline <tkline@goldwingair.com>
From: Mira Khan <mira.khan@firemark.com>
Date: December 4
Subject: Re: Your Flight with Goldwing Air

Dear Mr. Kline,

I am sorry to inform you that my experience on a recent trip was quite different from what was promised in your e-mail. I faced a number of delays before reaching my hotel.

The first of which was at the baggage collection area, where my suitcase was not waiting for me. Instead, I had to wait for around 30 minutes. [6]The shuttle bus was also delayed, so I was forced to take a taxi at an exorbitant price. When I finally got settled in, it was after 10 P.M.

I did like the passenger lounge, although I should say that it could use some more seating. I had nowhere to sit when I entered, and [7]one of the kind staff explained that if I waited a few minutes, a personal desk would become available. I ended up waiting 20. So, all in all, I would have been just as content sitting in the waiting area by the departure gate. [8]I had wanted to make use of the other facilities, especially the mobile phone charger, but they too were overcrowded.

On the positive side, the dinner I was served in the hotel restaurant was excellent and [9]the room was certainly more luxurious and relaxing than what we can usually expect for such a price.

Sincerely,
Mira Khan

［メール1］● entitle 〜に資格を与える　● perks 特典　● ticket stub チケットの半券
［メール2］● exorbitant（値段が）法外な、とても高い　● overcrowded ひどく混雑した　● luxurious 豪華な

17. What is the purpose of the first e-mail?
(A) To explain the conditions of air tickets
(B) To detail an upcoming itinerary
(C) To request feedback on a service
＊(D) To notify customers of benefits

解説 1つ目のメールの目的を問う問題。下線部1に「Goldwing Airのお客様特典についてお知らせします」という旨の文があり、また第2段落以降で、その特典の詳細が説明されている。よって、答えは(D)。notifyが文書中のinformの、benefitsが文書中のprivilegesの言い換えである。(A)の航空券の条件の説明や、(B)の旅程についての説明、(C)のサービスへの意見を募集するといった内容は書かれていない。

18. Who most likely is Mr. Kline?
(A) A hotel manager　　＊(B) A client liaison officer
(C) A travel agent　　(D) A survey administrator

● liaison 連絡係

解説 Kline氏は1つ目のメールの差出人。アドレスのドメイン、1文目の「Goldwing Airをご利用いただきありがとうございます」というあいさつ、署名の下の社名（5）から、Kline氏は航空会社の社員だとわかるので、(A)「ホテルのマネージャー」と(C)「旅行案内業者」は消去できる。(D)「アンケート管理者」に関しても、本文に記載がないので不適切。よって、答えは(B)「渉外担当者」。第4段落4で「私が弊社のカスタマーサービスチームのメンバー」と書かれているのも、(B)が正解であることの裏取りになる。

19. What benefit of the airline described in the first e-mail did Ms. Khan enjoy?
  (A) A shuttle bus service
  (B) A complimentary dinner
  (C) A mobile phone charger
  ＊(D) A private booth

解説 両文書参照問題。Khanさんは2つ目のメール第1段落6に、「シャトルバスも遅れていたのでタクシーを利用せざるをえなかった」と書いているので、(A)は誤り。(B)の「無料の夕食」に関する記述はない。(C)は第2段落8に「利用したかったが大変混雑していた（ので使えなかった）」とあることから誤り。一方で、7には「（個人用の机が利用できるまで）20分待った」とある。つまり、Khanさんは個人用の机がある場所を利用している。最初のメールの第3段落3から、机があるのは(D) private boothsだとわかる。

---

20. In the second e-mail, the word "content" in paragraph 2, line 4, is closest in meaning to
  (A) plentiful　　形 豊富な
  (B) keen　　　　形 熱心な、熱望して
  ＊(C) satisfied　　形 満足した
  (D) calm　　　　形 冷静な、落ち着いた

解説 contentの言い換えとして最も意味が近いものを選ぶ。「（乗客ラウンジの使い勝手が今一つだったので、）結局、出発ゲートの近くの待合室で座っていても同じくらい〜だっただろう」という文脈から考えると、「満足した」という意味の(C) satisfiedが適切。

---

21. What is indicated about Ms. Khan?
  (A) She managed to retrieve her lost baggage.
  (B) She arrived too late to eat at the hotel.
  (C) She did not plan to fly business class.
  ＊(D) She booked her hotel room online.

解説 1つ目のメール第2段落2に、インターネットでBeaumont Hotelを予約した場合の特典として「スタンダードルームの料金のまま部屋をアップグレードできる」と書いてある。2つ目のメール第3段落9でKhanさんが、「客室があのような値段で期待できるものより、ずっと贅沢で居心地が良かった」と述べていることから、Khanさんはこの特典を利用したことがわかる。よって、答えは(D)。(A)なくしたスーツケースをなんとか取り戻したこと、(B)ホテルに着くのが遅すぎて夕食を取れなかったこと、(C)Khanさんがビジネスクラスを利用するつもりがなかったことは、いずれも記述がないので不適切。

CHAPTER 5

言い換え対応力
PARAPHRASING

このスキルが足りない人は…

- ☐ 文書の内容は理解できているのに、答えが選べない
- ☐ 読んだ内容と選択肢の間に差があるように感じる
- ☐ 選択肢が文になっていると選ぶのに時間がかかる

CHAPTER 5
言い換え対応力
PARAPHRASING

➡️「具体」から「抽象」に変換する力
必要になるパート：Part 7

　TOEICでは言い換え表現が多用されます。出題者の観点からすると、文書中の単語がそのまま正解選択肢に現れるパターンのみでは、文意が理解できていなくても正解されてしまう可能性があるからです。TOEICで用いられる言い換えパターンは、**「具体から抽象へ」**と**「個別から一般へ」**が基本です。

　言語学者のサミュエル・I・ハヤカワが唱えた「抽象のはしご」(ladder of abstraction)という概念があります。ある弁護士がいたとしましょう。その人の名はMs. Johnsonですが、Johnson氏はa lawyer（弁護士）であり、a lawyerはa legal professional（法律の専門家）の一種です。また、a legal professionalはa specialist（専門家）に、さらに抽象化することが可能です。このように抽象度を上げていくと、具体的情報は削がれ、より普遍性が高まります。

　本来は議論の妥当性を高めるための概念ですが、TOEICの言い換えを見抜くためにも、この**「抽象のはしごを一段上がって考える力」**は重要です。もちろん、a commercial areaからa business districtのような、はしごでいうと同じ段にあるような語句への言い換えもありますが、こちらは語彙力と多少の発想力があれば対応できます。いずれの場合でも、言い換え表現がカギになる問題は多数存在します。診断テストの設問を例にとって、そのような問題パターンを見ていきましょう。

【Part 7】 p. 14, 17（抜粋。色字の選択肢が正解）

From: Joe Hope <jhope@geoline.com>
To: Mark Weinberg <mweinberg@gam.com>
Date: Tuesday, February 22
Subject: Position (associate producer)
Attachment: 📎 Résumé_JHope.doc

Dear Mr. Weinberg,

I have long been interested in working for Gauguin Advertising and Media and this is the second time I have applied for a position at your firm.
I am applying because of my strong desire to be involved in the creation of innovative marketing strategies for market leaders. （後略）

17. What is indicated about Mr. Hope?
(A) He has interviewed with GAM before.
(B) He is undertaking a course in Internet marketing.
＊(C) He is eager to take on creative challenges.
(D) He is sending his portfolio by regular mail.

言い換えフレーズを目印に正解候補を絞り込め

　この問題では、文書中のstrong desire to（～したいという強い願い）と、選択肢(C)のis eager to（～することを熱望している）が言い換えとして対応しており、これに気づけるかどうかが正解するための1つの条件です。もちろん、トラップとして用意された、文書の内容を部分的に言い換えた不正解選択肢もあるので、選択肢全文に目を通し、裏取りをする必要はあります。それでも、**言い換えフレーズを手掛かりにすると、解答プロセスを大幅にスピードアップさせることができます。**

【Part 7】 p. 12, 15（抜粋）

Dalton Air Finds New Direction

Sydney (August 10)—Since the leadership change in mid-May, there has been much speculation about how David Panetta, the new CEO, will make his mark on Australia's largest international airline. (中略)

Mr. Walker also mentioned that the undertaking might be achieved by merging with a smaller airline. Many experts in the industry speculate that because there is little time for them to hire and train staff before the first flights, it would be a logical step for the rapidly growing company. In that scenario, the new chief's business contacts from his time leading two other aviation companies might come in handy in finding an ideal partner.

15. According to the article, what is Mr. Panetta expected to do?
  ＊(A) Use his personal ties
  (B) Extend a deadline
  (C) Adopt a new practice
  (D) Appoint a board member

単語単位の発想に縛られず、本質を捉えよ

　直接的な言い換え表現を探すと、文書の最終行のfinding（〜［人］を見つける）と(D)のAppoint（〜［人］を任命する）が意味的に近いですが、この問題で用いられている言い換えは、そのような部分的・表面的な読み方では見抜くことができません。「新しいチーフの、これまでの仕事上のコネが役に立つだろう」→「Panetta氏は個人的なつながりを使うことを期待されている」という、**より本質的な内容理解**が試されます。

　単語・フレーズ単位の言い換えであれば、表面的な理解だけでも解答できますが、センテンス単位となると、より高い次元での読解力が要求されます。こういったハイレベルな問題を攻略するには、第3章で触れた**「要約力」の強化**が重要になってきます。文書を頭の中で要約し、主旨をしっかりと把握できていれば、自分の想定をやや外れるような言い換えにも対応できるからです。

　「言い換え対応力」を身につけるためには、TOEIC式の言い換えパターンの感覚をつかむことが必要です。そこで単語・フレーズ単位からセンテンス・段落単位ま

でさまざまな言い換えのパターンを習得できるトレーニングを2種類用意しました。パズルのような構成になっているので、楽しみながらトライしてください。

> **POINT**
> - 「具体から抽象へ」と「個別から一般へ」がTOEIC式言い換えの主流。
> - 言い換えフレーズをマスターし、解答の手掛かりにしよう。
> - センテンス単位のハイレベルな言い換えは、本質的な読解がカギ。

CHAPTER 5
言い換え対応力 PARAPHRASING

➡ トレーニング

Menu 1

　Part 7では、文書中の語句が、設問や選択肢の中で、より抽象的な語に言い換えられていることが多い。ここでは巧妙なパラフレーズを見抜くトレーニングをしよう。
　左欄(1)〜(20)の言い換えとなる語句を、右欄(A)〜(T)から選んで解答欄に書き入れよう。**制限時間は各7分。**

各7分

1.

(1) a vacant position
(2) three meters
(3) a magazine
(4) a decision to act
(5) a tentative plan
(6) airplane
(7) an age requirement
(8) a bill for services
(9) survey results
(10) a product designer
(11) dents and scratches
(12) a set of instructions
(13) main office
(14) an unforeseen termination
(15) a pianist
(16) a claim form
(17) a product launch
(18) illustrations
(19) a stapler
(20) a performance review

(A) an event
(B) headquarters
(C) a position
(D) an unexpected cancellation
(E) information
(F) an operational procedure
(G) an appraisal
(H) artwork
(I) a talent
(J) office equipment
(K) transportation
(L) a provisional arrangement
(M) a condition
(N) intent
(O) a publication
(P) an employment opportunity
(Q) an application
(R) damage
(S) a measurement
(T) an invoice

【 解答欄 】

(1) → _____　(2) → _____　(3) → _____　(4) → _____
(5) → _____　(6) → _____　(7) → _____　(8) → _____
(9) → _____　(10) → _____　(11) → _____　(12) → _____
(13) → _____　(14) → _____　(15) → _____　(16) → _____
(17) → _____　(18) → _____　(19) → _____　(20) → _____

2.

(1)　make an assessment
(2)　respond to an e-mail
(3)　go to a conference
(4)　have arranged ～ previously
(5)　compare alternatives
(6)　give a talk
(7)　take instruction for many years
(8)　say whether ～ or ...
(9)　be absent from work
(10)　supply an address
(11)　send a parcel
(12)　talk over a proposal
(13)　take more orders than one can fill
(14)　change the date of a meeting
(15)　reveal a plan
(16)　stop producing a product
(17)　meet potential partners and associates
(18)　search for an error in a document
(19)　open a new office
(20)　call an applicant

(A)　make an address
(B)　reschedule a gathering
(C)　take a vacation
(D)　proofread
(E)　indicate a location
(F)　ship a package
(G)　make business contacts
(H)　undergo extensive training
(I)　exceed capacity
(J)　discontinue an item
(K)　expand a business
(L)　contrast options
(M)　perform an evaluation
(N)　have experience organizing ～
(O)　attend an event
(P)　indicate a preference
(Q)　make contact
(R)　discuss an idea
(S)　state intentions
(T)　provide a reply

【 解答欄 】

(1) → _____　(2) → _____　(3) → _____　(4) → _____
(5) → _____　(6) → _____　(7) → _____　(8) → _____
(9) → _____　(10) → _____　(11) → _____　(12) → _____
(13) → _____　(14) → _____　(15) → _____　(16) → _____
(17) → _____　(18) → _____　(19) → _____　(20) → _____

Menu 1の解答・解説

1.

(1)	a vacant position 欠員ポスト	=	(P)	an employment opportunity 雇用の機会
(2)	three meters 3メートル	=	(S)	a measurement 寸法
(3)	a magazine 雑誌	=	(O)	a publication 出版物
(4)	a decision to act 行動する決意	=	(N)	intent 意図
(5)	a tentative plan 暫定的な計画	=	(L)	a provisional arrangement 仮の手配
(6)	airplane 航空機	=	(K)	transportation 輸送機関
(7)	an age requirement 年齢制限の条件	=	(M)	a condition 条件
(8)	a bill for services サービスの請求書	=	(T)	an invoice 請求明細書
(9)	survey results 調査結果	=	(E)	information 情報
(10)	a product designer 製品設計者	=	(C)	a position 職
(11)	dents and scratches へこみと傷	=	(R)	damage 損傷
(12)	a set of instructions 一連の指示	=	(F)	an operational procedure 操作（運用）手順
(13)	main office 本社	=	(B)	headquarters 本社、本部
(14)	an unforeseen termination 不測の（契約）終了	=	(D)	an unexpected cancellation 予期せぬ取り消し
(15)	a pianist ピアニスト	=	(I)	a talent 才能ある人
(16)	a claim form 請求用紙	=	(Q)	an application 申込書
(17)	a product launch 製品の発売	=	(A)	an event イベント
(18)	illustrations イラスト	=	(H)	artwork 芸術作品
(19)	a stapler ホチキス	=	(J)	office equipment オフィス用品
(20)	a performance review 人事考課	=	(G)	an appraisal 評価

解説 言い換えを見抜くには語句の核に着目する。(4)は a decision（決意）が核なので(N) intent（意図）に、(9)は results（結果）というデータが核なので(E) information（情報）に対応する。

2.

(1) make an assessment / 査定する = (M) perform an evaluation / 評価を行う

(2) respond to an e-mail / メールに返信する = (T) provide a reply / 返事をする

(3) go to a conference / 会議に行く = (O) attend an event / イベントに出席する

(4) have arranged 〜 previously / 以前に〜を手配した = (N) have experience organizing 〜 / 〜を組織した経験がある

(5) compare alternatives / 代案を比較する = (L) contrast options / 選択肢を対比する

(6) give a talk / 講演をする = (A) make an address / 演説をする

(7) take instruction for many years / 長年にわたり訓練を受ける = (H) undergo extensive training / 広範囲にわたる訓練をする

(8) say whether 〜 or ... / 〜か…かを言う = (P) indicate a preference / 好みを示す

(9) be absent from work / 欠勤する = (C) take a vacation / 休暇を取る

(10) supply an address / 住所の情報を与える = (E) indicate a location / 場所を知らせる

(11) send a parcel / 小包を送る = (F) ship a package / 荷物を発送する

(12) talk over a proposal / 提案について議論する = (R) discuss an idea / 考えを話し合う

(13) take more orders than one can fill / 受注可能な限度以上に受注する = (I) exceed capacity / 生産能力を超える

(14) change the date of a meeting / 会議の日程を変更する = (B) reschedule a gathering / 集会の予定を変更する

(15) reveal a plan / 計画を明らかにする = (S) state intentions / 意図を述べる

(16) stop producing a product / 製品の製造を中止する = (J) discontinue an item / 品物が製造中止になる

(17) meet potential partners and associates / パートナーになる可能性がある人に会う = (G) make business contacts / 仕事上のつてを作る

(18) search for an error in a document / 書類の間違いを探す = (D) proofread / 校正する

(19) open a new office / 新しいオフィスを開く = (K) expand a business / ビジネスを拡大する

(20) call an applicant / 応募者に電話する = (Q) make contact / 連絡を取る

解説 ▶ 動詞句の言い換えは、語句だけでなく構造が変わり、違う発想で表現される場合もある。(4)は「以前に〜したことがある」が「〜した経験がある」という表現になっている。(10)のan addressは「住所」で(E)のa location(所在地)に対応するが、(A)のan addressは「演説」だ。(Q) make contactと(G) make business contactsは単複の違いに留意すること。

Menu 2

語句ではなく文や段落単位のパラフレーズを見抜く練習をする。ボックス内の文書の内容の言い換えとして最も適切な文を、(A) 〜 (D)から選ぼう。**制限時間は各5分。**

● 各5分

1.

If you are planning on buying a new dishwasher, read this offer first. The current Dishpro models all come with a 10-year warranty on parts and labor. It should be mentioned that the longest warranty provided by any of our competitors is five years. Furthermore, you can trade in your old washer and receive up to $50 off the purchase price.

(A) Dishpro is the oldest manufacturer of dishwashers.
(B) Dishpro dishwashers come with the longest warranty on the market.
(C) Replacement parts are reasonably priced.
(D) All traded-in appliances will save the buyer $50.

2.

As you have been made aware in the weekly employee newsletter, Wilson Furniture is about to expand and we will be creating a large number of new positions. Additionally, several new supervisor positions will become available. You are all welcome to apply, but only staff members who have completed the training course will be considered for the new management positions.

(A) Wilson Furniture has recently hired new staff.
(B) Employees are encouraged to seek a promotion.
(C) New locations have already been announced in a bulletin.
(D) All supervisors are required to take a training course.

3.

> We are grateful for your input regarding the packaging of FruityPops. If it is put into practice, we will be sure to send you a complimentary carton of this popular product. In the meantime, we hope you enjoy the exciting new flavors we have developed. Please find enclosed a packet of banana and cherry FruityPops for you to try.

(A) The company rewards people who make suggestions that are adopted.
(B) There were some defects in the FruityPops packaging.
(C) Selected customers are regularly contacted to test potential products.
(D) The company offers its products for free only when they are newly released.

4.

> Hello Ms. Rosenthal,
>
> I am sorry to inform you that I will be unable to attend the workshop on Wednesday. Unfortunately, I have received a last-minute appointment request from a client on that day. I will be available to meet you at your office or in Ascot the following day, if you can make some time before your flight.
>
> Thanks,
>
> Malcolm Handy

(A) A workshop must be postponed.
(B) Mr. Handy's client has asked to change a date.
(C) Ms. Rosenthal's office is located in Ascot.
(D) Ms. Rosenthal is leaving on Thursday.

Menu 2 の解答・解説

※**色字**の選択肢が正解。
※問題文の訳文は紙面では省略（訳文の入手方法はp. 7をご覧ください）。

1.

> If you are planning on buying a new dishwasher, read this offer first. The current Dishpro models all come with a 10-year warranty on parts and labor. It should be mentioned that the longest warranty provided by any of our competitors is five years. Furthermore, you can trade in your old washer and receive up to $50 off the purchase price.

(A) Dishpro is the oldest manufacturer of dishwashers.
* (B) Dishpro dishwashers come with the longest warranty on the market.
(C) Replacement parts are reasonably priced.
(D) All traded-in appliances will save the buyer $50.

- dishwasher 食洗機　● parts and labor 交換部品と修理　● trade in ~ ～を下取りに出す

解説 ▶ 文書はDishproというブランドの食洗機の広告。「どの競合他社の保証も最長で5年」のところを、Dishproは「10年保証」を提供している。よって「Dishpro食洗機には市場で最も長い保証が付いている」という(B)が正解。下取り値引きはup to $50（最大50ドルまで）とあるので、一律50ドル引きとする(D)は不正解。

2.

As you have been made aware in the weekly employee newsletter, Wilson Furniture is about to expand and we will be creating a large number of new positions. Additionally, several new supervisor positions will become available. You are all welcome to apply, but only staff members who have completed the training course will be considered for the new management positions.

(A) Wilson Furniture has recently hired new staff.
＊(B) Employees are encouraged to seek a promotion.
(C) New locations have already been announced in a bulletin.
(D) All supervisors are required to take a training course.

● bulletin 社内報

解説 ▶ 「社内週報でご存じのように」とあるので、社員に向けた通知だとわかる。「いくつかの新たな管理職のポジション」が設けられ、研修を修了した人限定という条件付きではあるが、「皆さんの応募を歓迎します」とあるので、(B)「社員は昇進を希望するよう勧められている」が正解。apply for supervisor positions（管理職のポジションに応募する）＝ seek a promotion（昇進を希望する）の言い換えがポイントだ。

3.

We are grateful for your input regarding the packaging of FruityPops. If it is put into practice, we will be sure to send you a complimentary carton of this popular product. In the meantime, we hope you enjoy the exciting new flavors we have developed. Please find enclosed a packet of banana and cherry FruityPops for you to try.

＊(A) The company rewards people who make suggestions that are adopted.
(B) There were some defects in the FruityPops packaging.
(C) Selected customers are regularly contacted to test potential products.
(D) The company offers its products for free only when they are newly released.

● be put into practice 実現する　● carton 大箱　● defect 欠陥

解説 ▶ FruityPopという商品の製造会社が顧客からの「提案に感謝」するために書いたレターだ。「ご提案が実現すれば、この人気商品を必ず1箱無料でお送りします」とあるので、(A)「その会社は採用される提案をする人々に謝礼をする」が正解。send a complimentary ~（無料の~を送る）＝ reward（~に謝礼する）が言い換え表現として対応している。

4.

> Hello Ms. Rosenthal,
>
> I am sorry to inform you that I will be unable to attend the workshop on Wednesday. Unfortunately, I have received a last-minute appointment request from a client on that day. I will be available to meet you at your office or in Ascot the following day, if you can make some time before your flight.
>
> Thanks,
>
> Malcolm Handy

(A) A workshop must be postponed.
(B) Mr. Handy's client has asked to change a date.
(C) Ms. Rosenthal's office is located in Ascot.
＊(D) Ms. Rosenthal is leaving on Thursday.

- last-minute 直前の、間際の

解説 ▶ Rosenthal氏に宛てたメールの中でHandy氏は「水曜日の研修会に出席できない」と述べている。その理由はa last-minute appointment request（直前の面談依頼）があったからだが、「日程の変更を依頼」されたとは書いていないので(B)は不正解。the following day（翌日）、つまり木曜日、Rosenthal氏が「飛行機に乗る前」であれば会えるということは、(D)「Rosenthal氏は木曜日に出発する」ということなので、これが正解。間接的な言い換えが使われているが、文書や選択肢の中で曜日がキーになっていることに気づくことができれば、曜日を起点にし、情報を関連付けて解答を導くことができる。

Ted流 TOEICの泳ぎ方 ………長続きする英語自己学習法………

続かない原因その5　No reflection

「こんなにやっているのに、全然目標に届かない」と思うと、今までの努力が無駄だったように感じ、あきらめてしまいそうになります。その日の練習が終わったら、まずはやったことを振り返って自分の頑張りを認めましょう。そしてうまくいったこと、うまくいかなかったことを確認し、それに応じて次の日からのトレーニングメニューを工夫しましょう。

続かない原因その6　No fun

結果だけを追い求め、日々の練習ノルマを機械的にこなしていくのはつらいものです。しかし、プロセス自体を楽しめるようになると、練習に対する感情が、がらりと変わります。私が水泳をするときは、まず気持ちよく泳ぐこと、そしてルーティンワークの後、普段やらない泳法を試してみるなど、ちょっとした遊びの要素を取り入れることを心掛けています。あなたのTOEIC対策・英語学習における楽しみ・遊びは何ですか。

CHAPTER 5　言い換え対応力 PARAPHRASING

実践問題

仕上げに、本番形式の難問にチャレンジ。巧妙な言い換え表現を見抜けるか、試してみよう。

Part 7

文書に関する設問の解答として、最も適切なものを1つずつ選ぼう。

（解答・解説はpp. 192〜199）

3分

Questions 1-3 refer to the following advertisement.

Kyle's Books comes to Reed

This weekend the grand opening of Kyle's Books' 20th store in the New Hampshire area will be held at the Twin Pines Mall in Reed. Come in and pick out some of our books marked at far below retail price.

Kyle's Books is New Hampshire's fastest growing chain of bookstores. In addition to a wide variety of fiction and nonfiction books, we also have graphic novels, paper goods and toys. Whether you are looking for the latest novel, a stimulating science book or a practical guide to home landscaping, you are sure to find it here. The chief reason for our success is our dedication to customer service. If you need a book that we do not have in stock, we guarantee that we will have it for you within three business days.

All day on Saturday November 1, we will have various activities for people to enjoy. You can sign up for one of our book clubs and discuss books with other readers while enjoying free coffee and snacks. We have children's story times where toddlers and anyone who likes a good story exuberantly told are welcome. There is ample room for these events, and we will frequently be visited by authors on book-signing tours. To commemorate the opening of the store, we have asked Reed's own best-selling novelist Steve Turner to come in and read one of his books for the crowd. The television news will be covering the event and we are expecting a massive turnout, so be sure to come in nice and early. By all means, get to know our friendly, experienced staff, and see why Kyle's Books will soon be your favorite bookstore.

1. What is indicated about the event?
   (A) It will be held over two days.
   (B) Space will be set up temporarily.
   (C) Books will be discounted.
   (D) It is limited to book club members.

2. What is suggested about Kyle's Books?
   (A) It has started using a new ordering system.
   (B) It has food and beverages available for purchase.
   (C) It is the largest book chain in New Hampshire.
   (D) It offers literature from several genres.

3. Who most likely is Steve Turner?
   (A) A local resident
   (B) A book publisher
   (C) A television reporter
   (D) A charity organizer

Questions 4-6 refer to the following advertisement.

El Capo's
Home-style Mexican cooking at its best

2010 Armada St., Santa Fe, NM 87505
Phone 555-473-1131
www.elcapos.com

"... the most authentic Mexican dining experience in all of Santa Fe."
— Brian Denning, *What's on? Santa Fe*

"... excellent food and service. I'll be back."
— Joan Robbins, *Dining Out Magazine*

El Capo's serves the finest Mexican cuisine in Santa Fe and quite possibly the entire state. Our chefs pride themselves on the authenticity of their dishes. "Home-style Mexican cooking at its best" is the motto we all live by. Serving a largely Mexican clientele, we are confident that we live up to our claim.

We use locally grown, fresh ingredients and herbs and spices imported from traditional suppliers. The restaurant is open for lunch and dinner daily between the hours of 11 A.M. and 10 P.M. Dinners on Saturday and Sunday are always very popular and making a reservation is strongly advised. For large groups, we have a partitioned room that sits up to 20 comfortably. This is an ideal location for company events or large family gatherings. We can provide Mexican entertainment by traditional Mexican musicians as well as other amusements such as piñata and various games.

El Capo's has ample parking and public transport within three minutes' walk. Why not try something new and exciting the next time you eat out?

4. What is the purpose of the advertisement?
   (A) To announce a cruise dinner
   (B) To publicize popular menu items
   (C) To draw attention to an eatery
   (D) To promote a new banquet hall

   Ⓐ Ⓑ Ⓒ Ⓓ

5. Who most likely is Brian Denning?
   (A) A local farmer
   (B) A correspondent
   (C) A restaurateur
   (D) A media critic

   Ⓐ Ⓑ Ⓒ Ⓓ

6. What is NOT mentioned about El Capo's?
   (A) It is more crowded on weekends.
   (B) It imports some of its ingredients.
   (C) It can accommodate corporate functions.
   (D) It is located in downtown Santa Fe.

   Ⓐ Ⓑ Ⓒ Ⓓ

Questions 7-10 refer to the following article.

Douglas, June 1—Many residents of the small seaside community of Douglas are expressing concern about a council plan to build a toll road between there and Greenhaven. Unlike other public works, this one is not to be funded by taxpayers. Instead, it is a project of the Macintyre Infrastructure Group, and therefore some of the usual opportunities for people in the community to voice concern are not on offer. The biggest objections come from those who do not want to attract a larger population or additional visitors from the Greenhaven region. It seems that many in this tiny seaside village want to keep it that way. "We don't want tourism or big shopping malls here. We moved all the way to Douglas to avoid those things," said one disgruntled resident.

However, there are many in the community who welcome the new highway. One resident by the name of Genevieve Clementine said, "I think that the new road between Greenhaven and Douglas is going to shorten my commute time by a significant amount. That means I will have more time to spend with my family, and need to spend less on fuel."

Community leader, Des Linton says that he needed to balance the community's commercial and lifestyle needs in making the executive decision. "It may be rather disappointing for some that the town will probably never be as quiet as it is now, but the council and I have agreed that many local businesses need the extra traffic this will bring." Care has been taken to ensure that congestion levels are not affected greatly in the town center, and the new road's route will be well outside town in order to reduce noise levels as much as possible. Other possible concerns such as safety and environmental effects have been largely rejected based on the findings of an impact report published by the construction company that won the contract.

The project will be given an official go-ahead at the regular town council meeting on June 5. The highway is expected to open to traffic in four years' time and lead to a projected increase of 200,000 visitors annually. Toll rates are still under consideration and will have to be negotiated with the Douglas council before they are officially announced.

7. Why are many people in Douglas opposed to the plan?
   (A) The cost of construction is too high.
   (B) The environmental impacts are uncertain.
   (C) They want to preserve the town's character.
   (D) It requires a merger with another municipality.

8. What is suggested about Ms. Clementine?
   (A) She is concerned about rising fuel prices.
   (B) She has family members residing in Greenhaven.
   (C) She wants an opportunity to discuss the project.
   (D) She works outside the town of Douglas.

9. Who most likely is Des Linton?
   (A) A local business owner
   (B) The mayor of Douglas
   (C) A company spokesperson
   (D) An environmental activist

10. According to the article, how will the new highway affect the town of Douglas?
    (A) It will attract greater visitor numbers.
    (B) It will create work for the residents.
    (C) It will reduce damage to the environment.
    (D) It will improve the town's traffic safety.

● 4分

Questions 11-14 refer to the following e-mail.

	E-Mail Message
To:	Yuko Nakamori <ynakamori@onenet.com>
From:	Trevor Coleman <tcoleman@davidsoncc.com>
Date:	19 March
Subject:	Davidson Community Center Fair, March 25 to 28

Dear Ms. Nakamori,

Thank you for contacting me about the Davidson Community Center Fair. I understand you are interested in bringing a group of elderly guests to the fair on its second or third day. The fair has plenty of things to do for people of all ages, so I think your plan is an excellent idea.

Seeing as you are bringing such a large group, I wonder if there are any special accommodations we can make for them. I anticipate that we will be experiencing some high temperatures from next week, regardless of the weather. You may need to make sure they have somewhere to rest when they get tired. As it happens, we have a spare tent which we would be happy to make available for your group should they need it. At present, it is designated for storage purposes, so if you are likely to utilize it, I would ask that you give us notice a day ahead of your arrival. As to the best day to come, the earlier of your suggestions would be preferable, as we anticipate crowding on Saturday.

You already have my contact details, so I hope you will let me know if there is anything else we can do to make your outing more enjoyable.

Sincerely,
Trevor Coleman

11. What is the purpose of the e-mail?
   (A) To attract people to a fair
   (B) To offer advice to visitors
   (C) To seek assistance with an event
   (D) To confirm a reservation

12. What is suggested about the fair?
   (A) The venue is warm all year round.
   (B) It has attractions for senior visitors.
   (C) It will take place over two days.
   (D) There is a shortage of space for groups.

13. What does Mr. Coleman offer to Ms. Nakamori?
   (A) Group rates
   (B) Transport assistance
   (C) Contact information
   (D) Outdoor shelter

14. When most likely will Ms. Nakamori's group attend the fair?
   (A) On March 25
   (B) On March 26
   (C) On March 27
   (D) On March 28

実践問題の解答・解説

※**色字**の選択肢が正解。
※問題文の訳文は紙面では省略（訳文の入手方法はp. 7をご覧ください）。

Part 7

問題 1-3 は次の広告に関するものです。

Kyle's Books comes to Reed

[1]This weekend the grand opening of Kyle's Books' 20th store in the New Hampshire area will be held at the Twin Pines Mall in Reed. [2]Come in and pick out some of our books marked at far below retail price.

Kyle's Books is New Hampshire's fastest growing chain of bookstores. [3]In addition to a wide variety of fiction and nonfiction books, we also have graphic novels, paper goods and toys. Whether you are looking for the latest novel, a stimulating science book or a practical guide to home landscaping, you are sure to find it here. The chief reason for our success is our dedication to customer service. If you need a book that we do not have in stock, we guarantee that we will have it for you within three business days.

All day on Saturday November 1, we will have various activities for people to enjoy. You can sign up for one of our book clubs and discuss books with other readers while enjoying free coffee and snacks. We have children's story times where toddlers and anyone who likes a good story exuberantly told are welcome. There is ample room for these events, and we will frequently be visited by authors on book-signing tours. To commemorate the opening of the store, [4]we have asked Reed's own best-selling novelist Steve Turner to come in and read one of his books for the crowd. The television news will be covering the event and we are expecting a massive turnout, so be sure to come in nice and early. By all means, get to know our friendly, experienced staff, and see why Kyle's Books will soon be your favorite bookstore.

- graphic novel 漫画 ● stimulating 刺激的な ● landscaping 造園 ● dedication 献身、熱心さ
- toddler （よちよち歩きの）幼児 ● exuberantly 華麗に、意気揚々と ● ample 十分な、広々とした
- commemorate ～を祝う ● massive かなりの ● turnout 出席者数、動員 ● by all means ぜひとも、どうぞ

1. What is indicated about the event?
   (A) It will be held over two days.
   (B) Space will be set up temporarily.
   ∗ (C) Books will be discounted.
   (D) It is limited to book club members.

解説 Kyle's Booksの開店記念イベントについて述べられていることを選ぶ。第1段落2、Come in and pick out some of our books marked at far below retail price（小売価格よりかなり安く値付けされた本を買いに来てください）を言い換えた (C) Books will be discounted.（本が割引される）が正解。(A)は第3段落冒頭で1日限定イベントとわかるので不可。(B)のイベントスペースについては、同じ第3段落5〜6行目に「イベント用に豊富なスペースがあり」とは書かれているが、これが「一時的に設営される」かどうかは述べられていない。(D)の読書クラブメンバーについても第3段落で述べられているが、イベント参加の条件ではない。

2. What is suggested about Kyle's Books?
   (A) It has started using a new ordering system.
   (B) It has food and beverages available for purchase.
   (C) It is the largest book chain in New Hampshire.
   ∗ (D) It offers literature from several genres.

解説 第2段落3に着目。この書店は、フィクション、ノンフィクション、漫画など、さまざまなジャンルの本を取り扱っていることがわかる。この言い換えとしては、(D)の「さまざまなジャンルの本を提供している」がふさわしい。literature（印刷物、文献）は不可算名詞で、publicationの言い換え表現だ。第2段落冒頭に「Kyle's Booksはニューハンプシャー州で最も急速に成長している書店チェーン」とあるが、これは(C)の「最大の書店チェーン」とイコールではない。

3. Who most likely is Steve Turner?
   ∗ (A) A local resident
   (B) A book publisher
   (C) A television reporter
   (D) A charity organizer

解説 設問中のキーワード、Steve Turnerを文書内で探すと、第3段落4にReed's own best-selling novelist Steve Turner（Reed在住のベストセラー小説家、Steve Turner）という記述が見つかる。つまり、Turner氏はReedに住んでいるということだ。Reedは、第1段落1からイベントを開催する新店舗の所在地だとわかる。「イベントが開かれる地域に住んでいる」ということは「地元の住民」だと言い換えることができるので、正解は(A)。

問題4-6 は次の広告に関するものです。

[1] El Capo's
Home-style Mexican cooking at its best

2010 Armada St., Santa Fe, NM 87505
Phone 555-473-1131
www.elcapos.com

[2] "… the most authentic Mexican dining experience in all of Santa Fe."
— Brian Denning, *What's on? Santa Fe*

"… excellent food and service. I'll be back."
— Joan Robbins, *Dining Out Magazine*

[3] El Capo's serves the finest Mexican cuisine in Santa Fe and quite possibly the entire state. Our chefs pride themselves on the authenticity of their dishes. "Home-style Mexican cooking at its best" is the motto we all live by. Serving a largely Mexican clientele, we are confident that we live up to our claim.

[4] We use locally grown, fresh ingredients and herbs and spices imported from traditional suppliers. The restaurant is open for lunch and dinner daily between the hours of 11 A.M. and 10 P.M. [5] Dinners on Saturday and Sunday are always very popular and making a reservation is strongly advised. For large groups, we have a partitioned room that sits up to 20 comfortably. [6] This is an ideal location for company events or large family gatherings. We can provide Mexican entertainment by traditional Mexican musicians as well as other amusements such as piñata and various games.

[7] El Capo's has ample parking and public transport within three minutes' walk. Why not try something new and exciting the next time you eat out?

- at its best 最も良い状態の、最高の ● authentic 本物の ● cuisine 料理 ● clientele（集合的に）顧客、常連 ● live up to ~ ~（期待など）に応える ● ingredient 材料 ● partitioned 分割した、分けられた ● gathering 集まり ● piñata ピニャータ ※景品等を入れたつぼを天井からつるして割る、余興の一種。

4. What is the purpose of the advertisement?
　(A) To announce a cruise dinner
　(B) To publicize popular menu items
　＊(C) To draw attention to an eatery
　(D) To promote a new banquet hall

解説 広告の目的を問う問題。広告の見出し**1**のEl Capo's ／ Home-style Mexican cooking at its best（最高のメキシコ家庭料理）、第1段落**3**のserves the finest Mexican cuisine（最高のメキシコ料理を提供する）という記述から、El Capo'sは飲食店であることがわかる。正解は(C)「食堂に関心を集めるため」。eateryは「軽食堂、飲食店」で、restaurantの同義語。

5. Who most likely is Brian Denning?
　(A) A local farmer
　＊(B) A correspondent
　(C) A restaurateur
　(D) A media critic

解説 Brian Denningは**2**の「最も本格的なメキシコ料理体験」というコメントをした人物だ。名前の後の*What's on? Santa Fe*は、イタリック体で書かれていることと、その下のコメントの提供者名に続く*Dining Out Magazine*と並列になっていることから、Denning氏が所属する雑誌か新聞の名前だと推測できる。レストランのレビューをそうした媒体に載せる職業として最もふさわしいのは、(B) A correspondent（記者）。(C) A restaurateurは「レストラン経営者」。メディアを評論しているわけではないので、(D) A media critic（メディア批評家）は誤り。

6. What is NOT mentioned about El Capo's?
　(A) It is more crowded on weekends.
　(B) It imports some of its ingredients.
　(C) It can accommodate corporate functions.
　＊(D) It is located in downtown Santa Fe.

解説 El Capo'sについて述べられていないことを答える問題。(A)は第2段落**5**の「土日のディナーはとても人気」という情報が合致する。(B)は**4**の「輸入されたハーブとスパイス」（herbs and spices = ingredients）、(C)は**6**の「会社のイベントに最適な場所」（company events = corporate functions）と一致する。(C)のaccommodateは「〜の要求を満たす、〜に対応する」の意。第3段落**7**に「公共交通機関から徒歩3分」とあるが、これは「サンタフェの中心街にある」の言い換えとは言えない。よって、正解は(D)。

問題 7-10 は次の記事に関するものです。

Douglas, June 1—Many residents of the small seaside community of Douglas are expressing concern about a council plan to build a toll road between there and Greenhaven. Unlike other public works, this one is not to be funded by taxpayers. Instead, it is a project of the Macintyre Infrastructure Group, and therefore some of the usual opportunities for people in the community to voice concern are not on offer. [1]The biggest objections come from those who do not want to attract a larger population or additional visitors from the Greenhaven region. It seems that many in this tiny seaside village want to keep it that way. "We don't want tourism or big shopping malls here. We moved all the way to Douglas to avoid those things," said one disgruntled resident.

However, there are many in the community who welcome the new highway. [2]One resident by the name of Genevieve Clementine said, "I think that the new road between Greenhaven and Douglas is going to shorten my commute time by a significant amount. That means I will have more time to spend with my family, and need to spend less on fuel."

[3]Community leader, Des Linton says that he needed to balance the community's commercial and lifestyle needs in making the executive decision. "It may be rather disappointing for some that the town will probably never be as quiet as it is now, but [4]the council and I have agreed that many local businesses need the extra traffic this will bring." Care has been taken to ensure that congestion levels are not affected greatly in the town center, and the new road's route will be well outside town in order to reduce noise levels as much as possible. Other possible concerns such as safety and environmental effects have been largely rejected based on the findings of an impact report published by the construction company that won the contract.

The project will be given an official go-ahead at the regular town council meeting on June 5. [5]The highway is expected to open to traffic in four years' time and lead to a projected increase of 200,000 visitors annually. Toll rates are still under consideration and will have to be negotiated with the Douglas council before they are officially announced.

- infrastructure 基盤、基本的施設　● disgruntled 不満な　● resident 住民　● significant かなりの
- congestion 渋滞　● go-ahead 開始の許可　● projected 予測される、計画される　● toll 使用料

7. Why are many people in Douglas opposed to the plan?
   (A) The cost of construction is too high.
   (B) The environmental impacts are uncertain.
   ∗ (C) They want to preserve the town's character.
   (D) It requires a merger with another municipality.

解説 第1段落1に、「人口の増加やGreenhavenからの観光客の増加を望まない人からの反対の声が最も大きい。この小さな海辺の村を今のままに保ちたいというのが、多くの住人の意見だ」との記述がある。よって、正解は(C)「町の特色を残したい」。文書中のkeep it that way（そのままに保つ）が、(C)ではpreserve（維持する）に言い換えられている。

8. What is suggested about Ms. Clementine?
   (A) She is concerned about rising fuel prices.
   (B) She has family members residing in Greenhaven.
   (C) She wants an opportunity to discuss the project.
   ∗ (D) She works outside the town of Douglas.

解説 第2段落2で、Douglasの住民であるClementine氏は、「GreenhavenとDouglas間に新道ができたら、私の通勤時間はかなり短くなると思う」と述べている。ここから、彼女は普段からDouglas外で仕事をしているとわかる。よって、答えは(D)「Douglasの外で働いている」。

9. Who most likely is Des Linton?
   (A) A local business owner   ∗ (B) The mayor of Douglas
   (C) A company spokesperson   (D) An environmental activist

解説 Linton氏の名前は第3段落3に登場する。そこにあるCommunity leader（地域のリーダー）という記述と、4のthe council and I have agreed …（議会と私は…について同意した）という発言から推論すると、正解は(B) The mayor of Douglas（Douglas市長）だ。(A)も(D)も「地域のリーダー」である可能性はあるが、どちらも市議会と共に意思決定をする立場にはない。

10. According to the article, how will the new highway affect the town of Douglas?
    ∗ (A) It will attract greater visitor numbers.
    (B) It will create work for the residents.
    (C) It will reduce damage to the environment.
    (D) It will improve the town's traffic safety.

解説 第1段落1の計画反対の理由や、第4段落5の「この幹線道路により、年間20万人の訪問者増が見込める」という記述から、正解は(A)「より多くの訪問者を引き付ける」となる。他の選択肢に関する記述はない。

問 11-14 は次のメールに関するものです。

E-Mail Message

To:	Yuko Nakamori <ynakamori@onenet.com>
From:	Trevor Coleman <tcoleman@davidsoncc.com>
Date:	19 March
Subject:	[1] Davidson Community Center Fair, March 25 to 28

Dear Ms. Nakamori,

[2] Thank you for contacting me about the Davidson Community Center Fair. I understand you are interested in bringing a group of elderly guests to the fair on its second or third day. [3] The fair has plenty of things to do for people of all ages, so I think your plan is an excellent idea.

Seeing as you are bringing such a large group, I wonder if there are any special accommodations we can make for them. I anticipate [4] that we will be experiencing some high temperatures from next week, regardless of the weather. [5] You may need to make sure they have somewhere to rest when they get tired. As it happens, [6] we have a spare tent which we would be happy to make available for your group should they need it. At present, it is designated for storage purposes, so if you are likely to utilize it, I would ask that you give us notice a day ahead of your arrival. [7] As to the best day to come, the earlier of your suggestions would be preferable, as we anticipate crowding on Saturday.

You already have my contact details, so I hope you will let me know if there is anything else we can do to make your outing more enjoyable.

Sincerely,
Trevor Coleman

- anticipate 〜を予期する ● designate 〜を指定する ● storage 保管 ● utilize 〜を利用する
- crowding 混み合うこと

実践問題の解答・解説

11. What is the purpose of the e-mail?
(A) To attract people to a fair
∗ (B) To offer advice to visitors
(C) To seek assistance with an event
(D) To confirm a reservation

解説 ▶ 第1段落2から、メールの受信者であるNakamori氏が、以前、「Davidsonコミュニティーセンターのフェアに年配の方たちを連れていきたい」という旨の連絡をしたことがわかる。そして送信者であるColeman氏は、第2段落5、7など、いくつかの提案をしている。この内容をまとめて言い換えた(B)「来場者にアドバイスをするため」が正解。

12. What is suggested about the fair?
(A) The venue is warm all year round.
∗ (B) It has attractions for senior visitors.
(C) It will take place over two days.
(D) There is a shortage of space for groups.

解説 ▶ 第1段落3の「あらゆる年齢の人に楽しんでもらえることがある」という記述から、正解は(B)「年配の訪問者向けのアトラクションがある」。「年配の人」は「あらゆる年齢の人」に含まれるので、言い換えとして成立する。第2段落4に「来週から高温になる」とあるので、(A)「会場は1年中暖かい」は不適切。

13. What does Mr. Coleman offer to Ms. Nakamori?
(A) Group rates   (B) Transport assistance
(C) Contact information ∗ (D) Outdoor shelter

解説 ▶ 第2段落6に「予備のテントがあるので、あなたのグループが必要とするなら使えるようにします」とある。このa spare tentを言い換えた(D) Outdoor shelterが正解。shelterは日よけ、雨よけになるもの全般を指す語だ。

14. When most likely will Ms. Nakamori's group attend the fair?
(A) On March 25
∗ (B) On March 26
(C) On March 27
(D) On March 28

解説 ▶ 件名1によると、イベント開催日は3月25日から28日まで。第1段落2から、Nakamori氏の一行はフェアの2日目か3日目に会場を訪れようとしていることがわかる。そして、第2段落7に、「最も良い来場日は、あなたが提案した日のうち早い方」とある。つまり、Nakamori氏はイベント2日目の3月26日に来るように勧められている。よって、正解は(B)。

CHAPTER 5

Ted's Talks ❹

TOEICを超越する人3タイプ — 2. Expert（達人）

> *They absorb TOEIC. They try to master English.*
> （TOEICから英語を吸収したい。英語を極めたい。）

　英語に純粋に興味がある人や、TOEIC以外の入り口から英語学習をスタートした人に多いタイプです。彼らは、趣味の洋楽や洋画に接するのと同じようなアプローチでTOEICの問題に取り組んでいます。彼らの姿勢から、何を学べるでしょうか。

● 完璧さ

英語の歌を1曲歌えるようになるためには、歌詞を覚えたり不自然な発音を矯正したり、いろいろな努力が必要です。TOEICにも同様のアプローチで挑むのが達人タイプの人たちです。彼らはPart 7では長文をスラスラと読めるようになろうとし、Part 5では選択肢以外にも目を向け、不明なことがあれば辞書を引きます。正解するだけでは飽き足らず、問題文を徹底的に掘り下げて、完璧にマスターしようとするのが彼らの特徴です。一見遠回りのようでも、同じような語句やトピックが繰り返し登場するTOEICでは、このやり方が一定の効果をもたらします。

● 反復

完璧さに対する欲求が強いので、反復練習をいといません。何十回、何百回と繰り返し音読することで、考えなくても口がコロケーションを覚えている状態になります。常人離れした練習量は普通の人には真似できませんが、彼らのストイックな姿勢には学ぶべきものがあります。

● 指導

このタイプの人には、英語講師になったり、結果的に指導者的な立場になったりする人が多いようです。人に教えることは、最高の学習方法です。人に説明することによって知識が整理され、人の模範となるためにスキルが磨かれるからです。実際に講師にはならなくても、誰かに教えているつもりで問題解説や音読をしてみる「エア指導」は効果的な学習法です。

　何事も上達するとさらに意欲がかき立てられるものです。できるだけ楽をしたい、効率的にやりたいという意識を一度取り払ってしまえば、そこに道が開けてくるでしょう。最後にアメリカのオペラ指揮者、Sarah Caldwellの言葉をご紹介します。

Learn everything you can, anytime you can, from anyone you can; there will always come a time when you will be grateful you did.
（何でも、いつでも、誰からでも学ぶようにしなさい。いつか必ず、そうして良かったと思う時がくるから）

CHAPTER 6

語法・語感力
SENSITIVITY TO WORDS/USAGE

このスキルが足りない人は…

- [ ] 勘で解くとたいてい間違える
- [ ] 文法の基礎は押さえたけれど、例外によく引っ掛かる
- [ ] 語彙問題はつい訳して考えてしてしまい、正解を絞り込めない

CHAPTER 6
語法・語感力
SENSITIVITY TO WORDS/USAGE

➡ ディテールへの注意力
必要になるパート：Part 5／6／7

　TOEICの語彙問題には、意味に加えて語句の使い方、いわゆる「語法」も押さえておかないと解けない問題があります。このような問題は、語句の日本語訳を根拠に解こうとすると間違えることがあります。例えば、reserve a ------- の空所に入る語を選ぶ問題で、「ホテルを予約する」という日本語に引きずられると、hotelを選んでしまいそうになります。しかし、英語にはreserve a hotelという用法はなく、目的語にはa (hotel) roomのような語句が適切です。

　place an order（注文する）やstrictly confidential（極秘の）のような、よく一緒に用いられる語句の組み合わせのことを、**「コロケーション」**と言います。TOEICには、意味や文法的な観点から選択肢を消去していくことでも解けるけれど、コロケーションの知識があれば一瞬で解ける問題が多く出題されています。

　コロケーションの知識は、語句の使われ方に着目しながら英文を読んだり聞いたりすることで身についていきます。その経験が積み重なったものが「語感」です。実は、**英語力の高い人が言う「カンで解いた」は、たいてい「（語）感で解いた」という意味**です。彼らは単なるヤマ勘ではなく、経験記憶から解いているのです。

　語法・語感力を問う問題を攻略するためには、日頃から英文の細部に注意を払い、細かな違いを意識しておくことが大事です。では、診断テストの中で「語法・語感力」が正解のカギとなった問題を見てみましょう。

【Part 5】 p. 10, 7（色字の選択肢が正解）

7. Since the customer service department was taken over by Ms. White, it has been far more ------- to requests for assistance from customers.
   (A) helpful　　　　　形 役に立つ
   (B) pleasant　　　　形 気持ちのいい
   (C) understanding　形 思いやりのある
   ＊(D) responsive　　形 すぐに反応する

Part 5、6：和訳には表れない違いがカギになる

　空所までの文脈から考えると、複数の選択肢が入るように見えますが、ポイントは空所直後のto requestsとのつながりです。正解は(D) responsive to requestsで、「依頼にすぐに対応する」という意味になります。

　helpful to ~ やpleasant to ~ という形を覚えていたために(A)や(B)を選んだという人は、語法への注意力を高める必要があります。helpfulもpleasantも、to customersのようにto＋人（〜[人]にとって）の形でしかtoを取りません。「この形容詞の後ろに付く前置詞はto」のような限定的なルールしか覚えていないと、上級者向けの語法問題には太刀打ちできません。語法の知識を蓄積するためには、英文を読む際に、形容詞＋前置詞のような狭い範囲に注目するのではなく、もう少し視野を広げ、その後ろにどんな語が来ているか、どういう文脈で使われているかなどを観察しましょう。セットフレーズは音や韻で覚えるようにすると、効率的に記憶に定着します。

【Part 6】 p. 11, 9 (抜粋)

Many sports fans are reluctant to buy a season pass because they are concerned that they may be unable to make full use of their purchase. Unexpected work commitment and interstate transfers are commonly ------- reasons for underutilized passes, resulting in a

9. (A) insisted
(B) accessed
＊(C) cited
(D) neglected

huge waste of money.

Part 5、6：コロケーション記憶による取捨選択

　頭の中のコロケーションのデータベースを常に更新・拡張していくことで、読解や解答の速度は向上します。この問題は、空所直後のreasonsとよく一緒に用いられる(C) citedが正解です。cite（～を引用する、～を挙げる）は、giveやprovideと並び、reasonと相性の良い動詞です。多くの上級者はこうした問題を、「既視感」を利用して素早く処理できるので、リーディングセクションでも時間に余裕ができます。

　コロケーションや語句の使い分けは、もちろん、一朝一夕にはマスターできません。ですから、語法問題は英語学習者にとって、攻略すべき最後の砦のような手ごわい存在です。あきらめずにコツコツ対策していきましょう。

【Part 7】 p. 14, 19 (抜粋)

I am a competent computer user and will take any courses needed to bring me up-to-speed on the software GAM uses. As I mention in the attached résumé, I am also an expert photographer having won a number of local awards. My degree in international business had a marketing component and that, combined with my five years' experience at De La Care, makes me well suited to this position.

19. In the e-mail, the word "component" in paragraph 3, line 4, is closest in meaning to
 ＊(A) element
 (B) prospect
 (C) certificate
 (D) ingredient

Part 7：同義語知識に頼りすぎず、文脈把握に基づく語感で解く

　Part 7の同義語問題は、単語単体の意味だけでなく、文脈をも手掛かりにして解かなければなりません。指定された語句が文中で担っている意味を引き継いで、そのまま置き換えることができる選択肢を選びます。**19**で問われているcomponentは、単体では(D) ingredient（成分、構成要素）の同義語と捉えることが可能です。しかし、この文は大学における専攻の説明で、「マーケティングの『要素』を持っていた」という文脈なので、(A) elementを選ぶのが適切です。このように、単体では同義語になり得るが、文脈にそぐわないので不正解という選択肢が含まれている問題は、よく出題されます。**対で覚えた同義語の知識だけに頼らず、文脈把握と語感を軸に判断することが重要**です。

　「語法・語感力」を獲得するためには、似て非なる語句の使い分けを認識し、「fill outと来ればa form」と言えるように、**知識を能動化する（自発的にアウトプットできる状態にする）**ことが必要です。ここでは、紛らわしい2択問題と、文脈から能動的に語句を発想するためのトレーニングの2種類を用意しました。チャレンジしてみてください。

● POINT

- ☐ **Part 5、6では語句の意味だけではなく「使い方」も問われる。**
- ☐ **Part 7の同義語問題で多義語が出たら、文脈を把握して語感で解こう。**
- ☐ コロケーションの知識は経験記憶で蓄積し、能動化しよう。

CHAPTER 6
語法・語感力 SENSITIVITY TO WORDS/USAGE

→ **トレーニング**

Menu 1

　問題文を読んで、空所に入り得る語を想像できれば、正解は瞬間的に選べる。解答時間が短縮でき、集中力もPart 7のために温存できる。ここではそういった解き方を習得するために、選択肢のないPart 5に取り組もう。前後関係や文脈から空所に入る語を考え、記入しよう。空所には1語しか入れてはいけない。**制限時間は1問20秒、合計3分40秒**。厳しめだが、直感的に解くコツをつかむために挑戦してほしい。

● 3分40秒

1. Although Balani Industries originally planned to build it locally in Yorkdale, its first domestic plant will likely be constructed -------.

2. Staff at the exhibition booth should ensure that the batteries of the tablet computers are charged to ------- prior to the software demonstration.

3. This voucher ------- the bearer to two nights' stay at the Wilshire Hotel, including dinner and breakfast at the hotel restaurant.

4. Staff members assigned a company car are expected to maintain it in a clean condition as dirty vehicles ------- poorly on our brand image.

5. Department managers are required to provide an ------- of their spending over the coming year based on previous years' figures.

   _____

6. The company presented Tom Peralta with a watch as a ------- of appreciation for his many years of hard work.

   _____

7. Kimura Corporation is under ------- from consumers to update the software in its phones.

   _____

8. Marathon participants are required to ------- their race-day packets at City Hall by presenting their identification at the marathon administration desk.

   _____

9. Hu Yang Electronics has discontinued its line of electronic dictionaries as maintaining it would be nothing ------- a drain on resources.

   _____

10. Tim Cleminson played an important ------- in obtaining the distribution rights for D&F Cola in the state.

    _____

11. Oliveira Media Advertising will be required to make a ------- lower than the competition's in order to secure the contract for Stallard Airlines.

    _____

Menu 1の解答・解説

※問題文の訳文は紙面では省略（訳文の入手方法はp.7をご覧ください）。

1. Although Balani Industries originally **planned to build it locally in Yorkdale, its first domestic plant will likely be constructed** elsewhere.

   解説 初の国内工場をYorkdaleに建てる予定だったが、それを「どこかよそに」建設するとするelsewhereが正解。工場以外の「代わりに」なるものを提示していないので、insteadは不適。

2. Staff at the exhibition booth should ensure that the batteries of **the tablet computers are charged to** capacity **prior to the software demonstration.**
   - ensure ～を確かにする ● tablet computer タブレット型のコンピューター

   解説 「コンピューターのバッテリーを充電する」という文意から、toを伴い「容量いっぱいに」という成句を作るcapacity（容量）が正解。maximumやfullは文法的には除外できないが、英語としては不自然なので、不正解とする。

3. **This voucher** entitles **the bearer to two nights' stay** at the Wilshire Hotel, including dinner and breakfast at the hotel restaurant.

   解説 引換券がそのbearer（所持者）に2泊分の宿泊の「権利を与える」という文意から、entitlesが正解。entitle A toの後ろは名詞と不定詞の両方を置くことができる。be entitled to ～の受け身の形でもよく用いられる。能動的にこれが使えるのはBEYOND 990erレベル。

4. Staff members assigned a company car are expected to maintain it in a clean condition as **dirty vehicles** reflect **poorly on our brand image.**
   - assign ～を割り当てる、与える

   解説 汚れた車はブランドイメージに悪い「影響を与える」という意味のreflectが正解。「（水面などに）映る」という意味もあり、こちらはPart 1で重要。affectやinfluenceは他動詞なのでonが不要で、かつ副詞はpoorly（みすぼらしく）ではなくnegatively（マイナスに）が適切。

5. Department managers are required to **provide an** estimate **of their spending over the coming year** based on previous years' figures.

   解説 前年実績を踏まえて提出すべきものは次年度の「見積もり・概算」なので、正解はestimate。この語は「見積書」だけでなく、さまざまな数量などの「概算、推定」に用いることができる。もし空所前がaであればprediction（予測）が正解になる。

6. The company presented Tom Peralta with a watch as a token of appreciation for his many years of hard work.

解説 「〜の印として」という意味のas a token ofを作るtokenが正解。sign（表れ、兆し）にはtokenのような「気持ちの印」という意味はなく不適。as a way of saying thank you（感謝の意を述べる方法として）という、似た意味を持つフレーズもある。

7. Kimura Corporation is under pressure from consumers to update the software in its phones.

解説 underと合わさって「圧力を受けている」という意味の成句を作るpressureが正解。日本語の「圧力下にある」という表現と同じ発想だ。underには「影響などを受けて、〜の最中で」という意味がある。

8. Marathon participants are required to claim their race-day packets at City Hall by presenting their identification at the marathon administration desk.

● race-day packet レース日用のパケット ※ゼッケンなどのセット。

解説 レース日用パケットを「（権利として）請求する、要求する」という意味のclaimが正解。receiveやobtain、collectも空所に入れることができるが、このパケットはマラソンに参加する各人が当然受け取るべきものという文意からclaimがベストアンサーだ。ちなみに日本語の「クレーマー」は「しつこく苦情を言う」人だが、本来、claimにはそのような意味はない。

9. Hu Yang Electronics has discontinued its line of electronic dictionaries as maintaining it would be nothing but a drain on resources.

解説 前置詞のbutに「〜以外」という意味があるので、nothing butは「〜以外の何物でもない」=「〜だけ」となる。onlyと置き換え可能。a drain on resourcesは「資金の流出」。

10. Tim Cleminson played an important role in obtaining the distribution rights for D&F Cola in the state.

解説 play a roleで「役割を果たす」の意。空所にはpartも可能だが、roleの方がplayとの相性が良い。

11. Oliveira Media Advertising will be required to make a bid lower than the competition's in order to secure the contract for Stallard Airlines.

解説 契約を獲得するために必要とされるのは、より低い「入札価格、付け値」なので、bidが正解。「入札者」はbidderだ。priceはofferやgiveの目的語にはなれるが、makeは不可。

Menu 2

　Part 5、6には、2択までは簡単に絞れるが、最後の決め手が意味や用法の微妙な違いという難問がある。ここではPart 5形式の2択問題を解いて、自分の語法知識の深さ、または勝負運の強さをチェックしよう。
　(A) (B)どちらが空所に適切かを選ぼう。**制限時間は1問20秒、計4分40秒**。

4分40秒

1. Factory managers pointed to the reduced staff numbers as the reason for the ------- rate of production.
(A) diminished　　(B) declined

2. The chief executive argued that the company had become too ------- on its existing customers for income, and needed to expand the customer base.
(A) dependent　　(B) dependable

3. Mr. Peters' contributions to the marketing research team are highly ------- by the company because of his years of experience.
(A) valued　　(B) valuable

4. A ------- will be issued by the office manager for employees who need to park their private vehicles in the company parking garage.
(A) permission　　(B) permit

5. The ------- of the product launch was carefully planned to make the most of the holidays, when many people would be exchanging gifts.
(A) timing　　(B) timeliness

6. An awards ceremony has been organized to honor Ralph Wiggins, who has long been a ------- to the arts in Chicago.

(A) supporter (B) contributor

7. Many mobile phone subscribers have requested ------- of the contracts provided by telephone companies.
(A) simplicity (B) simplification

8. Much of the production process has been ------- in order to reduce costs, although the initial outlay was great.
(A) automatic (B) automated

9. 3-D printing technology has made ------- parts much easier for vintage vehicle restorers to obtain.
(A) duplication (B) duplicate

10. Mr. Remolds made a very ------- speech about the need for staff training with regard to negotiation skills and interaction with customers.
(A) persuasive (B) advisory

11. The factory's maximum output capacity will be ------- in weeks resulting in certain stock shortages at many retailers.
(A) achieved (B) reached

12. In many cases, clothing made by modern machines can hardly be ------- from that produced by skilled tailors.
(A) recognized (B) distinguished

13. After adopting the new shipping system, processing the usual volume of orders was more ------- than most people had predicted.
(A) manageable (B) managerial

14. Olson Design is the Copenhagen-based producer of some of the most ------- ergonomic furniture in the world.
(A) emerging (B) innovative

Menu 2の解答・解説

※色字の選択肢が正解。

---

1. Factory managers pointed to the reduced staff numbers as the reason for the ------- rate of production.

　＊(A) diminished　　　(B) declined

解説　「減少した、低下した」の意の(A) diminishedが正解。diminishはdecrease同様、自動詞「減る」、他動詞「～を減らす」両方の用法がある。declineは自動詞では「減る」の意だが、他動詞では「～を丁寧に断る」の意なので、(B) declinedの形で空所に入れると「断られた生産率」となってしまう。

---

2. The chief executive argued that the company had become too ------- on its existing customers for income, and needed to expand the customer base.

　＊(A) dependent　　　(B) dependable

解説　「依存している、頼っている」の意の(A) dependentが正解。(B) dependableはreliableの同義語で「信頼できる、頼れる」という意味。(A)と(B)は一見似ているが意味は対照的だ。

---

3. Mr. Peters' contributions to the marketing research team are highly ------- by the company because of his years of experience.

　＊(A) valued　　　(B) valuable

解説　空所後ろのby the companyが決め手となり、空所には受動態を作る過去分詞(A) valuedが入るとわかる。空所後ろの部分がなければ(B) valuable（役に立つ、貴重な）も可能。

---

4. A ------- will be issued by the office manager for employees who need to park their private vehicles in the company parking garage.

　(A) permission　　＊(B) permit

解説　私用車を会社の駐車場に止めるための「許可証」の意なので、(B) permitが正解。(A) permissionは、もっぱら「許可」という抽象的な意味の不可算名詞として用いられるので、空所前の冠詞Aと合わず、issue（発行する）の意味上の目的語としても不適。

---

5. The ------- of the product launch was carefully planned to make the most of the holidays, when many people would be exchanging gifts.

　● make the most of ~　～を最大限利用する

　＊(A) timing　　　(B) timeliness

解説　「慎重に計画された」とあるので、(A) timing（タイミング）が正解。(B) timelinessは「タイミングがいいこと、適時性」の意味で、計画できるものではないので不適。

6. An awards ceremony has been organized to honor Ralph Wiggins, who has long been a ------- to the arts in Chicago.
   (A) supporter　　　＊(B) contributor

   解説 空所後ろのtoとの組み合わせで使われる(B) contributor(貢献者)が正解。contribute to ~ (~に貢献する)の動詞句を覚えていれば応用で解ける。(A) supporter(支持者)は後ろにofを取る。

7. Many mobile phone subscribers have requested ------- of the contracts provided by telephone companies.
   (A) simplicity　　　＊(B) simplification

   解説 契約者が求めるのは契約書の「簡素化」なので、正解は(B) simplification。(A) simplicity (簡素、単純)は性質を表す語なので、すでに存在する契約書について、これを求めるとするのは不自然。

8. Much of the production process has been ------- in order to reduce costs, although the initial outlay was great.
   ● outlay 支出、出費

   (A) automatic　　　＊(B) automated

   解説 空所に入るのは経費を削減するため(in order to reduce costs)の意図的な行為なので「自動化された」の意の(B) automatedが正解。(A) automatic (自動の)は形容詞で、意図的な行為ではなく単に状態を表しているだけなので文意に不適。

9. 3-D printing technology has made ------- parts much easier for vintage vehicle restorers to obtain.
   ● vintage vehicle restorer ヴィンテージ車の修復家

   (A) duplication　　　＊(B) duplicate

   解説 空所後ろのparts (部品)を修飾する語としては「複製の」という意味の形容詞(B) duplicateが適切。(A) duplicationは「複製を作ること」の意なので、partsとの複合名詞では意味を成さない。

10. Mr. Remolds made a very ------- speech about the need for staff training with regard to negotiation skills and interaction with customers.
    ＊(A) persuasive　　　(B) advisory

    解説 空所後ろのspeechを形容する(A) persuasive (説得力のある)が正解。(B) advisoryは形容詞で「助言の、顧問の」、名詞で「勧告、状況報告」の意味だが、程度を表す副詞veryがこの語を修飾するのは不自然。

11. The factory's maximum output capacity will be ------- in weeks resulting in certain stock shortages at many retailers.
   (A) achieved   ∗ (B) reached

解説 どちらも「工場の最大生産能力が数週間中に -------」という文脈には合うが、後半でこれが「在庫不足につながる」と述べられているので、「(望ましいことを)達成する」という意味の(A) achievedは不適。これ以上生産できない状態に「達し」、在庫不足を起こすという文意になる(B) reachedが正解。

---

12. In many cases, clothing made by modern machines can hardly be ------- from that produced by skilled tailors.
   (A) recognized   ∗ (B) distinguished

解説 近代的な機械で作った衣類と熟練した仕立て職人に作られたものとは見分けがつかないという文意から(B) distinguished(見分けられた)が正解。distinguish A from Bで「AをBと区別する」の意。recognize A from Bは「BによりAだとわかる」という意味になる。

---

13. After adopting the new shipping system, processing the usual volume of orders was more ------- than most people had predicted.
   ∗ (A) manageable   (B) managerial

解説 空所にはvolume of orders(注文量)について説明する形容詞が入るので、「処理しやすい」の意の(A) manageableが適切。(B) managerialは「管理の、経営の」という意味なので不適。TOEICではmanagerial experience(管理職の経験)でよく出る。

---

14. Olson Design is the Copenhagen-based producer of some of the most ------- ergonomic furniture in the world.
   ● ergonomic 人間工学に基づく
   (A) emerging   ∗ (B) innovative

解説 ergonomic furniture(人間工学に基づく家具)という製品を修飾する空所には、(B) innovative(革新的な)が入る。(A) emergingは「新興の」というカテゴリーを表し、程度の比較ができないので、比較級・最上級の変化がない。また、もっぱら「技術、市場、国」などを修飾する語で、「製品」とは相性が悪い。

CHAPTER 6 語法・語感力 SENSITIVITY TO WORDS/USAGE

実践問題

仕上げに、本番形式の難問にチャレンジ。語法知識、語感を総動員して挑もう。

Part 5

空所に入る語句として、最も適切なものを1つ選ぼう。(解答・解説はpp. 224〜227)

● 5分

1. Goldster's one-year warranty does not cover products that have been damaged or rendered ------- by improper handling.
   (A) more useless
   (B) uselessly
   (C) uselessness
   (D) useless　　　　　　　　　　　　　　　Ⓐ Ⓑ Ⓒ Ⓓ

2. ------- you need to make an amendment to your booking, do not hesitate to call the hotel at any time.
   (A) Although
   (B) Should
   (C) Might
   (D) Before　　　　　　　　　　　　　　　Ⓐ Ⓑ Ⓒ Ⓓ

3. The key to ------- new company policies smoothly is the involvement of employees in the decision-making process.
   (A) implementing
   (B) be implemented
   (C) implement
   (D) have implemented

4. Omissions and errors in instruction manuals have always been ------- followed by an increase in telephone calls from customers requiring assistance.
   (A) closely
   (B) nearly
   (C) exactly
   (D) early

5. As entry positions are limited, the Edmonton Bicycle Fun Race Committee recommends ------- registration to ensure a place.
   (A) advanced
   (B) advancing
   (C) advance
   (D) advancement

6. The new laptop from PowerOn, Inc., is ------- thinner than the current model, yet its battery capacity is 20 percent greater.
   (A) profusely
   (B) highly
   (C) significantly
   (D) importantly

7. Stallard Financial has a new motto which will feature on signage and the corporate letterhead to better reflect our updated -------.
   (A) objection
   (B) objectively
   (C) objectiveness
   (D) objective

8. With regard to office devices such as photocopiers, lease only ------- is necessary because running costs are also high.
   (A) as many as
   (B) whatever
   (C) that
   (D) whereas

9. ------- that her department was under budget, Ms. Carter decided to refurbish the entrance and waiting room.
   (A) So
   (B) Owing
   (C) Provided
   (D) Relieved

10. Morello Landscape will provide free consultations and special discounts to customers who sign up for the ------- by the end of this month.
    (A) contract
    (B) service
    (C) terms
    (D) fees

11. Pierson Instruments was denied ------- to build a new shopping center on James Street because the land had been set aside for a nature reserve.
(A) permitted
(B) to permit
(C) permission
(D) permitting

12. The decision to raise concert ticket prices to the Avalon Festival had ------- to do with the popularity of this year's main acts at all.
(A) what
(B) nothing
(C) others
(D) something

13. The list of speakers to appear at the event has been decided ------- not all of them have accepted their invitations.
(A) but
(B) unless
(C) whereas
(D) in order that

14. Those canceling their tickets within seven days ------- the concert date are only eligible for a refund of 50 percent.
(A) for
(B) of
(C) by
(D) prior

15. The Rubin Foundation was established with the ------- purpose of raising funds for the development of career education programs.
(A) express
(B) expressing
(C) expressive
(D) expression

Part 6

空所に入る語句として、最も適切なものを1つずつ選ぼう。(解答・解説はpp. 228〜229)

Questions 16-18 refer to the following review. 1分30秒

Editor's Choice: Summer DVD Selection

This month's Editor's Choice is *Hillbilly Jack*. This is a film that has attracted ------- attention from reviewers or the public. Nevertheless, many of those

16. (A) little
    (B) some
    (C) due
    (D) full

who do see it end up recommending it to friends and family.

The main character, Jack, is a retired man who lives in a cabin in the wilderness with a bear named Boris. The story involves Jack's -------

17. (A) struggle
    (B) attempt
    (C) dedication
    (D) compatibility

for survival and a seemingly unrelated plot about a group of hikers searching for something in the forest. Everything is revealed when the two stories intersect and the excitement starts. This low-budget film is a touching human drama with great humor.

It is quite a pity that the film has not received the praise it is ------- of, but

18. (A) entitled
    (B) ahead
    (C) capable
    (D) worthy

perhaps through word of mouth, more people will be encouraged to rent it on DVD.

Part 7

文書に関する設問の解答として、最も適切なものを1つずつ選ぼう。

(解答・解説はpp. 230〜233)

Questions 19-22 refer to the following excerpt from a report.

● 4分

This is a summary of the outcomes of the Montgomery Analytics Company's market research for the Slater Beverages product BFT171, which is code-named Sweetwater (as hereafter referred to.) The research has been commissioned by Marketing Director Max Lucarelli of the Slater Company. The objective of the study is to identify how each age group will respond to the product and which characteristics of the product will be appealing to its potential consumers in those groups.

Sweetwater was best accepted among the Young Adult group (ages 20 to 34), who generally favored its taste over the competition's. However, the Teenage group (ages 13 to 19) showed a preference for the budget alternatives that are prevailing on the market. Cost calculation and pricing should merit further consideration.

The packaging was perceived as "immature" rather than "trendy" or "fresh" almost uniformly by the groups. Montgomery Analytics submits that an immediate redesign of the package should be implemented.

19. The word "characteristics" in paragraph 1, line 6, is closest in meaning to
   (A) experiments
   (B) possessions
   (C) attributes
   (D) advantages

20. The word "budget" in paragraph 2, line 3, is closest in meaning to
   (A) economy
   (B) allowance
   (C) quality
   (D) rival

21. The word "merit" in paragraph 2, line 5, is closest in meaning to
   (A) enhance
   (B) prohibit
   (C) grant
   (D) deserve

22. The word "uniformly" in paragraph 3, line 2, is closest in meaning to
   (A) regularly
   (B) unanimously
   (C) overwhelmingly
   (D) unidentifiably

Questions 23-26 refer to the following article.

A fast-growing chain of pie stores, known as Pie Face, has been springing up all over the state of Oregon. They are hugely successful, and this is mainly owing to the unmatched customer service provided by the most agreeable staff. The owner of the chain, Anita Mosley explains that she has achieved this high morale by making every worker a part-owner of the store.

Unlike other shops and restaurants, Pie Face is owned by a trust on behalf of its employees, each of whom has a voice in its operation and a share in its profits. This means that wages are directly linked to each store's profitability. Instead of asking management for pay raises, Pie Face workers can expect the efforts and contributions they make to pay off. "We would often lose good people when they found work at larger companies," Ms. Mosley explains. "Since we introduced the employee ownership scheme, our staff have started to stay twice as long as the industry average."

As a result of this benevolent system, revenue has been growing steadily and Ms. Mosley is happy to share the profits with her co-owners. She also has a special arrangement for people who leave. They are allowed to either sell their ownership back to the company or sell it on to their replacement. The business model has been such a resounding success that it seems likely to inspire other business owners to subscribe to the idea of co-ownership.

23. The word "agreeable" in paragraph 1, line 4, is closest in meaning to
   (A) sufficient
   (B) qualified
   (C) compliant
   (D) courteous

24. The word "morale" in paragraph 1, line 5, is closest in meaning to
   (A) enthusiasm
   (B) turnover
   (C) earnings
   (D) authority

25. The word "voice" in paragraph 2, line 2, is closest in meaning to
   (A) opinion
   (B) influence
   (C) debt
   (D) status

26. The phrase "subscribe to" in paragraph 3, line 7, is closest in meaning to
   (A) advocate
   (B) approve
   (C) endorse
   (D) underwrite

実践問題の解答・解説

※問題文の訳文は紙面では省略（訳文の入手方法はp. 7をご覧ください）。

Part 5

1. Goldster's one-year warranty does not cover products that have been damaged or rendered ------- by improper handling.

   (A) more useless 　形 より使い物にならない
   (B) uselessly 　副 無駄に、無用に
   (C) uselessness 　名 無用なこと
   ＊(D) useless 　形 使い物にならない

   ● warranty 保証　● cover ～を補てんする　● render (人・物を)～の状態にする

   解説 動詞 render は SVOC の文型で「O を C の状態にする」という意味を持つ。受動態になっている that 節内の主語 that は、先行詞 products を指す。空所には、「製品」が「どういう状態」になるかを表す形容詞を入れるのが適切なので、正解は(D) useless (使い物にならない)。動詞を修飾する副詞だと早合点して (B) uselessly を選びそうになっても、「無駄に～された」という文意は不自然だと気づくことができれば、不正解を回避できる。

2. ------- you need to make an amendment to your booking, do not hesitate to call the hotel at any time.

   (A) Although 　接 ～だけれども
   ＊(B) Should 　助動 ～ならば
   (C) Might 　助動 ～かもしれない
   (D) Before 　接 ～する前に

   解説 If you should ~ は、if を省略する倒置構文で、Should you ~ の形にすることができる。よって、正解は (B) Should。(A) Although や (D) Before のような接続詞を入れると、文法的にはつながるが、意味に不具合が出る。Should you ~, (please) do not hesitate to ...は定番の表現だ。

3. The key to ------- new company policies smoothly is the involvement of employees in the decision-making process.

   ＊(A) implementing
   (B) be implemented
   (C) implement
   (D) have implemented

   解説 key to + 名詞／動名詞という語法の知識を問う問題だ。正解は動名詞である(A)の implementing。key to ~ は「～へのカギ、秘訣」という意味。key to success (成功へのカギ) というフレーズで覚えておこう。

実践問題の解答・解説

4. Omissions and errors in instruction manuals have always been ------- followed by an increase in telephone calls from customers requiring assistance.

* (A) closely　副 ぴったりと、接近して
  (B) nearly　副 ほぼ、ほとんど
  (C) exactly　副 ちょうど
  (D) early　副 早く

● omission 脱落、抜け落ち

解説 空所直後のfollowedにかかる副詞を選ばせる問題。A be followed by Bは「Aに続いてBが起こる」の意で、それを「すぐに」という意味で強調できる(A) closelyが正解。選択肢にはないが、空所にはsoon（すぐに）も可。exactly（ちょうど）はat the same timeやwhenなどの、時を表す語句を修飾する。

---

5. As entry positions are limited, the Edmonton Bicycle Fun Race Committee recommends ------- registration to ensure a place.

  (A) advanced　形 最新の、先進の
  (B) advancing　形 前進する
* (C) advance　形 事前の
  (D) advancement　名 前進

解説 空所には直後のregistration（登録）を修飾する語が入る。文法的にはどの選択肢も空所に入れることができるので、語法がポイントになる。正解は「事前の」という意味の(C) advance。advance notice（事前告知）というコロケーションも重要だ。(A) advancedはadvanced technology（先端技術）のように使う。

---

6. The new laptop from PowerOn, Inc., is ------- thinner than the current model, yet its battery capacity is 20 percent greater.

  (A) profusely　副 過度に
  (B) highly　副 大いに
* (C) significantly　副 かなり
  (D) importantly　副 重要なことには

解説 空所直後の形容詞（比較級）thinnerを「かなり」という意味で修飾できる(C) significantlyが正解。considerablyやsubstantiallyは類義語だ。(B) highly（大いに）は、veryと同じく比較級を修飾できない副詞なので、空所には不適切だ。

---

7. Stallard Financial has a new motto which will feature on signage and the corporate letterhead to better reflect our updated -------.

  (A) objection　名 異議
  (B) objectively　副 客観的に
  (C) objectiveness　名 先入観に影響されない判断
* (D) objective　名 目標、目的

● motto モットー　● signage 表記、看板　● corporate letterhead 社用箋

解説 空所には所有格代名詞ourがかかる名詞が入る。「当社の最新の『目標』をよりよく反映するため」という意味になるべきなので、正解は(D) objective。(A) objectionは動詞object（反対する）が名詞化されたもので、「異議」の意。(C) objectivenessは形容詞objective（客観的な）から派生した名詞だ。

8. With regard to office devices such as photocopiers, lease only ------- is necessary because running costs are also high.

　＊(A) as many as　〜するだけの数のもの
　(B) whatever　[代名] 〜するのは何でも
　(C) that　[関代] 〜する、〜である
　(D) whereas　[接] 〜である一方で

解説 空所には動詞lease（〜をリースする）の目的語となる節を作り、かつ、is necessaryの主語になれる語が必要だ。正解は(A) as many as。このmanyは代名詞で、as many as is necessaryで「必要な数」という意味のイディオム的表現だ。(B) whateverは「〜なものは何でも」という制限がないことを表す語なので、空所前のonlyと合わない。(C) thatには先行詞となる名詞が直前に必要。

---

9. ------- that her department was under budget, Ms. Carter decided to refurbish the entrance and waiting room.

　(A) So　[接] 〜するように
　(B) Owing　[形]（owing toの形で）〜のせいで
　(C) Provided　[接] もし〜なら
　＊(D) Relieved　[動] 安心した

● refurbish 〜を改装する

解説 カンマ以前が「（Carter氏は）安心したので」という理由を表すと、文後半とのつながりがいい。よって、正解は(D) Relieved（安心した）。(As she was) relieved that ... のカッコ内を省略した分詞構文になっている。(A)を用いたSo that（…するために）は文意に不適。(C)を用いたProvided that（もし…であるならば）は仮定を表すが、カンマの後（Carter氏は決めた）は、その条件に対する帰結になっていない。

---

10. Morello Landscape will provide free consultations and special discounts to customers who sign up for the ------- by the end of this month.

　(A) contract　[名] 契約
　＊(B) service　[名] サービス
　(C) terms　[名]（契約の）条項
　(D) fees　[名] 料金

解説 sign up forを「サインする」と考えてしまい、さらに「契約書にサインする」という和訳に引きずられると、(A) contractを選びたくなるが、sign up for 〜は「〜に申し込む」という意味で、後ろには、例えば「講座」や「ニュースレター」など、申し込む対象や目的を表す語が来る。よって、正解は(B) service。「契約書に署名する」はsign a contractとするのが正しい。

---

11. Pierson Instruments was denied ------- to build a new shopping center on James Street because the land had been set aside for a nature reserve.

　(A) permitted
　(B) to permit
　＊(C) permission
　(D) permitting

● nature reserve 自然保護区

解説 deny A Bは「A（人など）に対しB（要求など）を与えない」という意味の、SVOO文型の用法だ。問題文はこのAが主語になった受動態の文で、空所は2つ目の目的語Bにあたる。

よって、名詞の(C) permission（許可）が正解。deny doing（～したことを否定する）の用法では目的語を2つ取れないので、(D) permittingは不可。

---

12. The decision to raise concert ticket prices to the Avalon Festival had ------- to do with the popularity of this year's main acts at all.

(A) what　　代名 何
＊(B) nothing　代名 何も～ない
(C) others　　代名 他のもの
(D) something　代名 何か

解説 ▶ 文末のat allと共に用いることができるのは(B) nothingだけなので、これが正解。have nothing to do with ~ (at all)で「～とは（まったく）無関係だ」の意。(D) somethingを入れてhad something to do with ~ とすると、逆に「～と何らかの関係があった」という意味になる。これは文末のat allと合わない。

---

13. The list of speakers to appear at the event has been decided ------- not all of them have accepted their invitations.

＊(A) but　　　接 しかし
(B) unless　　接 もし～でなければ
(C) whereas　 接 ～である一方で
(D) in order that　～するために

解説 ▶ 選択肢には接続詞が並んでいるので、空所前後の意味のつながりを考えよう。空所の前は「イベントに出演する講演者のリストは決定した」、後ろは「そのうちの全員が招待に応じたわけではない」だ。よって、逆接を表す(A) butが正解。(C) whereasは2つの事実を対比・比較するが、問題文は「講演者」という1つの対象について述べているだけなので不適。

---

14. Those canceling their tickets within seven days ------- the concert date are only eligible for a refund of 50 percent.

(A) for　　前 ～のために
＊(B) of　　前 ～の、～から起算して
(C) by　　前 ～までに
(D) prior　前 前の

解説 ▶ 「公演日『から』7日以内」という意味になる(B) ofが正解。公演後には通常は返金ができないコンサートチケットの話なので、within seven days of the concert dateは「公演日からさかのぼって7日以内」と解釈すべきだが、文脈によってはofが「～の後から」を意味する場合もある。(C) by（～までに）は、within seven daysのような期間を表す語句との併用はできないので不適。(D) priorは、後ろにtoを足せば、空所に入れることができる。

---

15. The Rubin Foundation was established with the ------- purpose of raising funds for the development of career education programs.

＊(A) express　　形 明確な、特別な
　　　　　　　　動 表現する
(B) expressing　動 表現する（現在分詞）
(C) expressive　形 表現が豊かな、表現の
(D) expression　名 表現

解説 ▶ 空所直後のpurpose（目的）を適切に修飾する語を選ぶ問題。正解は「特別な」という意味を持つ形容詞(A) express。(C) expressiveも肯定的な意味合いを持つ形容詞だが、これは「表現が豊かな」という意味で、例えば言葉や芸術作品を褒めるようなときに用いられる語だ。

Part 6

問題 16-18 は次のレビューに関するものです。

Editor's Choice: Summer DVD Selection

This month's Editor's Choice is *Hillbilly Jack*. This is a film that has attracted ------- attention from reviewers or the public. Nevertheless, many of those

16. (A) little
   (B) some
   (C) due
   (D) full

who do see it end up recommending it to friends and family.

The main character, Jack, is a retired man who lives in a cabin in the wilderness with a bear named Boris. The story involves Jack's -------

   17. (A) struggle
      (B) attempt
      (C) dedication
      (D) compatibility

for survival and a seemingly unrelated plot about a group of hikers searching for something in the forest. Everything is revealed when the two stories intersect and the excitement starts. This low-budget film is a touching human drama with great humor.

It is quite a pity that the film has not received the praise it is ------- of, but

   18. (A) entitled
      (B) ahead
      (C) capable
      (D) worthy

perhaps through word of mouth, more people will be encouraged to rent it on DVD.

- wilderness 荒野 ● seemingly 見たところ、表面上 ● plot (物語の) 筋 ● intersect 交わる
- touching 人を感動させる ● word of mouth 口コミ

16. ＊(A) little 形 ほとんど〜ない
　　(B) some 形 いくらかの
　　(C) due 形 正当な、当然の
　　(D) full 形 たくさんの

解説 空所を含む文の後にNeverthelessという逆接を表す副詞があることに注目しよう。この副詞の後には、「それを見た人の多くは友人や家族に薦めることになる」というポジティブな内容が書かれているので、その前の文は「注目されていなかった」というネガティブな内容になるのが適切だ。よって、「ほとんど〜ない」という(A) littleが正解である。

---

17. ＊(A) struggle 名 奮闘
　　(B) attempt 名 試み
　　(C) dedication 名 献身
　　(D) compatibility 名 適合性、互換性

解説 空所後ろのfor survival（生き残るための）との組み合わせで意味を考えると、(A) struggle（苦労、格闘）が正解。(B) attempt（試み）は後ろにforを取れず、atなどが続く。(C) dedication（献身、熱心さ）の後ろにはto work（仕事への）のような句が、(D) compatibility（適合性）の後ろにはwith the system（システムとの適合性）のような句が続く。

---

18. (A) entitled 動 〜に資格を与えた
　　(B) ahead 副 前方に
　　(C) capable 形 有能な
　　＊(D) worthy 形 〜に値する

解説 空所前のitはthe film（映画）を指していて、空所にはそれを形容する語が入る。正解は(D) worthy。the praise it is worthy ofで、「(その映画)が受けるに値する称賛」という意味だ。(A)はbe entitled to benefits（福利厚生を受ける権利がある）、(B)はahead of schedule（予定より早く）、(C)はbe capable of doing（〜する能力のある）のようなフレーズで語法を押さえておこう。

Part 7

問題 19-22 は次の報告書からの抜粋に関するものです。

This is a summary of the outcomes of the Montgomery Analytics Company's market research for the Slater Beverages product BFT171, which is code-named Sweetwater (as hereafter referred to.) The research has been commissioned by Marketing Director Max Lucarelli of the Slater Company. The objective of the study is to identify how each age group will respond to the product and which ¹characteristics of the product will be appealing to its potential consumers in those groups.

Sweetwater was best accepted among the Young Adult group (ages 20 to 34), who generally favored its taste over the competition's. However, the Teenage group (ages 13 to 19) showed a preference for the ²budget alternatives that are prevailing on the market. Cost calculation and pricing should ³merit further consideration.

The packaging was perceived as "immature" rather than "trendy" or "fresh" almost ⁴uniformly by the groups. Montgomery Analytics submits that an immediate redesign of the package should be implemented.

- outcome 結果 ● commission 委託する ● objective 目的 ● prevail 普及する
- immature 子どもっぽい

19. The word "characteristics" in paragraph 1, line 6, is closest in meaning to
　(A) experiments　名 実験
　(B) possessions　名 所有
　＊(C) attributes　名 特性
　(D) advantages　名 長所

解説 下線1のcharacteristicsは「特性」という意味で使われている。これと置き換えられるのは(C) attributesだ。(D) advantages（長所）は特性の中でも良い点だけを指す語なので、characteristicsの同義語としては不適切。

---

20. The word "budget" in paragraph 2, line 3, is closest in meaning to
　＊(A) economy　形 経済的な、安い
　(B) allowance　名 手当、小遣い
　(C) quality　形 上質の
　(D) rival　形 競争する

解説 budgetは名詞では「予算」だが、下線2のような形容詞用法では「手頃な値段の」という意味を持つ。正解は(A) economy（経済的な）。(C) qualityは名詞では「質」だが、「上質の」という形容詞用法でもよく用いられる。

---

21. The word "merit" in paragraph 2, line 5, is closest in meaning to
　(A) enhance　動 ～を高める
　(B) prohibit　動 ～を禁止する
　(C) grant　動 ～を許可する
　＊(D) deserve　動 ～に値する

解説 下線3のmeritは「～に値する」という意味の他動詞だ。この語と同様の意味を持つ(D) deserveが正解。meritの意味がわからなくても、その位置に選択肢の語を当てはめてみると、deserve further consideration（さらなる検討に値する）が最も意味が通ると判断できるはずだ。

---

22. The word "uniformly" in paragraph 3, line 2, is closest in meaning to
　(A) regularly　副 定期的に
　＊(B) unanimously　副 満場一致で
　(C) overwhelmingly　副 圧倒するように
　(D) unidentifiably　副 正体不明で

解説 下線4のuniformlyは「一様に」という意味なので、同様の意味を持つ選択肢(B) unanimously（満場一致で）が正解。uniformlyのuni-、unanimouslyのun-にはいずれも「単一」という意味がある。

問題 23-26 は次の記事に関するものです。

A fast-growing chain of pie stores, known as Pie Face, has been springing up all over the state of Oregon. They are hugely successful, and this is mainly owing to the unmatched customer service provided by the most ¹agreeable staff. The owner of the chain, Anita Mosley explains that she has achieved this high ²morale by making every worker a part-owner of the store.

Unlike other shops and restaurants, Pie Face is owned by a trust on behalf of its employees, each of whom has a ³voice in its operation and a share in its profits. This means that wages are directly linked to each store's profitability. Instead of asking management for pay raises, Pie Face workers can expect the efforts and contributions they make to pay off. "We would often lose good people when they found work at larger companies," Ms. Mosley explains. "Since we introduced the employee ownership scheme, our staff have started to stay twice as long as the industry average."

As a result of this benevolent system, revenue has been growing steadily and Ms. Mosley is happy to share the profits with her co-owners. She also has a special arrangement for people who leave. They are allowed to either sell their ownership back to the company or sell it on to their replacement. The business model has been such a resounding success that it seems likely to inspire other business owners to ⁴subscribe to the idea of co-ownership.

- spring up 現れる ● pay off 実を結ぶ、報われる ● scheme 構想、計画 ● benevolent 善意ある
- replacement 後任者 ● resounding 際立った

実践問題の解答・解説

23. The word "agreeable" in paragraph 1, line 4, is closest in meaning to
(A) sufficient　形 十分な
(B) qualified　形 資格のある
(C) compliant　形 従順な
＊(D) courteous　形 礼儀正しい

解説 下線1のagreeableという形容詞は、人を修飾する場合、「感じの良い、愛想がいい」という意味。(D) courteousは「親切で礼儀正しい」というポジティブなニュアンスを含む語で、これが正解。日本語に訳すと同じ性質を指すとは思えないagreeable、courteous、friendlyは、TOEICではすべて同義語として扱われる。

24. The word "morale" in paragraph 1, line 5, is closest in meaning to
＊(A) enthusiasm　名 熱意
(B) turnover　名 離職（率）、売上高
(C) earnings　名 利益
(D) authority　名 権限

解説 選択肢に並ぶ語は、すべて形容詞highと相性の良い名詞ではあるが、下線2のmorale（士気）と同じ意味になるのは、(A) enthusiasmだけだ。enthusiastは「愛好家、ファン」。

25. The word "voice" in paragraph 2, line 2, is closest in meaning to
(A) opinion　名 意見
＊(B) influence　名 影響力
(C) debt　名 借金
(D) status　名 地位

解説 下線3のvoiceは「発言権、影響力」の意。よって、(B) influenceが正解。

26. The phrase "subscribe to" in paragraph 3, line 7, is closest in meaning to
(A) advocate　動 〜を提唱する、擁護する
(B) approve　動 〜を承認する
＊(C) endorse　動 〜を支持する
(D) underwrite　動 〜を引き受ける

解説 選択肢には難語が多く、問題になっている下線4のsubscribe toも、よく知られている「〜を購読する」とは別の意味で用いられているので、難しい問題だ。このsubscribe to 〜は「〜（意見など）に賛同する」の意なので、正解は(C) endorse（〜を支持する）。

Ted's Talks ❺

TOEICを超越する人3タイプ ── 3. Practitioner（実務家）

> *They live TOEIC. They use English.*
> （彼らはTOEICの英語を体験している。英語を使っている。）

　仕事や海外生活を通じて、幅広い語彙を覚えてきたタイプの人です。彼らはTOEICに十分対応できる英語力をすでに持っているので、模試を数冊こなすだけで高得点を取れます。海外経験がない学習者が、彼らから学べることはあるのでしょうか。

● 必要性

　仕事で英語を使っている人たちも、楽をして英語を習得したわけではありません。英語でメールを書いたりプレゼンテーションをしたりなど、生活や業務上の必要に迫られて、徐々に身につけてきたのです。一般の学習者も、実際に英語を使う場面をイメージし、そのための学習を行うことで、同じ効果が期待できます。

● 速度と強度

　仕事には必ず締め切りや納期があり、それを守るためにはスピードが必要です。報告書作成のために短期間で大量の英語を読んだり、会議直前にスピーチの手直しをしたりということは仕事の現場では日常茶飯事です。このように差し迫った状況で英語に接していると、当然英語力も鍛えられます。自己学習においても時間を区切り、「1時間で何ページ」というような密度の濃い学習を行うと効果的でしょう。

● フィードバック

　メールで意図を誤解されたら、フォローが必要になります。会議で意見をうまく述べられなかったら、企画が承認されません。実務家たちはそうした周囲からのフィードバックを受けて、英語力をさらに磨く必要性を認識します。TOEICのスコアシートも、私たちの英語力に対するフィードバックです。スコアの数字やAbilities Measuredのパーセンテージは、上司や同僚よりむしろ口うるさくミスを指摘してくれます。自分の伸びしろを知る指標として利用しましょう。

　TOEICが2時間で200問というタイトな時間制限を設けているのは、時間的制約の中で緊迫感を持って英語を使わなければならない、仕事の現場を再現するためではないでしょうか。実務英語もTOEIC対策も、入り口こそ違えど、極めた人がたどり着く頂上は同じ所だと私は思います。最後に心理言語学者Frank Smithの言葉を紹介して、この項を終わりとします。

One language sets you in a corridor for life. Two languages open every door along the way.（1つの言語はあなたを人生の通路に立たせてくれる。2つの言語はあなたの行く先々ですべてのドアを開けてくれる）

CHAPTER 7

難語対応・忍耐力
ADVANCED VOCABULARY / ENDURANCE

このスキルが足りない人は…

- [ ] 選択肢に難しい語句が並んでいると戦意喪失する
- [ ] 苦手な分野のトピックだと文書を読む気がうせる
- [ ] テストが終わった後は、達成感よりむしろ疲労感が残る

CHAPTER 7
難語対応・忍耐力
ADVANCED VOCABULARY / ENDURANCE

➡ 持てる知識でベストを尽くせる力
必要になるパート：Part 5／6／7

　Part 5の最後の1列（135～140番辺り）やPart 7のシングルパッセージ、ダブルパッセージそれぞれの終盤は、リーディングセクションの山場です。骨が折れる問題が出やすく、「もうダメだ」と弱音を吐きそうになる人も多いでしょう。

　満点レベルの上級者にとっても、こうした山場は決して楽ではありません。しかし、彼らは漠然と「難しい」と思うのではなく、問題を解くに当たって、自分が何を知っていて何を知らないかを冷静に切り分けます。そして、知らないことがあったとしても、自分の持てる力を総動員し、最善の判断を下します。「自分は、TOEICで出題される範囲の知識は十分に押さえている」という自信があるから、例外的な難問に遭遇しても、「ベストを尽くすのみ」と覚悟できるのです。

　例外的な難問とは、例えば、Part 5で選択肢に難度の高い語句が2つ以上並んでいるような問題です。超難語が正解になるケースはまれですが、TOEIC頻出語とは言えない語句が正解になることはあります。また、難語を含む不正解選択肢を排除しなければ正解できない場合もあります。第4章で訓練した**消去法や、文脈や語幹からの推測など、使えるテクニックはすべて使い、わかるところからアプローチする**必要があります。

　Part 6やPart 7では、マイナーな業界・分野のトピックや、契約書、文芸評論など、なじみのない文書は難度が高いでしょう。**イマジネーションを最大限に働かせ、文書の書き手や受け取り手になったつもりで辛抱強く読み進める**ことが求められます。それでは、診断テストの例を見てみましょう。

【Part 5】 p. 10, 8（色字の選択肢が正解）

8. The council decided to remove trees used in the ------- of the park boundaries because they were dropping leaves onto neighboring property.
   * (A) delineation　　　名 縁取り、線描写
   (B) mediation　　　　名 仲介、調停
   (C) solidification　　名 凝固、団結
   (D) consolidation　　名 合併

Part 5：文脈、語幹、消去法などからベストな解答をせよ

　選択肢の中でTOEIC必修語と言えるのは(D) consolidation（合併）くらいで、残りの3語、特に(A)は未知の単語である可能性が高いでしょう。このように、**選択肢が難語ばかりの場合は、文脈、接頭・接尾辞、語幹などの知識を総動員して意味を推測し、消去法を使って解答する**しかありません。正解はその(A) delineation（縁取り、線描写）で、文意は「近隣の建物に葉を落としていたので、議会は公園の境目の縁取りに使われていた木を取り除くことを決定した」というものです。delineationの意味を、line（線）やlinear（線の）から連想できれば、解答に役立ったでしょう。(B) mediationはmedium（中間の）、(C)solidificationはsolid（固体の）の派生語で、意味的にも関連します。

　実際のテストでも、これに近いレベルの難問は出題されています。頻度にすれば数回受験して1問出くわすかどうかですが、リーディングセクションはノーミスでないと満点が出ないことも多く、パーフェクトスコアを狙うなら、こういう「非常事態的」問題にも対応する必要があります。次はPart 6の例です。

【Part 6】 p. 11, 11（抜粋）

... To put minds at ease, GameOne is offering an insurance package that ensures you get true value for money.
Should you be unable to use your ticket for an extended period, GameOne will refund the value of the unused portion.

The cost of this insurance is only 10 percent of the purchase price and could potentially save you hundreds of dollars. The terms and conditions and a detailed list of acceptable ------- are included in the brochure.

11. (A) locations
   *(B) circumstances
   (C) withdrawals
   (D) consequences

Part 6、7：TOEICの世界に入り込めれば勝機が見えてくる

11はPart 6の文脈型問題です。保険のパンフレットにThe terms and conditions（条件）と共に掲載されているものとして適切なのは、払い戻しが適用される「事態、状況」の詳細なリストなので、(B) circumstancesが正解です。この保険商品が不測の事態に対処するためのものであるという文意が理解できれば、(A) location（場所）は排除できます。

Part 6やPart 7では、背景知識がなく、読むのがつらいと感じる文書が出題されることもあるでしょう。しかし、TOEICには特定の業界の専門知識や特殊な用語を知らなければ解けないような問題は出ません。**必要なのは忍耐力だけ**です。一見難しそうな文書も、辛抱強く読み進めていくうちに、登場人物の姿や商品の特長などが少しずつ見えてきます。**文書中のストーリーを疑似体験するように読んでいれば、正解の糸口がつかめる**はずです。

難語対応・忍耐力を鍛えるためには、難度の高い問題に触れるしかありません。この章では、TOEICレベルを超える語句をあえて採用し、推測力を強化するトレーニングと、難解な長文の正誤問題で忍耐力をつけるトレーニングを用意しました。ここまでたどり着いた皆さんなら、最後の章も完走できるはずです。全力で解いて、達成感を味わいましょう！

・POINT

- [ ] 「超上級問題」は満点達成へのカギを握る。天命を待つ前にベストを尽くせ。
- [ ] なじみのない文書は、意識的に臨場感を高めて読むことで理解しやすくなる。
- [ ] テスト中に実力は伸びない。
  持てる知識と力を最大限に発揮することに意識を集中せよ。

CHAPTER 7
難語対応・忍耐力 ADVANCED VOCABULARY / ENDURANCE

→トレーニング

Menu 1

　問題文中の未知の語が設問に絡んでいたり、文意把握のカギを握っていたりする場合、文脈からその意味を推測しなければならない。正確な意味はわからなくても、ポジティブな語なのかどうかさえつかめれば消去法が効くという場合もある。ここではそうした推測力を鍛えるトレーニングを行う。なお、問題にはあえてTOEIC頻出語ではない難語も使用している。**制限時間は各40秒、計13分。**
① 各問題文の下線部の語句が、客観的に考えて好ましいニュアンスなら「○」、好ましくないニュアンスなら「×」、どちらでもなければ「?」を [　] 内に記入しよう。
② 指定された語と**文中の意味で**置き換えられる語を(A)~(D)から選び、下線部に記入しよう。

13分

1. The positive reaction to the chef's menu was an auspicious beginning for Alphonso's Restaurant on the Pier.

    ① ニュアンス [　]
    ② auspicious = ＿＿＿
    (A) alluring　(B) encouraging　(C) enterprising　(D) assuring

2. Dubrocom allocates liberal financial resources to research and development to help ensure its long-term viability.

    ① ニュアンス [　]
    ② liberal = ＿＿＿
    (A) limited　(B) valuable　(C) distinct　(D) generous

3. Although the sales manager was glad to accept the role of banquet organizer, the size of the event posed a major problem for his team.

   ① ニュアンス [　]
   ② posed = ____
   (A) presented　(B) displayed　(C) straightened　(D) arranged

4. When Mr. Petrov leaves the company in April, his role will be assumed by a relatively inexperienced coworker.

   ① ニュアンス [　]
   ② assumed = ____
   (A) expected　(B) trusted　(C) acquired　(D) trained

5. Wagner Solicitors had the sign for their office remade because they felt it was not prominent enough when seen from the street.

   ① ニュアンス [　]
   ② prominent = ____
   (A) obvious　(B) remarkable　(C) famous　(D) outstanding

6. Greco Bicycles has sustained a lot of criticism in recent years for the declining quality of its products.

   ① ニュアンス [　]
   ② sustained = ____
   (A) proven　(B) denied　(C) admitted　(D) endured

7. The Clarendon Hotel perfectly embodies the atmosphere of the Victorian era and should delight lovers of history and antiques.

   ① ニュアンス [　]
   ② embodies = ____
   (A) seizes　(B) captures　(C) detains　(D) acquires

8. The preliminary results of tests on the Hobson GH565 helicopter show that its revolutionary design will lead to gains in both performance and economy.

① ニュアンス ［　］
② preliminary = ＿＿＿
(A) conclusive　(B) significant　(C) initial　(D) practical

9. Decisions regarding company policy must not be made arbitrarily but after careful consultation with department heads.

① ニュアンス ［　］
② arbitrarily = ＿＿＿
(A) deliberately　(B) freely　(C) calmly　(D) responsibly

10. Most of the procedures described in the employee manual are geared towards reducing risk while maximizing productivity.

① ニュアンス ［　］
② geared = ＿＿＿
(A) tailored　(B) equipped　(C) appointed　(D) distributed

11. Management's suggestion that the staff take a day off to recuperate after the exhibition was appreciated by the whole team.

① ニュアンス ［　］
② recuperate = ＿＿＿
(A) aggravate　(B) recover　(C) cultivate　(D) brief

12. Ms. Van Dyke asserted that it was a great surprise to hear that she was being offered the vice president's position.

① ニュアンス ［　］
② asserted = ＿＿＿
(A) complained　(B) recalled　(C) claimed　(D) corrected

13. Staff at the Danube Hotel apologized to guests whom they had inconvenienced by <u>inadvertently deleting their reservations</u>.

① ニュアンス [   ]
② inadvertently = ____
(A) repeatedly   (B) impatiently   (C) unintentionally   (D) necessarily

14. Mr. Kos decided to <u>initiate a meeting</u> with his predecessor in order to discuss some of the intricacies of his position.

① ニュアンス [   ]
② initiate = ____
(A) assemble   (B) allocate   (C) arrange   (D) launch

15. The council has decided to let parking garages in town <u>dictate their own prices</u>, depending on location and time of day.

① ニュアンス [   ]
② dictate = ____
(A) determine   (B) position   (C) appoint   (D) neglect

16. Many guests flying to Frankfurt have to <u>forgo the complimentary breakfast</u> included with the hotel room because their departure is too early in the morning.

① ニュアンス [   ]
② forgo = ____
(A) abandon   (B) obtain   (C) prescribe   (D) declare

17. Mr. Rowlinson <u>deemed his position</u> as chief editor a temporary one as he preferred working as a journalist in the field.

① ニュアンス [   ]
② deemed = ____
(A) examined   (B) contemplated   (C) admitted   (D) considered

18. People who have worked at Megatron for more than 10 years will be the beneficiaries of a new loyalty incentive.
① ニュアンス [　　]
② beneficiaries = ＿＿＿
(A) providers　(B) contributors　(C) associates　(D) recipients

19. The proliferation of Web sites offering maps and navigation services has led to a severe downturn in the quantity of printed maps being sold.
① ニュアンス [　　]
② proliferation = ＿＿＿
(A) distinction　(B) increase　(C) attribution　(D) leverage

20. The amount of money spent on the new headquarters is indicative of Nichol Enterprises' confidence in its own financial stability.
① ニュアンス [　　]
② indicative = ＿＿＿
(A) descriptive　(B) illustrative　(C) narrative　(D) definitive

Menu 1の解答・解説

※問題文の訳文は紙面では省略(訳文の入手方法はp. 7をご覧ください)

1. The positive reaction to the chef's menu was <u>an auspicious beginning</u> for Alphonso's Restaurant on the Pier.

① ニュアンス ［ ○ ］
② auspicious = (B) encouraging(有望な)
(A) alluring(魅惑的な)　(C) enterprising(進取の気性に富んだ)
(D) assuring(保証する)

解説 主語The positive reaction(肯定的な反応)の補語an auspicious beginning(幸先の良いスタート)は主語同様に好ましい意味を持つと推測可能。auspiciousの同義語は(B) encouraging(有望な)。(A)、(C)、(D)はいずれもbeginningのような「状況」を修飾しない。

2. Dubrocom <u>allocates liberal financial resources</u> to research and development to help ensure its long-term viability.

● viability 成長可能性

① ニュアンス ［ ○ ］
② liberal = (D) generous(寛大な)
(A) limited(限られた)　(B) valuable(役に立つ)　(C) distinct(はっきりした)

解説 to help ensure its long-term viability(長期的な成長性を確かなものにする援助をするために)というポジティブな目的から、allocates liberal financial resources(研究開発に寛大な財源を割り当てる)も好ましい行為だと推測できる。liberalは(D) generousと同じく「寛大な」の意。(A) limited(限られた)はliberalの反対の意味だ。

3. Although the sales manager was glad to accept the role of banquet organizer, the size of the event <u>posed a major problem</u> for his team.

① ニュアンス ［ × ］
② posed = (A) presented(〜を引き起こした)
(B) displayed(〜を示した)　(C) straightened(〜を矯正した)　(D) arranged(〜を手配した)

解説 the sales manager was glad to(営業部長は喜んで〜した)という好ましい状況がAlthoughで逆接になっているので、主節は好ましくない情報だと推測できる。posedは「(問題や危険)をもたらした」の意で、(A) presented(〜を引き起こした)が同義。

4. When Mr. Petrov leaves the company in April, his role will be assumed by a relatively inexperienced coworker.

　① ニュアンス ［ ? ］
　② assumed = (C) acquired（得られた）
　(A) expected（予想された）　(B) trusted（信用された）　(D) trained（訓練された）

解説 his role will be assumed（彼の任務は引き継がれる）の部分は事実を述べているだけで、好ましいかどうかの価値判断は含まない。「（役割など）を引き受けた」という意味のassumedは、(C) acquired（得られた）と置き換え可能。

5. Wagner Solicitors had the sign for their office remade because they felt it was not prominent enough when seen from the street.

　● had ~ remade 〜を作り直させた
　① ニュアンス ［ × ］
　② prominent = (A) obvious（すぐわかる）
　(B) remarkable（注目すべき）　(C) famous（有名な）
　(D) outstanding（優れた、未払いの、未解決の）

解説 not prominent enough（よく目立たない）という状態は一般的には好ましくないニュアンスだ。prominent（目立つ）は(A) obvious（すぐわかる）で置き換え可能。(B) remarkable（注目すべき）は物や事に価値があることを表す。(D) outstandingは「優れた、未払いの、未解決の」の意味があるが、いずれもこの文意には不適。

6. Greco Bicycles has sustained a lot of criticism in recent years for the declining quality of its products.

　① ニュアンス ［ × ］
　② sustained = (D) endured（〜を受け止めた）
　(A) proven（〜を証明した）　(B) denied（〜を否定した）　(C) admitted（〜を認めた）

解説 has sustained a lot of criticism（多くの批判を受けている）という状態は好ましくない。sustained（〜を受けた）の同義語は(D) endured（〜を受け止めた）。

7. The Clarendon Hotel perfectly embodies the atmosphere of the Victorian era and should delight lovers of history and antiques.

　● delight 〜を楽しませる
　① ニュアンス ［ 〇 ］
　② embodies = (B) captures（〜を［画像や言葉で］捉える）
　(A) seizes（〜をつかむ）　(C) detains（〜を拘束する）　(D) acquires（〜を得る）

解説 「雰囲気を完璧に体現した」という表現は出来栄えが良いことを表しており、好ましいことだと推測できる。embodiesは「〜を体現した、〜をはっきりと表現した」の意で、「〜をう

まく表現した」という意味において(B) capturesが同義語。

---

8. The preliminary results of tests on the Hobson GH565 helicopter show that its revolutionary design will lead to gains in both performance and economy.
   ① ニュアンス ［ ? ］
   ② preliminary = (C) initial（初期の）
   (A) conclusive（最終的な） (B) significant（重要な） (D) practical（実用的な）

   解説 ▶ The preliminary results of tests（テストの予備段階の結果）自体には好ましいかどうかの価値判断は含まれていない。preliminary（予備の、準備の）は(C) initial（初期の）で置き換え可能。

---

9. Decisions regarding company policy must not be made arbitrarily but after careful consultation with department heads.
   ① ニュアンス ［ × ］
   ② arbitrarily = (B) freely（自由に）
   (A) deliberately（意図的に） (C) calmly（静かに） (D) responsibly（責任を持って）

   解説 ▶ 問題文でmust notと「禁止」の表現が用いられていることから、be made arbitrarily（恣意的に決定される）は好ましくないことだと推測できる。arbitrarilyの同義語は(B) freely（自由に）。

---

10. Most of the procedures described in the employee manual are geared towards reducing risk while maximizing productivity.
    ① ニュアンス ［ ○ ］
    ② geared = (A) tailored（合うように変えられた）
    (B) equipped（装備された） (C) appointed（任命された） (D) distributed（配布された）

    解説 ▶ reducing risk（リスクを減らすこと）はポジティブなことで、towards（〜に向かって）も正方向を表している。よってare geared towards reducing risks（リスクを減らすよう整えられている）も好ましい意味だと推測可能。geared（合わせてある）は(A) tailored（合うように変えられている）と同義語。

---

11. Management's suggestion that the staff take a day off to recuperate after the exhibition was appreciated by the whole team.
    ① ニュアンス ［ ○ ］
    ② recuperate = (B) recover（回復する）
    (A) aggravate（〜を悪化させる） (C) cultivate（〜を耕す、高める） (D) brief（〜を説明する）

    解説 ▶ appreciated by the whole team（チーム全体に喜ばれた）から、recuperate（回復する）は好ましい行為だと推測できる。同義語は(B) recover。

12. Ms. Van Dyke asserted that it was a great surprise to hear that she was being offered the vice president's position.

① ニュアンス ［ ？ ］
② asserted = (C) claimed（〜を主張した）
(A) complained（苦情を言った）　(B) recalled（〜を思い出した、〜を回収した）
(D) corrected（〜を訂正した）

解説 ▶ assertedは「〜を断言した、〜を強く主張した」の意で、その語自体には好ましいかどうかの価値判断は含まない。同義語は(C) claimed（〜を主張した）。(A) complained（苦情を言った）の目的語のthat節は好ましくない内容になる。

---

13. Staff at the Danube Hotel apologized to guests whom they had inconvenienced by inadvertently deleting their reservations.

① ニュアンス ［ × ］
② inadvertently = (C) unintentionally（故意ではなく）
(A) repeatedly（繰り返して）　(B) impatiently（いらいらして）
(D) necessarily（必ず、どうしても）

解説 ▶ inconvenienced（迷惑をかけた）とあるので inadvertently deleting their reservations（予約をうっかり消してしまったこと）は好ましくない意味とわかる。inadvertently（うっかりして、不注意に）は(C) unintentionally（故意ではなく）と置き換え可能。

---

14. Mr. Kos decided to initiate a meeting with his predecessor in order to discuss some of the intricacies of his position.

● predecessor 前任者　● intricacies 複雑な事情

① ニュアンス ［ ？ ］
② initiate = (C) arrange（〜を手配する）
(A) assemble（〜を集める）　(B) allocate（〜を割り当てる）
(D) launch（〜を開始する、売り出す）

解説 ▶ initiate a meetingは「面談を設定する」の意で、好ましいかどうかの価値判断は含まない。(A) assemble（〜を集める）の目的語は、peopleやa groupのような人や団体。a meetingは「集める対象」ではないので、空所には不適。

---

15. The council has decided to let parking garages in town dictate their own prices, depending on location and time of day.

① ニュアンス ［ ？ ］
② dictate = (A) determine（〜を決定する）
(B) position（〜を置く、〜を位置付ける）　(C) appoint（〜を任命する）
(D) neglect（〜を放置する）

解説 ▶ dictate their own prices（独自に値段を決める）は、業者にとってはいい話だが、利用者にとってはどうかわからない。よって、このフレーズ自体に客観的な価値判断はない。同義語は(A) determine（〜を決定する）。(C) appointはもっぱら「〜を任命する」の意味で用いられ、その場合は目的語に人を取る。

---

16. Many guests flying to Frankfurt have to <u>forgo the complimentary breakfast</u> included with the hotel room because their departure is too early in the morning.

① ニュアンス ［ × ］
② forgo = (A) abandon（〜を放棄する、捨てる）
(B) obtain（〜を入手する）　(C) prescribe（〜を処方する）　(D) declare（〜を宣言する）

解説 ▶「出発が朝早すぎるので、無料の朝食をforgoしなければならない」という文脈から、forgo the complimentary breakfastは好ましくない意味を持つと推測できる。forgo（〜を我慢する、差し控える）は、(A) abandon（〜を放棄する）と置き換え可能。

---

17. Mr. Rowlinson <u>deemed his position</u> as chief editor a temporary one as he preferred working as a journalist in the field.

● temporary 一時的な　● in the field 現場の

① ニュアンス ［ ? ］
② deemed = (D) considered（〜だとみなす、考える）
(A) examined（〜を調べる、検討する）　(B) contemplated（〜を熟考する）
(C) admitted（〜を認める、採用する）

解説 ▶ deemed his position（職を〜だと考えた）という行為自体には、好ましいかどうかの判断は入っていない。deemed A Bは「AをBと考えた」の意で、(D) consideredが同じ意味と用法を持つ。

---

18. People who have worked at Megatron for more than 10 years will be the <u>beneficiaries of a new loyalty incentive</u>.

① ニュアンス ［ ○ ］
② beneficiaries = (D) recipients（受取人）
(A) providers（供給者）　(B) contributors（貢献者）　(C) associates（仲間、提携者）

解説 ▶「10年以上勤めた人がなる」というbeneficiaries of a new loyalty incentive（新しい勤労奨励金の受取人）は好ましい地位だと推測可能。beneficiariesは(D) recipientsと同義で「受取人」の意。

19. The proliferation of Web sites offering maps and navigation services has led to a severe downturn in the quantity of printed maps being sold.
   ① ニュアンス ［？］
   ② proliferation = (B) increase（増加）
   (A) distinction（区別）　(C) attribution（属性）　(D) leverage（影響力、てこの力）

   解説 ▶ a severe downturn（激しい低下）という、問題文で述べられている結果はネガティブなものだが、The proliferation of Web sites（ウェブサイトの急増）自体には、好ましいかどうかの価値判断は含まれない。proliferationは「急増」の意で、(B) increase（増加）が同義。

20. The amount of money spent on the new headquarters is indicative of Nichol Enterprises' confidence in its own financial stability.
   ① ニュアンス ［？］
   ② indicative = (B) illustrative（実例となる）
   (A) descriptive（記述的な、解説的な）　(C) narrative（物語の、語りの）
   (D) definitive（決定的な）

   解説 ▶ indicative of ~ は「～を示して、表して」の意で、これ自体に好ましいかどうかの価値判断は含まない。問題文中では(B) illustrative（実例となる）と置き換え可能。(A) descriptiveはdescribe（～を説明する）の派生語なので、「（言葉を用いて）記述的な、解説的な」という意味を表す形容詞だ。

Menu 2

　Part 7には、なじみのない機械の仕様書や、文字ぎっしりの記事など、読む前から戦意を喪失させるような文書がしばしば登場する。人はイヤなものからは逃げたい生き物なので、こういう文書ではつい読み飛ばしをしてしまい、解答のキーを見落としがちだ。ここでは忍耐力を持って英文を読むトレーニングをする。

　なじみのないトピック、難しい語彙・表現を含む長文を読み、設問に答えよう。文書が難しいので、設問は負荷が低い正誤問題を用意した。頑張ってチャレンジしてほしい。正しければ○、誤りなら×を記入しよう。**制限時間は1題5分。**

トレーニング Menu 2

Questions 1-6 refer to the following advertisement.   5分

PostagePro

Print your own stamps and shipping labels without setting foot in a post office.

This is a modern, reasonable alternative to an in-office postage meter supplied by the postal authorities. Postage meters are bulky machines that are used to mark letters and parcels with proof of payment and a postage date. They can save companies time, but not money. Typically, leasing a postage meter for a year will cost you hundreds of dollars and depending on the size of your operation, they can cause holdups because only one person can operate them at a time.

This is where PostagePro comes in. By creating a corporate account and installing our easy-to-use software, you can simultaneously print postage at multiple workstations in multiple offices. All without having to pay a cent in leasing. Furthermore, because it is managed via computer, keeping track of mailing and shipping outlay is a breeze.

Our reporting system gives you the following information at a glance.
• Postage expenses filtered according to user and/or office location
• Postage balances calculated according to day, week, month or even year
• A detailed breakdown of spending by mail class, weight, and mail type
• Trend analysis to identify even gradual changes in postage use
• Stationery, insurance and other incidental costs

PostagePro has a team of well-trained staff, ready to offer unlimited online technical assistance. No matter what time of day or night it is, you can submit a help request and expect a response within two business days.

As a special introductory offer for new customers, a set of postage scales that can be connected directly to your computer to completely automate the calculation of postage for large letters and parcels is included in the sign-up price.
The software is programmed according to the latest standards of usability and intuitive design so that your staff can switch over immediately, no training or orientation is necessary. Install the software and you're ready to go!

Call us today at 555-6355 and learn about our other special offers.

1. Postage meters are used by companies to reduce shipping costs.   ____
2. PostagePro customers can print postage stamps at their place of work.   ____
3. Postage meters cost less when purchased.   ____
4. With PostagePro, fluctuations in usage tendencies can be easily spotted. ____
5. PostagePro customers can request technical support by phone 24 hours a day. ____
6. Postage scales are provided at no additional cost.   ____

Questions 7-12 refer to the following contract.

Service Contract

Fairway Hauling, Inc., (hereafter referred to as "Contractor") has agreed to the following terms with regard to services to be provided for Bryant Foods, Inc., (hereafter referred to as "Client") starting September 1.

Service Outline
The Contractor will provide all shipping services for the Client from the production facility on Gladwell Street, North Halifax. All vehicles used in shipping are to be clean, well maintained, late model trucks. When providing service for the Client, they must feature a magnetic sign on each side featuring the logo and contact details of the Client prominently.
Drivers are responsible for the loading and unloading of vehicles as well as reporting any interaction with customers and undeliverable packages.

Payment
Payment is to be calculated on a price per kilometer basis, with the mileage of the vehicles determined by a GPS tracking system provided by the Client. Projected fuel costs will be calculated by the Client using the price of gasoline on the first day of each month, and paid in advance. This fuel compensation will be combined with the below mentioned fee from the previous month and issued altogether. The outstanding fee will be calculated by the Contractor and submitted as an invoice on the final day of the month. Payment for services will occur on the 10th of the following month unless that falls on a weekend, in which case payment will be due on the Friday before.

Additional Terms
The Client and Contractor may enter into discussions to find mutually beneficial solutions should unforeseen circumstances arise. Nevertheless, any deviations from the agreement described in this document must be agreed to in writing before changes to the original terms can be put into practice.

Contractor:

Peter Green	*General Manager* *Fairway Hauling, Inc.*	*August 11*
Signature	Title	Date

Client:

Rose Madden	Owner, Bryant Foods, Inc.	August 11
Signature	Title	Date

7. Bryant Foods is responsible for loading and unloading trucks. _____
8. The client company must be visually represented on the vehicles. _____
9. All payment is due by the 10th of the following month. _____
10. The contract is for an indefinite period. _____
11. Amendments may occur if there are unexpected complications. _____
12. There is a probationary period before the contract takes effect. _____

Menu 2の解答・解説

※文書中の番号＋_____部分は、同じ番号の問題のキーがある箇所を示している。

問題 **1-6** は次の広告に関するものです。

PostagePro

Print your own stamps and shipping labels without setting foot in a post office.

This is a modern, reasonable alternative to an in-office postage meter supplied by the postal authorities. Postage meters are bulky machines that are used to mark letters and parcels with proof of payment and a postage date. [1]They can save companies time, but not money. Typically, leasing a postage meter for a year will cost you hundreds of dollars and depending on the size of your operation, they can cause holdups because only one person can operate them at a time.

This is where PostagePro comes in. By creating a corporate account and installing our easy-to-use software, [2]you can simultaneously print postage at multiple workstations in multiple offices. All without having to pay a cent in leasing. Furthermore, because it is managed via computer, keeping track of mailing and shipping outlay is a breeze.

Our reporting system gives you the following information at a glance.
- Postage expenses filtered according to user and/or office location
- Postage balances calculated according to day, week, month or even year
- A detailed breakdown of spending by mail class, weight, and mail type
- [4]Trend analysis to identify even gradual changes in postage use
- Stationery, insurance and other incidental costs

[5]PostagePro has a team of well-trained staff, ready to offer unlimited online technical assistance. No matter what time of day or night it is, you can submit a help request and expect a response within two business days.

As a special introductory offer for new customers, [6]a set of postage scales that can be connected directly to your computer to completely automate the calculation of postage for large letters and parcels is included in the sign-up price.
The software is programmed according to the latest standards of usability and intuitive design so that your staff can switch over immediately, no training or orientation is necessary. Install the software and you're ready to go!

Call us today at 555-6355 and learn about our other special offers.

● set foot in ~ ～に足を踏み入れる　● postage meter 郵便料金別納証印刷機　● bulky かさばる、大きい　● holdup つまり、渋滞　● outlay 支出　● breeze たやすいこと　● incidental costs 雑費　● intuitive 直感的にわかる

解説 どんな製品やサービスが宣伝されているのかを理解するのが難しい広告。第1段落では、PostagePro社のソフトウエア製品が取って代わろうとしている従来の製品、postage meter（郵便料金別納証印刷機）のことしか述べられていない。本題であるPostagePro社の製品の紹介に入るのは、第2段落からだ。「問題提起→解決策の提案」という展開は広告文で多用されるので、意識しておこう。

1. Postage meters are used by companies to reduce shipping costs. ×
   postage metersは「時間を節約させることはできますが、お金を節約させることはできません」とあるので誤り。

2. PostagePro customers can print postage stamps at their place of work. ○
   PostageProの顧客が利用できるサービスとして、「複数のオフィス…で、郵便料金別納証を同時に印刷することができます」とあるので正しい。

3. Postage meters cost less when purchased. ×
   第1段落後半に、postage metersは「1年間リースすると何百ドルも」かかるとは書かれているが、「購入すれば安く済む」とは書いていないので、誤り。

4. With PostagePro, fluctuations in usage tendencies can be easily spotted. ○
   「緩やかな変化さえも見つけ出すトレンド分析」と述べられている部分が直接的なキーとなり正解。fluctuations（変動）はchangesの言い換えだ。

5. PostagePro customers can request technical support by phone 24 hours a day. ×
   「昼や夜のどんな時間でもヘルプの依頼をすることができる」とはあるが、「オンライン」のサポートしか言及されていない。よって、「電話で技術サポートを依頼できる」は×。

6. Postage scales are provided at no additional cost. ○
   「郵便料金計算用はかり1台が登録料金に含まれます」とあるので正しい。キーのある文は、長いthat節の中にto不定詞も入っており、読みにくい。主語と動詞をしっかりと特定することが求められる問題だ。

問題 **7-12** は次の契約書に関するものです。

Service Contract

Fairway Hauling, Inc., (hereafter referred to as "Contractor") has agreed to the following terms with regard to services to be provided for [7] Bryant Foods, Inc., (hereafter referred to as "Client") [10,12] starting September 1.

Service Outline

[7] The Contractor will provide all shipping services for the Client from the production facility on Gladwell Street, North Halifax. [8] All vehicles used in shipping are to be clean, well maintained, late model trucks. When providing service for the Client, [8] they must feature a magnetic sign on each side featuring the logo and contact details of the Client prominently.
[7] Drivers are responsible for the loading and unloading of vehicles as well as reporting any interaction with customers and undeliverable packages.

Payment

Payment is to be calculated on a price per kilometer basis, with the mileage of the vehicles determined by a GPS tracking system provided by the Client. Projected fuel costs will be calculated by the Client using the price of gasoline on the first day of each month, and paid in advance. [9] This fuel compensation will be combined with the below mentioned fee from the previous month and issued altogether. The outstanding fee will be calculated by the Contractor and submitted as an invoice on the final day of the month. [9] Payment for services will occur on the 10th of the following month unless that falls on a weekend, in which case payment will be due on the Friday before.

Additional Terms

[11] The Client and Contractor may enter into discussions to find mutually beneficial solutions should unforeseen circumstances arise. Nevertheless, any deviations from the agreement described in this document must be agreed to in writing before changes to the original terms can be put into practice.

Contractor:

Peter Green	General Manager Fairway Hauling, Inc.	[12] August 11
Signature	Title	Date

Client:

Rose Madden	Owner, Bryant Foods, Inc.	[12] August 11
Signature	Title	Date

- hereafter 以下、ここから先 ● magnetic sign 磁石付きの看板 ● prominently 目立つように
- interaction 交流 ● undeliverable 配達できない ● mileage 走行距離 ● fuel compensations 燃料費の支払い ● issue ～を支払う ● outstanding fee 未収料金 ● mutually beneficial 相互に利益のある ● unforeseen 不測の ● deviation それること、逸脱

解説 契約書を読む際には、hereafter referred to as "Contractor"/ "Client"（以下「請負人・受託業者」／「依頼人・委託者」とする）という文言を確認し、誰がサービスを提供し、誰が提供されるのかを頭の中で整理しよう。各条項には、業者の責任や支払いの期日などさまざまなことが書かれているが、ほとんど常識的なことばかりだ。どの辺りにどんな情報があるかを把握し、情報検索力＋局所的な精読力で問題を解こう。インターネットプロバイダーや携帯電話会社との契約など、自分に身近な例を思い起こすと、何が書かれているかイメージしやすい場合もある。

7. Bryant Foods is responsible for loading and unloading trucks. ×
Bryant Foods社は業務委託者。「車両からの荷物の積み降ろし」は、受託業者が手配する運転手の仕事なので×。

8. The client company must be visually represented on the vehicles. ○
「業務委託者のロゴと連絡先情報」を書いたマグネットをトラックの両サイドに貼ることになっているので○。

9. All payment is due by the 10th of the following month. ○
当月の予想燃料費は毎月1日に計算され、前月分の差額料金と合算で10日に支払われる。10日が週末の場合はその前の金曜日に支払うとあるので、「10日までに」は○。

10. The contract is for an indefinite period. ○
「9月1日」からという契約開始日のみ言及されていることと、毎月支払い請求が発生することになっていることから、「契約期間は無期限」は○。

11. Amendments may occur if there are unexpected complications. ○
予期せぬ事態が発生した場合は、協議して書面での合意を得れば契約内容を変更することができるとあるので、「修正が生じることがある」は○。

12. There is a probationary period before the contract takes effect. ×
契約書署名日（8月11日）と契約開始日（9月1日）の間が空いているが、これはprobationary period（試用期間）ではないので×。

CHAPTER 7 難語対応・忍耐力 ADVANCED VOCABULARY / ENDURANCE

実践問題

仕上げに、本番形式の難問にチャレンジ。最後まで粘り強く解ききろう。

Part 5

空所に入る語句として、最も適切なものを1つ選ぼう。(解答・解説はpp. 270〜275)

⏱ 6分40秒

1. Many of the devices carried around by service technicians have become ------- since the advent of smartphones.
   (A) redundant
   (B) resolute
   (C) obligatory
   (D) preferential   Ⓐ Ⓑ Ⓒ Ⓓ

2. A new farming innovation has been created, which will make crop quality far less ------- to the weather.
   (A) anchored
   (B) subject
   (C) substantial
   (D) resourceful   Ⓐ Ⓑ Ⓒ Ⓓ

3. A council meeting was held to discuss the likelihood of delays to the reconstruction of Rolston Public Library and what to do in that -------.
   (A) causality
   (B) eventuality
   (C) exclusivity
   (D) functionality

4. With fuel prices rising at an unprecedented rate, businesses and local authorities are exploring ways to reduce -------.
   (A) expenditure
   (B) drawbacks
   (C) fractions
   (D) redemption

5. Problems with the file server were ------- by having a service representative from the manufacturer replace some of the components.
   (A) deferred
   (B) restricted
   (C) stabilized
   (D) rectified

6. The manager cautioned that the company had become overly ------- on repeat customers and was not attracting new business.
   (A) perpetual
   (B) adverse
   (C) moderate
   (D) reliant

7. Due to an extended power outage, the organizing committee has been ------- additional time in which to finalize preparations for the opening ceremony.
   (A) fabricated
   (B) attested
   (C) accorded
   (D) stipulated

8. Wellbio Food's claims about the properties of its nutritional supplements had to be ------- after some data was shown to be erroneous.
   (A) intervened
   (B) retracted
   (C) acknowledged
   (D) disseminated

9. The keynote speech at the conference will be delivered by Mike Miller, one of the most ------- and acclaimed business leaders in the pharmaceutical sector.
   (A) mundane
   (B) variable
   (C) distinguished
   (D) retained

10. The $20 delivery fee will be ------- for orders of over $50 for members of our Premium Shoppers Club.
    (A) expended
    (B) waived
    (C) assigned
    (D) derived

11. We at Altan Pharmaceuticals expect management to be ------- role models to employees both in and out of the workplace.
(A) exemplary
(B) feasible
(C) customary
(D) discreet

12. Please be advised that maintenance work is being performed on part of the visitor parking lot ------- to the main entrance.
(A) extended
(B) demolished
(C) adjoined
(D) assimilated

13. A ------- of the malfunction on the assembly line revealed that the equipment lacked adequate lubrication causing its gears to grind to a halt.
(A) conclusion
(B) diagnosis
(C) probe
(D) neglect

14. FT Computers fulfills its ------- to customers by providing software updates whenever a shortcoming is identified.
(A) determination
(B) privilege
(C) conformity
(D) obligation

15. Megabuy has a fitness gym and a staff lounge on the ------- to help maintain the health, performance and engagement of its employees.
(A) resources
(B) premises
(C) facilities
(D) inference

16. When organizing the upcoming company banquet, Mr. Goodman took a ------- against poor weather by reserving a venue with both indoor and outdoor dining sections.
(A) strategy
(B) liability
(C) precaution
(D) foresight

17. The gardens of the Molton City Museum are ------- maintained by a team of experienced volunteer gardeners.
(A) recurrently
(B) exceedingly
(C) conversely
(D) meticulously

18. After the plenary meeting, employees ------- and took part in various workshops depending on their functions within the company.
(A) dispersed
(B) articulated
(C) isolated
(D) concentrated

19. A variety of products whose sales have been ------- will be consolidated at the Tucson store and sold at drastically reduced prices.
(A) jeopardizing
(B) lucrative
(C) sporadic
(D) versatile

20. Respondents to the survey expressed satisfaction concerning the current customer support system ------- it was always available and priced competitively.
(A) in order that
(B) for the sake of
(C) provided that
(D) inasmuch as

Part 7

文書に関する設問の解答として、最も適切なものを1つずつ選ぼう。

(解答・解説はpp. 276〜282)

Questions 21-25 refer to the following Web page. 6分

Hamilton Landscape Services

At Hamilton Landscape Services we consider not only the topography of your site, but also the climate and the particular region, including its wildlife and native plant species. In the long term, ongoing care costs are usually far higher than the landscaping itself. Our preliminary investigations and planning help us tailor projects to our clients' budgets by keeping ongoing care costs to a minimum. There is a 15 percent price reduction for public amenities, non-profit groups, and corporate clients registered with the Ridgemont Business Association.

- All plants are treated with organic fertilizers prepared at our own facilities.
- For pest control and weed reduction, we use only products that have been approved by both the council's environmental management division and the Nature Preservation Society of Ridgemont.
- When unavoidable, pesticides may be used after thorough consultation.
- Our lawn care crew uses specialized equipment that improves the quality of the soil to encourage root growth and leaf quality.
- Ongoing monitoring of irrigation systems is conducted using both remote and on-site methods to ensure minimal water waste.
- Fallen leaves and branches are mulched on-site and recycled into usable natural compost.
- Staff employ planting procedures that ensure fast growth and longevity.

Please explore other parts of our Web site to see our past clients and their testimonials. You may also check out our latest news on the blog. We provide a free landscape analysis for customers who do not qualify for other discounts. Please use the information in the contact section to get in touch with one of our customer support officers.

21. Which page of the Web site is most likely being shown?
   (A) Lawn and Plant Care
   (B) Environmentally friendly pesticides
   (C) About Hamilton Landscape Services
   (D) Customer Testimonials

22. What is indicated about Hamilton Landscape Services?
   (A) It always uses only the most effective pesticides.
   (B) It provides recommendations for clients to maintain their landscapes.
   (C) It recognizes security issues when designing environments.
   (D) It takes clients' fiscal concerns into consideration.

23. What does Hamilton Landscape Services undertake to do?
   (A) Confer with clients before using toxic substances
   (B) Select trees and shrubs native to the area
   (C) Conform to government regulations when clearing land
   (D) Remove all leaves and branches from worksites at completion

24. What benefit is NOT mentioned on the Web page?
   (A) Accelerated plant growth
   (B) Efficient water usage
   (C) Recycling of excavated soil
   (D) Customized landscape design

25. Who is eligible for a free site evaluation?
   (A) Charity organizations
   (B) Private home owners
   (C) Corporate clients
   (D) Council departments

Questions 26-30 refer to the following article.

Padovano's, Il Tragico Farfalla: A Favorite with Audiences

Although it was expected to have a run of only six weeks, Padovano's famous opera, Il Tragico Farfalla, has been asked to delay its conclusion to accommodate the hundreds of people still hoping to get tickets. Certainly, the show's star, Felicity Graham has been a huge draw for audiences but she is not all it has going for it.

From its opening night, the production has earned high praise, most of which has been for the outstanding work of Belinda Pierce, a well-known figure in the world of opera—just last year, she took the top prize for the fourth time at the International Critics' Award for Operatic Performance. However, Ms. Pierce has elected not to appear on stage in this production. This is her directorial debut, and in this capacity, she has demonstrated just as amazing a talent as she did in the spotlight.

The performers were to have a three-week break before the show reopens in Chicago in May, but they have agreed to forgo much of that to fulfill the wishes of the Boston Performing Arts Society, who are promoting the production. Unfortunately, Ms. Pierce and Ms. Graham will not be present for the final two weeks of performances, the former already laying the groundwork at the group's next destination and the latter being contractually entitled to a week's vacation in her hometown of Paris, France. In a recent interview though, she said she would be visiting London on her way back to attend a charity concert featuring her younger sister.

Audiences should not be too disappointed, however, because world-renowned opera singer, Sophie Melina has agreed to come out of retirement to fill Graham's shoes at the current venue. She made a name for herself in this very role, so there is a lot of public expectation attached to her performances. Consequently, there is some apprehension that this rare and likely final opportunity to see Ms. Melina perform may attract audiences from far and wide, once again denying local residents their chance to attend.

26. What is the main purpose of the article?
   (A) To report the extension of a performance
   (B) To provide a review of a production
   (C) To introduce an upcoming performance
   (D) To describe the career of a performer

27. Who is Ms. Pierce?
   (A) A cast member
   (B) A director
   (C) An association representative
   (D) An opera reviewer

28. What city will Ms. Graham visit next?
   (A) Chicago
   (B) Boston
   (C) Paris
   (D) London

29. The word "elected" in paragraph 2, line 9, is closest in meaning to
   (A) opted
   (B) voted
   (C) assigned
   (D) wished

30. What concern is mentioned about the performance?
   (A) People will not buy tickets unless Ms. Graham performs.
   (B) The cast of the production may be overworked.
   (C) Boston residents will have to compete for seats.
   (D) There is not enough time to prepare in Chicago.

Questions 31-35 refer to the following articles.

Bristol (January 5)—After less than five years of operation, the doors of Swansea Shopping Centre (SSC) in South Wales will close at the end of January. With a 12-screen cinema and international fashion chains, SSC was meant to be a one-stop destination for shoppers of all kinds. For the first few months, footfall was in line with management's expectations.

"The problem was in cultivating a customer base," regrets Paul Blease, managing director of SSC. Mr. Blease suspects the finger of blame should be pointed at the food court and it's not particularly appealing fare. According to customer surveys conducted by the Kemble Institute, an independent research firm, SSC's biggest drawback is its inconvenient location. People, especially younger generations, prefer to do their shopping around the city center.

No announcement has been issued yet as to whether SSC will seek a way to reopen the mall or find a buyer and sell the property altogether. The adverse effects of this closure will surely be felt in Swansea, where employment opportunities are in short supply.

Bristol (November 10)—Swansea Shopping Centre (SSC) has undergone a remarkable transformation that will be revealed to the public on December 10. After a renovation that has been in progress since February, SSC will soon be ready once again to welcome shoppers and their families, with over a hundred shops ranging from internationally renowned fashion retailers to grocery shops selling locally grown food.

Restarting the business all over again has required a substantial investment. It was made possible by real estate developer, Shahid Group. The Dubai-based company has acquired a significant part of SSC but states that it does not intend to take over the business. The owner and founder of Shahid Group, Mr. Abdul Shahid, spent his teenage years in Swansea, and apparently it was his attachment to the city rather than a desire to accomplish any business objectives that moved him. "I certainly see future profitability in SSC, but more than that, I wanted to give back to the local community where I grew up," the property tycoon explained.

Despite its impressive list of tenants, SSC was unable to attract enough traffic in the past, mainly due to its somewhat inconvenient location. From December, however, the management expects to be able to remove this obstacle by offering free shuttle buses every quarter of the hour to and from Central Station. In addition to the improved transportation, the food court offers a wide array of exciting cuisines including sushi, tacos and dim sum.

The mayor of Swansea, Sarah Jones, went on record saying that this would bring a lot of much needed jobs into the area. She accepted an invitation from SSC's managing director Paul Blease to cut the tape at the occasion held to mark the reopening. Visit the SSC Web site (www.swanseasc.co.uk) to find a list of discounts and specials available in the reopening week.

31. What problem does Mr. Blease mention?
　(A) Attracting a variety of stores
　(B) Raising funds for a restoration
　(C) Establishing regular customers
　(D) Hiring suitable staff

32. What is suggested about Abdul Shahid?
　(A) He predicts financial return on the investment.
　(B) His firm hired Kemble Institute to conduct research.
　(C) He is a native of the city of Swansea.
　(D) His company acquired full ownership of SSC.

33. What has been changed at Swansea Shopping Centre since its closure?
　(A) Its location
　(B) Its management
　(C) Its dining offerings
　(D) Its entertainment facilities

34. What does Ms. Jones say about the reopening?
　(A) Retail options in the area will be expanded.
　(B) It will provide employment opportunities.
　(C) It will lead to an improved transportation infrastructure.
　(D) There will be more entertainment venues for youth.

35. What will most likely happen on December 10?
　(A) Online promotions will commence.
　(B) A local politician will attend a ceremony.
　(C) Mr. Blease will announce his successor.
　(D) Mr. Shahid will sign an official agreement.

実践問題の解答・解説

※問題文の訳文は紙面では省略（訳文の入手方法はp. 7をご覧ください）。

Part 5

1. Many of the devices carried around by service technicians have become ------- since the advent of smartphones.

* (A) redundant　形 余分な
* (B) resolute　形 意志の固い
* (C) obligatory　形 義務的な、必須の
* (D) preferential　形 優先的な

● carry around 持ち歩く　● advent 出現、登場

解説 スマートフォンの出現により、多くの機器は「不必要」になる、という意味が適切なので、正解は (A) redundant。redundantは「余分な」という訳語だけを覚えている人もいるかもしれないが、redundant = not needed or useful という感覚で押さえておこう。

---

2. A new farming innovation has been created, which will make crop quality far less ------- to the weather.

* (A) anchored　動 固定された
* * (B) subject　形 影響を受ける
* (C) substantial　形 実体のある
* (D) resourceful　形 機知に富んだ

● farming innovation 農業の革新

解説 crop quality（農産物の品質）が「天候に左右されなくなる」という文意はつかみやすい。(A) anchoredは後ろに to ~を伴うことはできるが、「（物が）固定された」という意味が不適。正解は「影響を受ける」という意味の形容詞(B) subject。be subject to change without prior noticeは「予告なく変更される場合がある」という但し書きによく使われるフレーズ。

---

3. A council meeting was held to discuss the likelihood of delays to the reconstruction of Rolston Public Library and what to do in that -------.

* (A) causality　名 因果関係
* * (B) eventuality　名 万が一の事態
* (C) exclusivity　名 排他性
* (D) functionality　名 機能性

解説 各選択肢の意味は、(A) causality — cause（原因）、(B) eventuality — eventually（最終的に、結局）、(C) exclusivity — exclusive（排他的な）、(D) functionality — functional（機能的な）といった派生語を手掛かりにすれば、ある程度は推測できる。空所には、delays to the reconstruction（改築の遅れ）を指して「万が一の事態」と表現する(B) eventualityが適切。

実践問題の解答・解説

4. With fuel prices rising at an unprecedented rate, businesses and local authorities are exploring ways to reduce -------.

　＊(A) expenditure　［名］支出
　(B) drawbacks　［名］欠点
　(C) fractions　［名］かけら
　(D) redemption　［名］償還

● unprecedented 前例のない　● local authorities 地方自治体

解説 With fuel prices rising（燃料価格が上がっている）という状況で、businesses and local authorities（企業や地方自治体）が何を減らしたいかを考えれば、空所には「経費」のような意味を補うのが適切とわかる。expense（経費）と形や意味が似ている、(A) expenditure（支出）が正解。「経費、支出」の意味ではexpenseの方が一般的で、expenditureは支払いを伴う場合にのみ用いられる。

---

5. Problems with the file server were ------- by having a service representative from the manufacturer replace some of the components.

　(A) deferred　［動］延期された
　(B) restricted　［動］制限された
　(C) stabilized　［動］安定化された
　＊(D) rectified　［動］修正された

● component 部品

解説 問題文から、サーバーのトラブルはa service representative（サービス担当者）に部品を交換してもらうことによって解決した、という文意が推測できる。(B) restricted（制限された）、(C) stabilized（安定化された）は容易に排除できるだろう。残り二択のうち、正解は(D) rectified（修正された、是正された）。(A) deferredは「延期された」の意。de- という接頭辞にはdownやawayという意味がある。

---

6. The manager cautioned that the company had become overly ------- on repeat customers and was not attracting new business.

　(A) perpetual　［形］永遠の
　(B) adverse　［形］逆の
　(C) moderate　［形］過度な
　＊(D) reliant　［形］依存する

解説 that節はcautionedの目的語であり「注意した」内容なので、空所には会社にとって好ましくない状態を表す語を入れるのが適切だ。正解は、rely（頼る）の派生語で空所直後のonを取れる、(D) reliant（依存する）。(B) adverseも「逆の、不利な」というネガティブな意味を持つが、後ろにonを取れず、意味も合わない。

7. Due to an extended power outage, the organizing committee has been ------- additional time in which to finalize preparations for the opening ceremony.

(A) fabricated 動 ～をでっちあげた
(B) attested 動 ～を証明した
*(C) accorded 動 ～を与えた
(D) stipulated 動 ～を規定した

● power outage 停電

解説 問題文は、the organizing committee（組織委員会）が、空所直後の目的語 additional time（延長時間）を「与えられた」という文意になると推測できる。しかし、選択肢には難しい語が多い。正解できるか否かは、いくつの単語を知っていて消去できるかにもかかってくる。正解は (C) accord（～を与えた）。これは give や grant の同義語だ。

8. Wellbio Food's claims about the properties of its nutritional supplements had to be ------- after some data was shown to be erroneous.

(A) intervened 動 介入される
*(B) retracted 動 撤回される
(C) acknowledged 動 認められる
(D) disseminated 動 広められる

● property 特質、性質 ● erroneous 誤りのある

解説 文末の erroneous は error の派生語で、「間違った」の意。「データが間違っていたことが証明された」ので、食品メーカーの claims（主張）は「撤回される」べきだ、という文意から、正解は (B) retracted。接頭辞 re- には back の意味がある。

9. The keynote speech at the conference will be delivered by Mike Miller, one of the most ------- and acclaimed business leaders in the pharmaceutical sector.

(A) mundane 形 平凡な
(B) variable 形 気まぐれな
*(C) distinguished 形 著名な、優れた
(D) retained 動 保たれた

解説 空所に入る語は、acclaimed（高く評価された）と共に最上級で business leaders を修飾しているので、ポジティブな意味の単語であるはずだ。正解は (C) distinguished（著名な、優れた）。動詞 distinguish は「～を区別する」という意味なので、「他の人と区別された」＝「際立った」と関連付けて覚えよう。

10. The $20 delivery fee will be ------- for orders of over $50 for members of our Premium Shoppers Club.

(A) expended 動 消費される
*(B) waived 動 免除される
(C) assigned 動 割り当てられる
(D) derived 動 引き出される

解説 会員がまとまった注文をすると、配送料は無料になるという文意だ。正解は「免除される」という意味の (B) waived。waive a fee は「料金を免除する」、waiver clause は「免責条項」。

11. We at Altan Pharmaceuticals expect management to be ------- role models to employees both in and out of the workplace.

* (A) exemplary　形 模範的な
(B) feasible　形 実行可能な
(C) customary　形 習慣的な、通常の
(D) discreet　形 思慮深い、控えめな

解説 空所直後のrole models（手本となる人）にかかる適切な形容詞を考える。正解は「模範的な」という意味の(A) exemplary。example（例）と同じ語源なので、関連付けて覚えよう。(B) feasible（実行可能な）は計画や方法を修飾する語。(C) discreet（思慮深い）を入れると「控えめな手本」といった意味になるので、不適切。

---

12. Please be advised that maintenance work is being performed on part of the visitor parking lot ------- to the main entrance.

(A) extended　動 拡張された
(B) demolished　動 取り壊された
* (C) adjoined　動 隣接した
(D) assimilated　動 同化した

解説 the visitor parking lot（来客用駐車場）とthe main entrance（正面入口）という2つの場所を表す句をつなぐことができるのは、(C) adjoined（隣接した）。前置詞はnextと同じくtoを取る。(A) extendedを入れると「正面入口まで拡張工事された」という意味になるが、これはadjoinedのように明確な場所を表さず、文意に対して余計な情報となり不適切。

---

13. A ------- of the malfunction on the assembly line revealed that the equipment lacked adequate lubrication causing its gears to grind to a halt.

(A) conclusion　名 結論
* (B) diagnosis　名 診断
(C) probe　名 調査
(D) neglect　名 無視

● malfunction 故障　● lubrication 潤滑油の注入　● grind to a halt 急停止する

解説 revealed（明らかにした）の主語として適切な語を考える。明らかにされた内容は、that以下のthe assembly line（組み立てライン）の故障の原因だ。正解は「診断」という意味の(B) diagnosis。(A) conclusion（結論）は、ofの後ろに「診断」や「調査」などの語が必要。(C) probe（調査）は後ろにintoやforを取る。

---

14. FT Computers fulfills its ------- to customers by providing software updates whenever a shortcoming is identified.

(A) determination　名 決意
(B) privilege　名 特権
(C) conformity　名 順守
* (D) obligation　名 義務、責任

● shortcoming 欠陥

解説 動詞fulfillsは「（約束・任務など）を遂行する、果たす」という意味で、その目的語としては、(D) obligation（義務）が適切。(B) privilege（特権、特典）は顧客に与えるものなので不適切。(C) conformity（順守）は、toやwithの後ろに「法律・規則」などを伴う。

15. Megabuy has a fitness gym and a staff lounge on the ------- to help maintain the health, performance and engagement of its employees.

● engagement 仕事の契約

(A) resources 名 資金、資産
*(B) premises 名 敷地
(C) facilities 名 施設
(D) inference 名 推論

解説 空所には、Megabuy社が持つa fitness gym and a staff lounge（フィットネスジムと社員休憩室）がどこにあるかを表す語が入るべきだ。正解は(B) premises（敷地）。(A) resources（資金、資産）や(D) inference（推論）は場所ではない。(C) facilitiesはフィットネスジムや休憩室などの「施設」そのものを指す語なので不適切。

16. When organizing the upcoming company banquet, Mr. Goodman took a ------- against poor weather by reserving a venue with both indoor and outdoor dining sections.

(A) strategy 名 戦略
(B) liability 名 負債、法的責任
*(C) precaution 名 備え、対策
(D) foresight 名 将来の展望

解説 indoor and outdoor dining sections（屋内と屋外の食事場所の両方がある会場）を予約することは、poor weather（悪天候）に対する「対策」なので、正解は(C) precaution。(A)はadopt a strategy（戦略をとる）、(B)はaccept liability（責任を認める）、(D)はhave foresight（先見の明がある）のように使うが、いずれもtakeの目的語にはならない。

17. The gardens of the Molton City Museum are ------- maintained by a team of experienced volunteer gardeners.

(A) recurrently 副 反復的に
(B) exceedingly 副 非常に
(C) conversely 副 反対に
*(D) meticulously 副 細心の注意を払って

解説 experienced volunteer gardeners（経験豊かなボランティアの庭師）によって庭園が維持されている様子を適切に表す副詞を選ぶ。正解は(D) meticulously（細心の注意を払って、念入りに）。(A) recurrentlyはrecur（再発する）、(B) exceedingly（非常に、甚だしく）はexceed（〜を超える）という動詞から意味を推測できるだろう。なお、(B)の後ろにはwell-maintained（よく管理された）のように良しあしなどの程度を表す語句が必要。

実践問題の解答・解説

18. After the plenary meeting, employees ------- and took part in various workshops depending on their functions within the company.

● plenary meeting 全体会議 ● function 職務

* (A) dispersed　　動 解散した
(B) articulated　　動 はっきりと話した
(C) isolated　　　動 〜を分離した
(D) concentrated　動 集中した

解説 空所には、従業員の行動を表す動詞が入る。「さまざまなワークショップに参加した」につながる「解散した」という意味の(A) dispersedが正解。(C) isolated (〜を分離した)は他動詞なので、後ろに目的語を伴うか受動態にする必要がある。plenary meeting (全体会議)の後、職種によって個別のワークショップに分かれたという文意から、(C) concentrated (集結した、集中した)は排除できる。

---

19. A variety of products whose sales have been ------- will be consolidated at the Tucson store and sold at drastically reduced prices.

● consolidated 統合された

(A) jeopardizing　危うくする
(B) lucrative　　形 もうかる
* (C) sporadic　　形 散発的な
(D) versatile　　形 多目的な

解説 どのような売り上げの製品が集められ、大胆な割引価格で売られるかを考える。正解選択肢は頻出語ではないので、消去法で解くべき問題だ。(A) jeopardizingはjeopardy (危険)から「危うくする」という意味を連想できるだろう。(B) lucrativeは「もうかる」の意、(D) versatileは「多目的の、多才な」の意で、どちらも公開テストに出題されたことがある語だ。いずれも空所には当てはまらないので、残った(C) sporadic (散発的な、断続的な) が正解となる。

---

20. Respondents to the survey expressed satisfaction concerning the current customer support system ------- it was always available and priced competitively.

(A) in order that　　〜するために
(B) for the sake of　〜のために
(C) provided that　　もし〜ならば
* (D) inasmuch as　　〜だから

解説 空所には、その前後の節をつなぐ接続詞が入る。(B) for the sake of (〜のために) は前置詞なので排除できる。空所前にはRespondents to the survey (調査の回答者)が「現在の顧客サービスシステムに満足だと言った」とあり、空所後に述べられている「利便性と競争力のある料金」は、その理由だ。よって、空所には「理由」を表す接続詞が入る。(A) in order that (〜するために)は後ろに「目的」が来る。(C) provided thatは「条件」を表す。正解は残りの(D) inasmuch as (〜だから)だ。

Part 7

問題 21-25 は次のウェブページに関するものです。

Hamilton Landscape Services

¹At Hamilton Landscape Services we consider not only the topography of your site, but also the climate and the particular region, including its wildlife and native plant species. In the long term, ongoing care costs are usually far higher than the landscaping itself. ²Our preliminary investigations and planning help us tailor projects to our clients' budgets by keeping ongoing care costs to a minimum. ³There is a 15 percent price reduction for public amenities, non-profit groups, and corporate clients registered with the Ridgemont Business Association.

- All plants are treated with organic fertilizers prepared at our own facilities.
- For pest control and weed reduction, we use only products that have been approved by both the council's environmental management division and the Nature Preservation Society of Ridgemont.
- ⁴When unavoidable, pesticides may be used after thorough consultation.
- Our lawn care crew uses specialized equipment that improves the quality of the soil to encourage root growth and leaf quality.
- ⁵Ongoing monitoring of irrigation systems is conducted using both remote and on-site methods to ensure minimal water waste.
- ⁶Fallen leaves and branches are mulched on-site and recycled into usable natural compost.
- ⁷Staff employ planting procedures that ensure fast growth and longevity.

Please explore other parts of our Web site to see our past clients and their testimonials. You may also check out our latest news on the blog. ⁸We provide a free landscape analysis for customers who do not qualify for other discounts. Please use the information in the contact section to get in touch with one of our customer support officers.

● topography 地形 ● native plant species その土地固有の植物種 ● tailor ～に合わせる ● public amenity 公共施設 ● fertilizer 肥料 ● pest 害虫 ● pesticide 殺虫剤 ● irrigation 水やり ● mulch 根覆いをする、マルチングする ● compost 堆肥 ● employ ～（手段）を用いる ● longevity 寿命、長生きすること

---

21. Which page of the Web site is most likely being shown?
(A) Lawn and Plant Care
(B) Environmentally friendly pesticides
＊(C) About Hamilton Landscape Services
(D) Customer Testimonials

解説 1に続く部分の記述などから、Hamilton Landscape Services社の業務内容について書かれたページであることがわかる。よって(C)が正解である。

22. What is indicated about Hamilton Landscape Services?
   (A) It always uses only the most effective pesticides.
   (B) It provides recommendations for clients to maintain their landscapes.
   (C) It recognizes security issues when designing environments.
   * (D) It takes clients' fiscal concerns into consideration.

解説 ▶ 2に「初期調査と計画立案を行うことにより、お客様の予算に合わせることができます」という記述があるので、(D)「顧客の財務的懸念を考慮する」が正解。(B)については、第1段落1行目で「topography(地形)を考慮する」とは述べられているが、recommendations(助言)を提供するとは書かれていない。

---

23. What does Hamilton Landscape Services undertake to do?
   * (A) Confer with clients before using toxic substances
   (B) Select trees and shrubs native to the area
   (C) Conform to government regulations when clearing land
   (D) Remove all leaves and branches from worksites at completion

解説 ▶ 4に「やむを得ない場合、徹底した協議の上、殺虫剤を使用することもあります」という記述があるので、(A)の「毒性のある物質を使用する前には顧客と話し合う」が正解。文中のpesticides(殺虫剤)は選択肢でtoxic substances(毒性物質)に、consultation(協議)はconfer(話し合う)に言い換えられている。

---

24. What benefit is NOT mentioned on the Web page?
   (A) Accelerated plant growth   (B) Efficient water usage
   * (C) Recycling of excavated soil   (D) Customized landscape design

解説 ▶ (A)「早められた植物の生育」については、7に「スタッフは、早く生育し長持ちする植え付け方法を用います」という記述がある。(B)の「効率的な水の使用」については、5で「水の無駄使いを最小限にするため(中略)水やりシステムを監視しています」と述べられている。(D)の「カスタマイズされた造園設計」については、2の「お客様の予算に合わせて計画立案します」が対応している。よって、述べられていないのは(C)「掘り起こした土のリサイクル」。6に「落ち葉や枝はリサイクルされて堆肥にされます」という記述があるが、「土のリサイクル」ではない。

---

25. Who is eligible for a free site evaluation?
   (A) Charity organizations   * (B) Private home owners
   (C) Corporate clients   (D) Council departments

解説 ▶ 3に「公共施設、非営利団体、法人顧客には割引があります」との記述があり、8に「割引を受けられないお客様には無料で用地分析を提供します」との記述があるので、「無料で用地評価をしてもらえる人」は(B)「個人宅所有者」である。(A)は3のnon-profit groupsの言い換えであり、(D)「市の部局」は同じく3のpublic amenities(公共の設備)に含まれている。

問題 26-30 は次の記事に関するものです

Padovano's, Il Tragico Farfalla: A Favorite with Audiences

[1]Although it was expected to have a run of only six weeks, Padovano's famous opera, Il Tragico Farfalla, has been asked to delay its conclusion to accommodate the hundreds of people still hoping to get tickets. Certainly, the show's star, Felicity Graham has been a huge draw for audiences but she is not all it has going for it.

From its opening night, the production has earned high praise, most of which has been for the outstanding work of Belinda Pierce, a well-known figure in the world of opera—just last year, she took the top prize for the fourth time at the International Critics' Award for Operatic Performance. However, [2]Ms. Pierce has elected not to appear on stage in this production. This is her directorial debut, and in this capacity, she has demonstrated just as amazing a talent as she did in the spotlight.

[3]The performers were to have a three-week break before the show reopens in Chicago in May, but they have agreed to forgo much of that to fulfill the wishes of the Boston Performing Arts Society, who are promoting the production. Unfortunately, [4]Ms. Pierce and Ms. Graham will not be present for the final two weeks of performances, the former already laying the groundwork at the group's next destination and [5]the latter being contractually entitled to a week's vacation in her hometown of Paris, France. In a recent interview though, she said [6]she would be visiting London on her way back to attend a charity concert featuring her younger sister.

Audiences should not be too disappointed, however, because world-renowned opera singer, Sophie Melina has agreed to come out of retirement to fill Graham's shoes at the current venue. She made a name for herself in this very role, so there is a lot of public expectation attached to her performances. Consequently, [7]there is some apprehension that this rare and likely final opportunity to see Ms. Melina perform may attract audiences from far and wide, once again denying local residents their chance to attend.

- draw 呼び物 ● forgo（楽しみを）慎む ● lay the groundwork 下準備をする ● contractually 契約により ● fill ~'s shoes ～（人）の代役を果たす ● apprehension 懸念

26. What is the main purpose of the article?
* (A) To report the extension of a performance
 (B) To provide a review of a production
 (C) To introduce an upcoming performance
 (D) To describe the career of a performer

解説 1の「6週間の公演予定だったが、最終公演を延ばすよう要請されている」との記述から、この記事の目的は(A)の「公演延長を知らせるため」だ。a review（評論）を提供するためではないので(B)は不適切。(C)は、公演はすでに行われているので、an upcoming（来る）という部分が合わない。(D)の内容は記事に含まれているが「主な目的」ではない。

実践問題の解答・解説

27. Who is Ms. Pierce?
(A) A cast member
∗ (B) A director
(C) An association representative
(D) An opera reviewer

解説 ▶ 2に「Pierce氏はこの作品の舞台に立たないことに決めた。これは彼女の監督としてのデビュー作である」との記述があるので、(B) A directorが正解である。

---

28. What city will Ms. Graham visit next?
(A) Chicago
(B) Boston
(C) Paris
∗ (D) London

解説 ▶ 4に「Graham氏は公演の最後の2週間は出演しない」との記述がある。5のthe latterはGraham氏を指し、「故郷のパリで1週間の休暇を取る」と述べている。しかし、6に「故郷へ戻る途中にロンドンを訪れるつもりだ」と書かれているので、次に訪れる町は(D) London。

---

29. The word "elected" in paragraph 2, line 9, is closest in meaning to
∗ (A) opted
(B) voted
(C) assigned
(D) wished

解説 ▶ electedは「～を選んだ」という意味で使われている。(A) opted、(B) votedはともに「～を選んだ」と訳せるが、(B)は「投票で選ぶ」という意味なので、ここでは不適切。自由意思で選ぶという意味を含んだ(A)が正解。optの名詞形がoption、形容詞形がoptionalであることを考えると、「選択自由なものから選ぶ」というニュアンスが推測できるだろう。

---

30. What concern is mentioned about the performance?
(A) People will not buy tickets unless Ms. Graham performs.
(B) The cast of the production may be overworked.
∗ (C) Boston residents will have to compete for seats.
(D) There is not enough time to prepare in Chicago.

解説 ▶ 7に「いくらかのapprehension（懸念）がある」との記述がある。that以下で「この公演にはあちこちから観客が来るだろうから、地元住民が鑑賞する機会は今回もないかもしれない」と述べている。この「地元」とは、3から延長公演が行われるボストンのことだとわかる。よって(C)の「ボストンの住民は席を争わなくてはならない」が正解。

問題31-35 は次の記事に関するものです。

Bristol (January 5)—After less than five years of operation, the doors of Swansea Shopping Centre (SSC) in South Wales will close at the end of January. With a 12-screen cinema and international fashion chains, SSC was meant to be a one-stop destination for shoppers of all kinds. For the first few months, footfall was in line with management's expectations.
¹"The problem was in cultivating a customer base," regrets Paul Blease, managing director of SSC. ²Mr. Blease suspects the finger of blame should be pointed at the food court and it's not particularly appealing fare. According to customer surveys conducted by the Kemble Institute, an independent research firm, SSC's biggest drawback is its inconvenient location. People, especially younger generations, prefer to do their shopping around the city center.
No announcement has been issued yet as to whether SSC will seek a way to reopen the mall or find a buyer and sell the property altogether. The adverse effects of this closure will surely be felt in Swansea, where employment opportunities are in short supply.

Bristol (November 10)—³Swansea Shopping Centre (SSC) has undergone a remarkable transformation that will be revealed to the public on December 10. After a renovation that has been in progress since February, SSC will soon be ready once again to welcome shoppers and their families, with over a hundred shops ranging from internationally renowned fashion retailers to grocery shops selling locally grown food.

Restarting the business all over again has required a substantial investment. It was made possible by real estate developer, Shahid Group. The Dubai-based company has acquired a significant part of SSC but states that it does not intend to take over the business. The owner and founder of Shahid Group, Mr. Abdul Shahid, spent his teenage years in Swansea, and apparently it was his attachment to the city rather than a desire to accomplish any business objectives that moved him. "⁴I certainly see future profitability in SSC, but more than that, I wanted to give back to the local community where I grew up," the property tycoon explained.

Despite its impressive list of tenants, SSC was unable to attract enough traffic in the past, mainly due to its somewhat inconvenient location. From December, however, the management expects to be able to remove this obstacle by offering free shuttle buses every quarter of the hour to and from Central Station. In addition to the improved transportation, ⁵the food court offers a wide array of exciting cuisines including sushi, tacos and dim sum.

⁶The mayor of Swansea, Sarah Jones, went on record saying that this would bring a lot of much needed jobs into the area. ⁷She accepted an invitation from SSC's managing director Paul Blease to cut the tape at the occasion held to mark the reopening. Visit the SSC Web site (www.swanseasc.co.uk) to find a list of discounts and specials available in the reopening week.

［記事1］● footfall 客数　● cultivate 育てる　● fare 料理　● adverse effect 負の影響
［記事2］● attachment 愛着　● business objective 経営目標　● tycoon 大物実業家　● obstacle 障害
● dim sum 点心

31. What problem does Mr. Blease mention?
(A) Attracting a variety of stores
(B) Raising funds for a restoration
＊(C) Establishing regular customers
(D) Hiring suitable staff

解説 忍耐力強化の仕上げに、TOEIC受験者の多くが苦手とする文書タイプ「記事」をあえて2つ並べたダブルパッセージ問題を用意した。Swansea Shopping Centre (SSC) のManaging Director (社長) であるBlease氏は、**1**で「顧客基盤の開拓において問題があった」と述べている。これを言い換えた(C)「常連客層を確立すること」が正解。第1段落で、SSCには大型映画館や世界的ファッションチェーンがあると述べられているので、(A)「さまざまな店を誘致すること」は問題にはなっていない。(B)「補修作業のための資金を集めること」や、(D)「適任のスタッフを雇うこと」は言及されていない。

32. What is suggested about Abdul Shahid?
＊(A) He predicts financial return on the investment.
(B) His firm hired Kemble Institute to conduct research.
(C) He is a native of the city of Swansea.
(D) His company acquired full ownership of SSC.

解説 Shahid氏は**4**で「SSCは将来確実に利益が見込めるだろう」と述べているので、(A)「彼はこの投資に対する経済的利益を予測している」が正解。2つ目の記事の第2段落3行目に「Shahid GroupはSSCを買収するつもりはない」とあるので、(D)は不適切。

33. What has been changed at Swansea Shopping Centre since its closure?
(A) Its location
(B) Its management
＊(C) Its dining offerings
(D) Its entertainment facilities

解説 SSCの以前の問題点について、**1**で「非難されるべき点はフードコートとその料理ではないか」との意見が述べられている。新装開店後のSSCについては、**5**で「フードコートは種類の豊富な、わくわくするような料理を提供する」と説明が一転している。これらの記述から、SSCにおける変化としては、(C) Its dining offerings (食事メニュー) が適切。

34. What does Ms. Jones say about the reopening?
　(A) Retail options in the area will be expanded.
　＊(B) It will provide employment opportunities.
　(C) It will lead to an improved transportation infrastructure.
　(D) There will be more entertainment venues for youth.

解説 SSCについて、6でSwansea市長のJones氏は、「たくさんの必要とされる仕事がこの地域に生まれるだろう」と発言したと述べられている。よって、Jones氏の発言として適切なのは(B)の「雇用機会を提供する」だ。

---

35. What will most likely happen on December 10?
　(A) Online promotions will commence.
　＊(B) A local politician will attend a ceremony.
　(C) Mr. Blease will announce his successor.
　(D) Mr. Shahid will sign an official agreement.

解説 3より、12月10日は、改装されたSSCが新装開店する日であるとわかる。7には「彼女(Swansea市長であるJones氏)はSSCの新装開店セレモニーでテープカットを行うことを引き受けた」と書かれているので、市長のことをlocal politicianと言い換えた(B)が正解。

Ted's Talks ❻

BEYOND対談 ── TOEIC講師 TEX加藤

> 連続満点講師に聞く、990点達成への最大の壁

Ted： TOEIC公開テストはほぼ毎回満点を取得されているTEXさんでも、「毎回のように知らない語句に出合う」というのは本当ですか。

TEX： はい。特にPart 7で知らない単語が出てきます。まあ、知らなくても解答には影響がないものばかりですが。私自身の語彙レベルはそんなに高くありません。英検1級の語彙問題なんてボロボロです。

Ted： 私も語彙力はそれほど高くないのですが、TOEICで満点を取る上ではあまり支障がありません。ただ、Part 5で知らない単語が正解選択肢というケースは、ごくまれにありますよね。そういう場合は消去法頼みになります。

TEX： それも語彙力ですよね。不正解選択肢3つを、自信を持って消去できるということは、根拠となる語彙・語法の知識があるということですから。

Ted： 確かに。消去法やテスト勘でなんとか切り抜けている問題もありますが、結果として安定的に満点を取ることができています。一方で、語彙力を含め、英語力は十分あるのに満点が安定的に取れない人、あるいはあと一歩で満点に届かない人もいます。特にリーディングがあと10〜20点足りないという人には、どんなアドバイスができますか。

TEX： やはり、たくさん受験するということは必要でしょうね。そして、問題を解くのが好きなら解きまくる、洋書を読むのが好きなら読みまくる。ただし、TOEICに直結する語句が出やすいビジネス書がお薦めです。自分の「好きな方法」で英語力を高めるということが有効だと思います。

Ted： 私たちの周りのBEYOND 990erを見ても、そこまでの道程は本当に人それぞれですよね。ただ、長いケースだと1年も2年も最高点が980のままという人もいるようで、それはさすがに長すぎるだろうと。

TEX： この本は、そういう人たちの満点獲得を阻んでいるであろう難問を凝縮していますよね。オリジナルBEYOND（『TOEIC®テスト BEYOND990 超

Ted's Talks ❻

上級の問題＋プロの極意』）も、難問演習と高地トレーニングで壁を越えようという本で、おかげさまで好評です。この続編も多くの人の役に立つでしょうね。

Ted： そう願っています。本書で取り上げた7つのスキルのうち、TOEICから英語学習に入った人にとって、どれが最も満点達成へのネックになりそうだと思われますか。

TEX： 語法・語感力でしょうか。ミスをするのはたいていPart 5の、上級者の間でも意見が分かれる問題ですよね。情報検索力も最初はネックになるでしょうが、慣れで克服できそうです。

Ted： なるほど。私も語法・語感は最後の難関だと思っています。

TEX： Part 5では迷ったら論理より直感を信じるといいかもしれません。

Ted： TEXさんがリーディングセクションで気をつけていることはありますか。

TEX： Part 7では必ず正解の根拠を見つけること。確信が持てなければすべての選択肢をチェックします。また、タイムマネジメントにも気をつけますね。170番まで来たら時計を見て、残り40分なら通常のペースで解き続け、それ以下なら少しペースを上げます。

Ted： Part 7を解いているときは、解答することに集中していますか、それとも登場人物や場面などが頭に浮かんでいますか。

TEX： 両方ですね。問題文を読む際は、実際にその文書を読む人の立場になって読んでいる感じです。文書を読み切ったら、初めて設問に意識が移ります。ただ、ダブルパッセージで文書を読んでいて不自然な箇所があると、「あ、これは両文書参照型問題のヒントだな」と問題に意識が飛ぶことはありますが。

Ted： 文書にリアリティーを感じる元サラリーマンの目と、設問を分析するTOEIC講師の目の両方が機能しているのかもしれませんね。

TEX： そうですね。仕事上、「受験者」「講師」「著者」と、複数の視点で解いています。

弱点スキル診断テスト 解答一覧

本章のスキル解説で触れられていない問題についてのみ、解説が付いている。
(診断テストの問題文の訳はダウンロードにて提供。詳細はp.7をご覧ください)

Part 5 (pp.9〜10)

1. (C) 情報検索力 語法・語感力 解説→Chapter 2、p. 59

---

2. (B) 精読力 語法・語感力

顧客の意見は、品質も向上するのであれば、値上げは容認できるというものだ。
(A) 名 決定　　＊(B) 名 感情、意見　　(C) 名 評判　　(D) 名 質問

解説 文の主語である空所は、補語のthat節によって説明されているので、that節の意味に合う選択肢が正解になる。「品質も向上するのであれば、値上げは容認できる」というのは顧客の「感情、意見」なので、正解は(B) feeling。値上げが「容認できるかどうか」は「容認するかしないか」という「決定」ではないので、(A) decisionは不適切。ここは精読力が試される。that以下は、過去の出来事や活動に起因する「評判」でもなく、また「質問」でもないので、(C) reputationや(D) questionも空所に当てはめることはできない。

---

3. (C) 精読力 裏取り力 解説→Chapter 1、p. 19

---

4. (A) 裏取り力 語法・語感力 解説→Chapter 4、p. 135

---

5. (D) 裏取り力 精読力 解説→Chapter 4、p. 136

---

6. (C) 情報検索力 語法・語感力

成功する事業を行う秘訣の1つは、直接的な監督指示がなくても働けると信頼できる人を雇うことだ。
(A) 動 励まされる　　(B) 動 信頼される　　＊(C) 動 (+onで)信頼される、期待される
(D) 動 権限を与えられる

解説 空所を含むwho節はpeopleを修飾し、事業を成功させるために必要な人材とはどういうものかを表している。空所直後のonを伴う用法を持ち、「信頼される」という意味も適切な(C) countedが正解。意味だけであれば(B) trustedも合うが、「(人や考え)を信頼する」の意味では他動詞で、ゆえに、後ろに前置詞のonを取らないことから不正解。count onとtrustの語法の違いが、この問題の主なポイントだ。(A) encouraged(励まされる)と(D) authorized(権限を与えられる)は意味的にふさわしくない上、後ろにonを伴わず直接to doを取ることからも不適切。

7. (D) 語法・語感力　精読力　解説→Chapter 6、p. 203

8. (A) 難語対応・忍耐力　解説→Chapter 7、p. 237

Part 6 （p. 11）

9. (C) 語法・語感力　裏取り力　解説→Chapter 6、p. 204

10. (A) 情報検索力　要約力　解説→Chapter 2、p. 60／Chapter 3、p. 97

11. (B) 難語対応・忍耐力　精読力　要約力　解説→Chapter 7、p. 238

Part 7 （pp.12〜13）シングル・パッセージ

12. (B) 裏取り力　情報検索力　解説→Chapter 4、p. 137

13. (C) 情報検索力　要約力　解説→Chapter 2、p. 61

14. (D) 要約力　難語対応・忍耐力　解説→Chapter 3、p. 98

15. (A) 言い換え対応力　要約力　難語対応・忍耐力　解説→Chapter 5、p. 172

ダブル・パッセージ（pp.14〜15）

16. (B) 情報検索力　要約力

　　その職についてどんなことが示されているか。
　　(A) 継続的なトレーニングが提供される。　　＊(B) 海外出張をすることが必要だ。
　　(C) アナリストとしての免許保有が望ましい。　(D) 応募書類が受領されると連絡がいく。

解説 広告の第1段落冒頭に「新しい副プロデューサーの採用を予定しています」と書かれているので、この文書は求人広告だ。同段落3〜4行目に、この職の説明として、full of challenges and opportunities to explore foreign countries（やりがいと外国を探索するチャンスに満ちている）という情報がある。よって、正解は「海外出張をすることが必要だ」という(B) Some overseas travel is required. だ。募集要項がまとめられている第2段落ではなく第1段落にあえて正解のキーを置き、情報検索力と要約力を試そうという問題だ。

17. (C) 言い換え対応力　要約力　裏取り力　解説→Chapter 5、p. 171

18. (D) 精読力　裏取り力　言い換え対応力　難語対応・忍耐力　解説→Chapter 1、p. 21

19. (A) 語法・語感力　精読力　言い換え対応力　解説→Chapter 6、p. 205

20. (D) 情報検索力

　　Hope氏はどのような方法で連絡を受けたいと思っているか。
　　(A) 電話で　　(B) ファクスで　　(C) 郵便で　　＊(D) メールで

解説 メールの第4段落1〜2行目で、Hope氏は、I would like to opt for the second contact option（2つ目の連絡方法を選びます）と述べている。連絡方法の選択肢はメールには書かれていないので、広告に戻って情報検索する。連絡方法などの事務連絡は広告の終盤で説明されることが多い。このメールも例に漏れず、第3段落2行目にApplicants will be replied to either by phone or by e-mail.（応募者には電話かメールのいずれかの方法で返事をします）という記載がある。ここから、Hope氏が言う「2つ目の連絡方法」はすなわち「メールで」を指すとわかる。よって、正解は(D) By e-mail。

TOEIC® テスト BEYOND 990 超上級リーディング 7つのコアスキル

発行日：2015年10月26日（初版）

著者：テッド寺倉、ロス・タロック
執筆協力：岩重理香、豊馬桃子、溝口優美子、ヒロ前田、TEX加藤
編集：英語出版編集部
校正：玉木史惠、Peter Branscombe

デザイン：伊東岳美
DTP：株式会社創樹
印刷・製本：シナノ印刷株式会社

発行者：平本照麿
発行所：株式会社アルク
　　　　〒168-8611　東京都杉並区永福2-54-12
　　　　TEL 03-3327-1101
　　　　FAX 03-3327-1300
　　　　Email：csss@alc.co.jp
　　　　Website：http://www.alc.co.jp/

地球人ネットワークを創る
アルクのシンボル
「地球人マーク」です。

落丁本、乱丁本は弊社にてお取り替えいたしております。
アルクお客様センター（電話：03-3327-1101、受付時間：平日9時〜17時）までご相談ください。
本書の全部または一部の無断転載を禁じます。
著作権法上で認められた場合を除いて、本書からのコピーを禁じます。
定価はカバーに表示してあります。

©2015 Ted Terakura / Ross Tulloch / ALC PRESS INC.
Printed in Japan.
PC：7015031
ISBN：978-4-7574-2656-6

TOEIC エキスパート三人衆が教える！

TOEIC®テスト
新形式問題
早わかりガイド

⬇ PCやスマホでダウンロードできる
　　無料音声あり　→詳しくはページ裏参照

ヒロ前田　テッド寺倉　ロス・タロック　著

2016年5月29日（日）の公開テストから、TOEICテストの出題形式の**一部が変更**になりました。TOEICテスト開発元によれば、テストの難易度、スコアが持つ意味は変わらないとのことです。つまり、**これまでの勉強や教材で十分戦える**ということです。
でも、不安ですよね（笑）。そこで、TOEIC指導に長年たずさわってきたボクら3人が、**どこがどのように変わるのか具体的に説明**していきます。
それでは、新形式問題をいっしょに見ていきましょう。
ヒロ前田

※本冊子は『TOEIC®テスト 非公式問題集 至高の400問』（アルク刊）の巻頭記事を再構成したものです。

TOEIC is a registered trademark of Educational Testing Service (ETS). This publication is not endorsed or approved by ETS.

⬇ 無料音声・電子テキストのダウンロード

本冊子の電子テキストやサンプル問題の音声は、以下のURLからダウンロードすることができます（要登録）。ダウンロードセンターでの検索の際は商品コード（9950059）をご利用ください。スマートフォンで音声を利用できるアプリ「語学のオトモ ALCO（アルコ）」もご案内していますので、ぜひご活用ください（電子テキストはPCでご利用ください）

[アルク・ダウンロードセンター]
http://www.alc.co.jp/dl

《「語学のオトモ ALCO」の使い方》

❶アルクID（メールアドレスID）を登録します。すでにお持ちの方は、上記URLを経由してスマホにALCOをインストールし、音声をダウンロードセンターから直接ダウンロードしていただけます。
❷ダウンロードした音声は、ALCOのプレーヤーですぐに聴けます。
❸プレーヤーは、巻き戻し／早送りの秒数を「2秒／4秒／8秒／16秒／30秒」の5段階で設定可能。聞き取れない個所の繰り返しリスニングに便利です。

※本サービスの内容は、予告なく変更する場合がございます。

目次

TOEICテスト、どこがどう変わる？.........P1

リスニングセクションの変更点.........P3
Part 3 サンプル問題........P6
Part 4 サンプル問題........P10

リーディングセクションの変更点.........P12
Part 6 サンプル問題.......P14
Part 7 サンプル問題.......P16

まとめ.........P24

2016年5月～

TOEIC®テスト、どこがどう変わる？

2016年5月29日（日）の公開テストから、TOEICテストの出題形式の一部が変更される。出題形式の変更は2006年以来10年ぶりのことだが、TOEICテスト開発元のETS（Educational Testing Services）によれば、今回の変更は大幅なものではなく、「今の時代の英語コミュニケーション状況をテストによりよく反映するための"アップデート"にとどまる」とのことだ。テストの難易度に変更はなく、従って、スコアが持つ意味も変わらないという。では、具体的にどこがどのように変わるのか。ここでは、TOEICテストの実施団体、国際ビジネスコミュニケーション協会（IIBC）のプレスリリースや、2015年11月に行われた「TOEIC® Test Updates発表会」、2016年2月発売の『TOEIC®テスト公式問題集 新形式問題対応編』をもとに、変更点をまとめてみた。

まずは、テストの構成（問題数）を比較してみよう。

問題構成の変更点

〈リスニングセクションの構成〉　部分が変更箇所

パート	名称 (旧 〜2016年4月)	問題数	名称 (新 2016年5月〜)	問題数
1	写真描写問題 Photographs	10問	写真描写問題 Photographs	6問
2	応答問題 Question-Response	30問	応答問題 Question-Response	25問
3	会話問題 Conversations	10会話・30問 (1会話3問)	会話問題 Conversations (with and without a visual image)	13会話・39問 (1会話3問)
4	説明文問題 Talks	10トーク・30問 (1トーク3問)	説明文問題 Talks (with and without a visual image)	10トーク・30問 (1トーク3問)

※ 計100問、約45分間、495点満点（変更なし）

〈リーディングセクションの構成〉

パート	名称 (旧 〜2016年4月)	問題数	名称 (新 2016年5月〜)	問題数
5	短文穴埋め問題 Incomplete Sentences	40問	短文穴埋め問題 Incomplete Sentences	30問
6	長文穴埋め問題 Text Completion	4文書・12問 (1文書3問)	長文穴埋め問題 Text Completion	4文書・16問 (1文書4問)
7	読解問題 1つの文書 Single passages 2つの文書 Double passages	9文書28問 (1文書2〜5問) 4組20問 (1組5問)	読解問題 1つの文書 Single passages 複数の文書 Multiple passages	10文書29問 (1文書2〜4問) 2つの文書:2組10問(1組5問) 3つの文書:3組15問(1組5問)

※ 計100問、75分間、495点満点（変更なし）

[リスニングセクションの変更点]
Part 3 の変化が大きい。
会話のパターンが増え、難化する可能性あり。

Part 1、2 は数が減るだけだが、Part 3、4 は問題文（会話・トーク）の形式と、設問の両方に変更がある。合計 23 の問題文のうち 7 ～ 9 つ、69 問のうち約 10 問が新形式になる。従来形式の問題もすべて残るとはいえ、印象はかなり変わるだろう。特に Part 3 の問題文は、「図表付きの会話」「3 人による会話」「2 人によるやり取りの多い会話」「2 人による 2 往復までの会話」の 4 種類となるので、変化が大きい。重視されているのは「複数の情報源から得られる情報をひもづける能力」。より本質的なリスニング能力が問われることになる。聞き取るべき文が短い Part 1、2 の設問数が減り、その分が長文の Part 3 に回ることで、リスニングセクションが難化すると感じる人も多いだろう。ただし、試験時間は約 45 分のままであるため、Part 3 が増えるといっても、全体として聞き取るべき分量が増えるわけではない。

それでは、パートごとに変更点を細かく見ていこう。

Part 1　写真描写問題

1 枚の写真について、4 つの短い説明文が 1 度だけ放送される。説明文はテスト冊子には印刷されていない。4 つの文のうち、写真を最も的確に描写しているものを選び、その記号を解答用紙にマークする。

- 設問数が減る（10 問 → 6 問）。出題形式には変更なし。

Part 2　応答問題

1 つの質問または発言と、それに対する 3 つの応答が、それぞれ 1 度だけ放送される。質問 / 発言・応答はテスト冊子には印刷されていない。3 つの応答のうち、質問 / 発言に対して最もふさわしいものを選び、その記号を解答用紙にマークする。

- 設問数が減る（30 問 → 25 問）。出題形式には変更なし。
- 質問・応答文に、省略形（going to → gonna、want to → wanna など）、言いよどみが用いられることがある。

Part 3　会話問題

2人または3人による会話が1度だけ放送される。会話はテスト冊子には印刷されていない。
会話を聞いて、テスト冊子に印刷された設問（設問は放送もされる）と4つの選択肢を読み、設問の答えとして最も適当なものを選んで、その記号を解答用紙にマークする。また、印刷された図表を見て答える設問もある。各会話には設問が3問ずつある。

- 会話数・設問数が増える（10会話・30問→13会話・39問）。
- 2者間の会話だけでなく、3者間の会話も加わる。
- 従来の会話は1.5往復（A→B→A）、または2往復（A→B→A→B）だったが、発言が短く、やり取りが3～4往復以上になる会話が加わる。
- 会話に、省略形、短縮形（will not→won'tなど）、文の一部（Yes, in a minute.など）が用いられることがある。
- 会話に、言いよどみや言い直しが出現する頻度が従来より高くなる。
- 会話内の情報と、テスト冊子に印刷された図や表を関連付けて答える設問が加わる。
- 会話の中の発言の意図を問う設問が加わる。

Part 4　説明文問題

1人によるトークが1度だけ放送される。トークはテスト冊子には印刷されていない。
トークを聞いて、テスト冊子に印刷された設問（設問は放送もされる）と4つの選択肢を読み、設問の答えとして最も適当なものを選んで、その記号を解答用紙にマークする。また、印刷された図表を見て答える設問もある。各トークには設問が3問ずつある。

- トーク数・設問数は変更なし（10トーク・30問）
- トークで、省略形、短縮形、文の一部が用いられる可能性がある。
- トークに、言いよどみや言い直しが出現する頻度が従来より高くなる。
- トーク内の情報と、テスト冊子に印刷された図や表を関連付けて答える設問が加わる。
- トークの中の発言の意図を問う設問が加わる。

[リスニングセクション全体について]

- Part 3、4 の、計 23 の会話・トークのうち、約 3 分の 1（7 ～ 9）が新形式のものになる。

  新形式の会話・トーク
  (1) 3 人による会話
  (2) 発言が短く、やり取りが多い会話
  (3) 図表付きの会話
  (4) 図表付きのトーク

- リスニングセクション計 100 問のうち、9 ～ 11 問が新形式の設問になる。

  新形式の設問
  (1) Part 3、4 の発言の意図を問う設問（本書では「意図問題」と呼ぶ）
  (2) Part 3、4 の会話・トークと図表を関連付けて答える設問（本書では「グラフィック問題」と呼ぶ）
  ※この他に、従来の Part 3、4 では出題されていなかった「What does the man / woman / speaker imply about ...」という設問が加わっており、これも「新形式問題」とみなすことができる（本書では「暗示問題」と呼ぶ。

- Part 3 の新形式の会話と設問の組み合わせについては、「3 者間の会話にグラフィック問題が付くことはない」と発表されている。また、1 つの会話にグラフィック問題と意図問題が両方付く可能性も低い。しかし、その他はいろいろな組み合わせが考えられる。

  Part 3 の新形式の会話と設問の組み合わせ
  2 者間 2 往復までの会話＋グラフィック問題／意図問題
  2 者間のやり取りの多い会話＋グラフィック問題／意図問題
  3 者間の会話＋意図問題
  ※暗示問題は従来の設問と同様、どのタイプの会話にも付く。

- Part 3、4 に意図問題が加わることによって、公式認定証のリスニングの Abilities Measured（項目別正答率、AM）に、「フレーズや文から、話し手の目的や暗示されている意味が理解できる」という項目が追加される＊。これにより、リスニングの AM は計 5 項目となる。

  ＊上記の「What does ～ imply about ...」などの設問は、この項目に分類されるものと考えられる。また、Part 1 や 2 の一部の問題がこの項目に分類される可能性もある。

Sample 1

Part 3 3者間の会話 ＋ 発言の意図を問う問題

会話は音声のみで、印刷はされていない。設問と選択肢は印刷されている。

MP3 001_Sample 1

Point 1

Questions 32 through 34 refer to the following conversation with three speakers.

女性1 The sales reports for our new music players have arrived. I've forwarded them to you both by e-mail. — Take a look when you have some time.
男性 Thanks, Kerry. Are sales up or down?
女性1 I haven't read them yet — what do you two think? **Point 2**
女性2 Well — the product reviews have been excellent. So, up, I guess.
男性 I don't know about that. **Point 3** I read that people haven't been upgrading because they're satisfied with the previous models.
女性1 I think we have to reduce the prices.
女性2 I agree. Ours is the most expensive brand on the market.
男性 OK — Let's discuss it all over lunch.

32. What is the main topic of the conversation?
 (A) Work allocation
 (B) Lunch menus
 (C) Sales results
 (D) Production schedules

Point 3

33. What does the man mean when he says, "I don't know about that"?
 (A) He is pleasantly surprised.
 (B) He is doubtful.
 (C) He is waiting on an update.
 (D) He is not an expert.

34. What do the women imply about the new music players?
 (A) They are too expensive.
 (B) They are low quality.
 (C) They are selling well.
 (D) They are heavily advertised.

Point 1　3者間の会話

3者間の会話の問題は、問題番号のコールの際に、"with three speakers" という文言が入る。3者が登場するといっても、同性ばかり3人では設問がきわめて作りづらいので、男性2人女性1人、女性2人男性1人の、いずれかのパターンになると予想される。2人の同性については、アクセントの違いも活用し、どちらが話しているかをわかりやすくする、との説明があった。

Point 2　Fragments（文の一部）

完全な文にはなっていない発話が入る。自然な会話の中ではよく起きることである。

Point 3　話者の発言の意図を問う問題

会話の中の発言（この場合は "I don't know about that"）がどのような意図で為されているかを問う問題。Why does ～ say "..."?（～はなぜ「…」と言ったか）と、What does ～ mean / imply when he/she says "..."?（～はどういう意図で「…」と言ったか）という形がある。

Sample 1【Part 3】　32. (C)　33. (B)　34. (A)

問題 32-34 は次の3人の話者による会話に関するものです。
女性1 新しい音楽プレーヤーの売上報告書が来たわよ。2人両方にメールで転送しておいたから。時間があるときに見ておいて。
男性 ありがとう、Kelly。売り上げは上がっていた、それとも下がっていた？
女性1 まだ読んでないのよ。2人はどう思う？
女性2 そうねえ、製品の評価は素晴らしいわ。だから、上がったんじゃないかしら。
男性 それはどうかな。ユーザーは前の機種に満足していて、買い替えをしていないという記事を読んだよ。
女性1 私は価格を下げないといけないと思うわ。
女性2 賛成。販売されている製品の中で、うちのブランドが一番高いのよね。
男性 よし。それについては昼食のときにしっかりと話し合おう。

32. この会話の主な話題は何ですか。
 (A) 仕事の割り当て
 (B) 昼食のメニュー
 (C) 売り上げの結果
 (D) 生産予定

33. 男性はどういうつもりで "I don't know about that" と言っていますか。
 (A) 彼は大喜びで驚いている。
 (B) 彼は疑いを持っている。
 (C) 彼は最新情報を待っている。
 (D) 彼は専門家ではない。

34. 女性たちは新しい音楽プレーヤーについて何を示唆していますか。
 (A) 高過ぎる。
 (B) 低品質である。
 (C) よく売れている。
 (D) 大々的に広告されている。

Sample 2

Part 3 2者間のやり取りが多い会話 ＋ 会話と図表を関連付ける問題

会話は音声のみで、印刷はされていない。図表、設問と選択肢は印刷されている。

MP3 002_Sample 2

Questions 41 through 43 refer to the following conversation and receipt.

男性	Hi, is this the help desk?
女性	Yes, it is.
男性	I've found a mistake in my receipt. I think I've been overcharged.
女性	Do you mind if I take a look at it?
男性	Sure. I didn't buy that packet of pens. I bought the notebook and the gloves and the other things. It isn't among the items in my shopping bag.
女性	Can I ask when you made the purchase?
男性	Just now. I haven't even left the store.
女性	Well, that makes it easy. Let's go and see the cashier who served you — I'll have them refund the amount immediately.

Receipt — Brown Mart	
Four-color pens	$3.00
Notebook	$4.00
Extension cable	$6.20
Gardening gloves	$21.00

41. Who most likely is the woman?
 (A) A cashier
 (B) A purchasing manager
 (C) A warehouse worker
 (D) A customer support officer

42. Look at the graphic. How much will the man be refunded?
 (A) $3.00
 (B) $4.00
 (C) $6.20
 (D) $21.00

43. What does the woman ask about?
 (A) The price of an item
 (B) The time of purchase
 (C) The location of a business
 (D) The type of a coupon

> **Point 1** 図表付きの会話

図表付きの会話は、最初にその図表が何であるかが放送される（この場合はレシート）。
図表は常に、3つの設問のセットの上に印刷される。
スケジュールや価格表、地図やクーポンなどさまざまなものが出題されるが、誰もがその図が持つ意味をすぐ理解できるような、単純なものしか出題されない（例えば、円グラフなどは出題されない）と説明されていた。

> **Point 2** 2人の「やり取りの多い」会話

従来と同様の2者間の会話だが、やり取りが2.5往復以上ある。やり取りは、4往復以上になる可能性もあると発表されている。

> **Point 3** 図表に関する設問

会話内の情報と、図表の情報を関連付けて解く設問については、設問の冒頭に、Look at the graphic.（図表を見てください）と言う文言がある（放送もされる）。

Sample 2【Part 3】 41. (D) **42.** (A) **43.** (B)

問題 41-43 は次の会話とレシートに関するものです。
男性 こんにちは。ここはサービスカウンターですか。
女性 はい、そうです。
男性 レシートに間違いを見つけたんです。実際よりも高く請求されていると思うんですが。
女性 見せてもらってもよろしいですか。
男性 もちろん。そのペン1箱は買っていないんです。ノートと手袋とその他のものは買いましたけど。それは買い物袋の中の商品には入っていません。
女性 いつご購入されたのか教えていただけますか。
男性 たった今です。まだお店を出てもいません。
女性 ああ、それなら簡単です。担当したレジ係のところへ一緒に行きましょう。すぐにその金額を返金させます。

領収書 — Brown Mart	
4色ペン	3.00ドル
ノート	4.00ドル
延長ケーブル	6.20ドル
園芸用グローブ	21.00ドル

41. 女性は誰であると考えられますか。
(A) レジ係
(B) 購買マネージャー
(C) 倉庫作業員
(D) 顧客サポート担当者

42. 図表を見てください。
男性はいくら返金を受けますか。
(A) 3.00ドル
(B) 4.00ドル
(C) 6.20ドル
(D) 21.00ドル

43. 女性は何について尋ねていますか。
(A) 商品の価格
(B) 購入の時期
(C) 会社の場所
(D) 割引券の種類

Sample 3

Part 4 トークと図表を関連付ける問題
会話は音声のみで、印刷はされていない。図表、設問と選択肢が印刷されている。

(MP3) 003_Sample 3

Questions 71 through 73 refer to the following telephone message and schedule.

男性 Hi, my name is Gavin Coleman. I'm calling about joining one of the college's evening courses. I work for a local theater and my employer requires that I complete some kind of training course every year. Um ... the deadline is July 1, so I'm interested in taking the course that commences on May 25. My employer is going to pay for the course and even give me some time off, so I just want to know if there are any seats left. Can you give me a call back at 555-2932? Thanks.

Upcoming Courses	
March 23 ~ April 14	Introductory Spreadsheets
April 16 ~ May 23	Public Speaking
May 25 ~ June 19	Web Design
July 1 ~ July 24	Leadership

71. Where does Mr. Coleman work?
 (A) At a college
 (B) At a tour company
 (C) At a restaurant
 (D) At a theater

72. Look at the graphic. Which course does Mr. Coleman want to take?
 (A) Introductory Spreadsheets
 (B) Public Speaking
 (C) Web Design
 (D) Leadership

73. What information does Mr. Coleman require?
 (A) Tuition fees
 (B) Start times
 (C) Course content
 (D) Seat availability

Point 1 図表付きのトーク

Part 3 と同様、図表付きのトークについては、最初にその図表が何であるかが放送される(この場合は schedule)。図表は常に 3 つの設問のセットの上に印刷される。

Point 2 言いよどみ、言い直し

従来のようにすらすらと話される正確なトークばかりでなく、「ええと」「あのう」のような言いよどみや、言い間違えて、「…じゃなくて」と訂正するような発話が混じる。このような言いよどみや言い直しは、Part 2 や Part 3 の会話にも入る可能性がある。

Point 3 図表に関する設問

トーク内の情報と、図表の情報を関連付けて解く設問については、設問の冒頭に、Look at the graphic.(図表を見てください)と言う文言がある(放送もされる)。

Sample 3【Part 4】 71. (D) **72.** (C) **73.** (D)

問題 71-73 は次の電話メッセージとスケジュールに関するものです。
男性 もしもし、Gavin Coleman と申します。大学の夜間講座の 1 つを履修することについてお電話しています。私は地元の劇場で働いていまして、雇い主に、毎年何らかの研修を修了するように言われているのです。ええと……締め切りは 7 月 1 日なので、5 月 25 日に始まる講座の受講を検討しています。雇い主が受講料を支払ってくれて、しかも休みもくれるので、残席があるかどうかだけ知りたいのです。555-2932 まで折り返し電話をもらえますか。どうも。

今後の講座	
3月23日~4月14日	表計算入門
4月16日~5月23日	プレゼンテーション
5月25日~6月19日	ウェブデザイン
7月1日~7月24日	リーダーシップ

71. Coleman 氏はどこで働いていますか。
(A) 大学
(B) 旅行会社
(C) レストラン
(D) 劇場

72. 図表を見てください。Coleman 氏はどのコースを受けたいですか。
(A) 表計算入門
(B) プレゼンテーション
(C) ウェブデザイン
(D) リーダーシップ

73. Coleman 氏はどんな情報を求めていますか。
(A) 授業料
(B) 開始時刻
(C) 講座内容
(D) 席の空き具合

[リーディングセクションの変更点]

Part 7 に新しい形の文書が加わる。
「位置選択問題」は、文脈の理解がカギ。

Part 5は問題数が減るだけで、出題形式に変更はない。変わるのはPart 6、7だ。まず、Part 6では、4文書が出題される点は変わらないが、1文書に付く設問が3問から4問に増える。追加される1問は、単語ではなく文を選ぶ設問(本書では「文選択問題」と呼ぶ)となるため、文法や語彙の力だけでなく、「文脈」の理解が求められる。

そして、Part 7で起きる変化は大きい。設問数が48問から54問に増え、チャットや「3つの文書」問題といった新しい文書スタイルが登場する。さらに、与えられた一文を挿入するために、最も適切な位置を問う設問(本書では「位置選択問題」と呼ぶ)が加わる。これもTOEICの歴史に見られなかった新タイプだ。

これらのPart 6とPart 7における変化は、TOEICが「文法・語彙」よりも「文脈理解」を重視しようとしていることを示している。

Part 5　短文穴埋め問題

テスト冊子に、空所を1つ含む英文が印刷されている。英文を完成させるために、空所に入れるべき最も適当な語句を、4つの選択肢から選び、その記号を解答用紙にマークする。

- 設問数が減る(40問→30問)。出題形式には変更なし。

Part 6　長文穴埋め問題

テスト冊子に、空所を4つ含む英語の文書が印刷されている。文書を完成させるために、空所に入れるべき最も適切な語句、あるいは文を、4つの選択肢から選び、その記号を解答用紙にマークする。

- 文書の数は4つのまま。
- 1つの文書に付く設問数が3問から4問に増え、計16問になる。
- 選択肢が文書の中ではなく、外に配置される(Part 7と同様になる)。
- 空所に、語句でなく文を挿入する設問(本書では「文選択問題」と呼ぶ)が加わる。

Part 7　読解問題

テスト冊子に、メールや広告、記事、テキストメッセージやチャットなどの英語の文書と、複数の設問・選択肢が印刷されている。各設問に対し、最も適切な答えを4つの選択肢から選び、その記号を解答用紙にマークする。前半で「1つの文書」問題、後半で「複数の文書」問題が出題される。

- 1つの文書問題（Single passage、SP）の問題数・設問数が増える。
  SPは、9文書28問（1文書につき2〜5問）から、10文書29問（1文書につき2〜4問）になる。
- 2つの文書問題（Double passages、DP）が、複数の文書問題（Multiple passages）に変更される。DPも残るが、3つの関連する文書を読んで解く問題（通称Triple passages、TP）が加わる。
  DPは2組10問、TPは3組15問（いずれも1組5問）になる。
- 複数名がやり取りを行う携帯テキストメッセージや、オンラインチャット形式の文書が加わる。
- 文書中の一文の、書き手の意図を問う設問（本書では「意図問題」と呼ぶ）が加わる。
- 文書中に新たな一文を挿入するために、最も適切な位置を選ぶ設問（本書では「位置選択問題」と呼ぶ）が加わる。

Sample 4

Part 6 文を挿入する問題

Questions 131-134 refer to the following e-mail.

Point 1

To: Gene Cummings <gcummings@starworldtours.com>
From: Monica Waters <mwaters@starworldtours.com>
Date: May 1
Subject: New World Games

Dear Gene,

I received an e-mail this morning from Vanderlay Bus Lines. It indicated that ---131.--- would be unable to supply enough vehicles and drivers to meet our needs during the New World Games in San Francisco.

Of course, the most pressing issue is finding another bus company that can handle the unassigned portion of the work. ---132.---, the group tour section is already busily contacting other transport companies and making the necessary reservations. I will get an update on the situation from Jim Nichol by noon today. If they are unable to find one ---133.---, we will be forced to rely on smaller regional companies or even rival firms.

---134.---. I propose that we seek partnerships with additional suppliers, not only bus and limousine companies, but also hotels, restaurants and even golf courses.

Monica Waters

---

131. (A) she
(B) we
(C) they
(D) you

132. (A) Accordingly
(B) Insomuch as
(C) Nevertheless
(D) In that case

133. (A) nearly
(B) locally
(C) generously
(D) largely

Point 2

134. (A) We should ask event organizers to assign us additional work.
(B) Staff will attend a series of training workshops to help them prepare.
(C) Let's take this opportunity to refurbish our offices before the busy period.
(D) I think that we are depending too heavily on a select few companies.

Point 1　空所の数・レイアウトの変更

空所が3つから4つになる。従来、文書中の空所のすぐ下に置かれていた選択肢が、文書の枠外に印刷される。

Point 2　文選択問題

指定の空所に入れるべき文を4つの選択肢から選ぶ。4問中1問は、この文選択問題になるが、何問目に出題されるかは定まっていない。

Sample 4【Part 6】 **131.** (C) **132.** (A) **133.** (B) **134.** (D)

問題 131-134 は次のメールに関するものです。
宛先：Gene Cummings<gcummings@starworldtours.com>
発信者：Monica Waters <mwaters@starworldtours.com>
日付：5月1日
件名：New World Games
Gene さん
Vanderlay Bus Lines から今朝メールを受け取りました。そのメールによると、San Francisco での New World Games の期間中に、われわれの要求に応えられるだけの車と運転手を供給できないとのことです。
もちろん、一番急を要することは、割り当てられていない仕事を担当できる他のバス会社を見つけることです。それを受けて、グループ旅行課はすでに熱心に他の交通会社を当たり、必要な予約をしてくれています。今日の正午までに、Jim Nichol から状況報告を受けることになっています。もし近くで見つからない場合は、小規模な地方の会社か、または競合他社にすら頼らざるを得なくなるでしょう。
私たちは、より抜きの少数の会社に強く依存しすぎていると思います。バス会社やリムジン会社だけでなく、ホテルやゴルフコースなど、さらに多くの業者との協力関係を模索することを提案します。
Monica Waters

131. (A) 彼女は
(B) 私たちは
(C) 彼らは
(D) あなたは

132. (A) それを受けて
(B) ～だから
(C) しかしながら
(D) その場合は

133. (A) ほとんど
(B) 近くで
(C) 気前よく
(D) 主に

134. (A) イベント主催者に追加の業務を割り当ててもらうよう頼むべきです。
(B) スタッフは彼らが準備するのを助けるために、一連の研修に参加すべきです。
(C) この機会を利用して、繁忙期の前に事務所を改装しましょう。
(D) 私たちは、より抜きの少数の会社に強く依存しすぎていると思います。

Sample 5

Part 7 テキストメッセージのやり取り

Questions 147-148 refer to the following text message chain. **Point 1**

MING CHANG   6:50 A.M.
Thanks for agreeing to come in and help me greet the guests. I know it's your day off.

BARRY HOLDEN   6:51 A.M.
Don't mention it. I'm on my way. I should be there in about 30 minutes. Do you want me to pick something up on the way?

MING CHANG   6:53 A.M.
Yeah! Could you get me a coffee from Joe's Café? It wasn't open when I passed by earlier.

BARRY HOLDEN   6:55 A.M.
Sure. I was planning on dropping in there, anyway.

BARRY HOLDEN   7:03 A.M.
The train has stopped. The driver just announced that the snow is causing some delays.

MING CHANG   7:40 A.M.
There's not much time left. Are you going to make it?

BARRY HOLDEN **Point 2**   7:42 A.M.
It doesn't look like it. You'll have to ask someone else to help you.

MING CHANG   7:45 A.M.
It'll be fine. Bob has just arrived. You can head home if you like.

---

147. What does Mr. Holden say about Joe's Café?
(A) He intended to go there.
(B) He does not know where it is.
(C) He will meet with a client there.
(D) He noticed that it was closed.

148. At 7:42 A.M., why does Mr. Holden write, "It doesn't look like it"?
(A) He does not recognize an object.
(B) He will probably arrive late.
(C) He thinks the store is still closed.
(D) He has not checked the time.

> **Point 1** 複数人によるテキストメッセージのやり取り、オンラインチャット形式の文書

この 10 年で当たり前のように使われるようになった、パソコンを使ったチャットや、スマートフォンでのテキストメッセージのやり取りが、問題文として出題されるようになる。こうした文書は 1 回のテストに 2 つ出題される。

> **Point 2** 書き手の意図を問う設問

Part 3、4 で出題される発言の意図を問う「意図問題」と同様、文書の流れから、指定の文がどういう意味を持つのかを問う「意図問題」が出題される。

Sample 5 【Part 7】 147. (A) **148.** (B)

問題 147-148 は以下のテキストメッセージに関するものです。

MING CHANG	6:50 A.M.
お客様をお出迎えするために快く出てきてくれてありがとう。今日はあなたの休みの日なのに。	
BARRY HOLDEN	6:51 A.M.
気にしないで。今、向かっているよ。あと 30 分くらいで着くはずだ。途中で何か買って行こうか。	
MING CHANG	6:53 A.M.
ええ！ Joe's Café でコーヒーを買ってきてくれる？ さっき前を通ったときは開いてなかったのよ。	
BARRY HOLDEN	6:55 A.M.
もちろん。いずれにせよ、そこに寄るつもりだったから。	
BARRY HOLDEN	7:03 A.M.
電車が止まった。雪で遅れていると、たった今、運転士がアナウンスしたよ。	
MING CHANG	7:40 A.M.
あまり時間がないわ。間に合う？	
BARRY HOLDEN	7:42 A.M.
そうは思わないね。誰か他の人を呼ばないといけないんじゃないかな。	
MING CHANG	7:45 A.M.
大丈夫。Bob が今到着したわ。もしよかったら帰宅していいわよ。	

147. Joe's Café について、Holden 氏は何と言っていますか？
(A) そこに行くつもりだった。
(B) それがどこなのか知らない。
(C) 顧客とそこで会う。
(D) 閉まっていたと気付いた。

148. 7 時 42 分に、Holden 氏はどういうつもりで "It doesn't look like it" と書いていますか。
(A) どういう物なのかがわからない。
(B) たぶん遅れて到着する。
(C) まだその店は閉まっていると思う。
(D) 時間を確認していない。

Sample 6

Part 7 位置選択問題

Questions 149-151 refer to the following e-mail.

From: Mark Hunt
To: All Staff
Subject: Next week
Date: June 19

Hi, everyone,

On Wednesday next week a team of plumbers will be visiting the restaurant to completely replace our outdated pipes and plumbing. This is a major job and it could take as long as three days.
— [1] — . We have decided to close the restaurant during that time. In preparation for the closure, I have a number of requests for staff. — [2] — .

— [3] — . Suppliers should be notified that we will not need any deliveries of ingredients on those dates. We should put a sign in the window and change the answering machine message so that callers and passersby can see that the closure is only temporary. Any food items that are likely to expire should be taken home for use by staff, or thrown away. Each employee will be assigned a task and held responsible for its completion. — [4] — .

If the plumbing work is unlikely to be finished by Friday afternoon, I will contact each of you by telephone with an update. I hope you will all take this opportunity to get some well-earned rest.

Mark Hunt

---

149. What is the purpose of the e-mail?
(A) To explain the use of a device
(B) To notify staff of upcoming repair work
(C) To recommend a marketing strategy
(D) To comment on the quality of a service

150. According to the e-mail, why might Mr. Hunt call staff members?
(A) To invite them to a celebration
(B) To request assistance with an event
(C) To announce a delay
(D) To inform them of a meeting venue

151. In which of the positions marked [1], [2], [3], and [4] does the following sentence best belong?

"Please advise our regular patrons that the restaurant will be closed Wednesday through Friday."

(A) [1]
(B) [2]
(C) [3]
(D) [4]

Point 文を挿入する適切な位置を選択する問題

提示された文を挿入するのに最も適切な位置を、文書中の [1] [2] [3] [4] から1つ選んで答える「位置選択問題」が出題される。この設問は、その文書に付いている設問の中で、必ず最後になる。

Sample 6【Part 7】 **149.** (B) **150.** (C) **151.** (C)

問題 149-151 は次のメールに関するものです。
発信者：Mark Hunt
宛先：全従業員
件名：来週
日付：6月19日
皆さん
来週の水曜日に、水道工事業者が当レストランを訪問し、古くなったパイプや配管設備を完全に交換します。これは大掛かりな作業で、3日間ほどかかるかもしれません。その期間中は、レストランを閉めることにしました。閉店の準備のために、従業員の皆さんにはいくつかのお願いがあります。
水曜日から金曜日の間は、レストランがお休みになるということを常連客に知らせてください。それらの日には食材の配達も不要であると納入業者に連絡してください。窓にお知らせを掲げ、留守番電話のメッセージも変えておき、電話をかけてきた人や通行人が、休業が一時的なものだとわかるようにしなければなりません。消費期限が切れそうな食材はスタッフが家に持ち帰って使うか、廃棄してください。すべての従業員で作業を分担し、その完了までの責任を持ってください。
金曜日の午後までに水道工事が終わりそうにない場合は、皆さんに電話で状況をお知らせします。この機会に、久々の休暇を取ってください。
Mark Hunt

149. メールの目的は何ですか。
(A) 装置の使用方法を説明するため
(B) 今度の修理作業について知らせるため
(C) マーケティング戦略を勧めるため
(D) サービスの質について見解を述べるため

150. メールによると、なぜ Hunt 氏は従業員に電話をするかもしれないのですか。
(A) 祝賀会に招待するため
(B) イベントの手伝いを頼むため
(C) 遅延について知らせるため
(D) 会議の場所について知らせるため

151. 次の文は [1][2][3][4] のどの位置に最もよく当てはまりますか。
「水曜日から金曜日の間は、レストランがお休みになるということを、常連客に知らせてください。」

Sample 7

Part 7 トリプルパッセージ問題

Questions 186-190 refer to the following information, online receipt, and e-mail.

Wally World is opening two exciting new attractions this summer, the Funhouse Roller Coaster and the Wipeout Waterslide. We are offering a preview for people who have season tickets for Wally World Amusement Park. The preview is scheduled for the evening of June 9. After the park's day visitors have gone home, we will reopen for four hours of nighttime fun from 6 P.M. The $60 admission fee includes dinner at one of the park's restaurants as well as unlimited use of the other attractions. Tickets for people under 13 years of age are $30. Only 300 tickets will be sold. They are available at the gate, or online through the Wally World Web site at www.wallyworld.com/preview.

---

www.wallyworld.com/tickets

WALLY WORLD
Atlanta's most famous family fun park!

Guest Name: Peter Bloomfield
Admission Time: Evening
Date: June 9
Tickets: 2 Adults / 2 Children
Discount Code: 82993 (15 percent off)
Total: $153
Purchased: May 2
Payment Type: Credit card

We look forward to welcoming you!

Click here to print your receipt. **CLICK**

To: Peter Bloomfield <pbloomfield@whitestar.com>
From: Customer Relations <cr@wallyworld.com>
Date: May 27
Subject: Your reservation

Dear Mr. Bloomfield:

Wally World regrets that one of its newest attractions, the Wipeout Waterslide, will be unavailable on the preview evening due to complications we have experienced in its construction. We would like to offer you the option of either a full or partial refund of the entrance fee. If you would like to cancel your tickets, please visit the Web site at any time before June 9. You can choose the cancel option on the ticketing section. Otherwise, you will be able to attend the event at the reduced rate of $45 for adults and $20 for children. Purchasers who paid in cash, can request a refund at the gate. If you paid using your credit card, your refund will be processed automatically.

Sincerely,

Gail Nguyen

186. What is the purpose of the information?
(A) To notify visitors of a change of policy
(B) To request assistance with preparations
(C) To attract guests to an event
(D) To apologize for an accounting error

187. What is NOT indicated about Wally World?
(A) It has some restaurants.
(B) It offers discounts for children.
(C) It is located in Atlanta.
(D) It offers group discounts.

188. What is implied about Mr. Bloomfield?
(A) He is an employee of Wally World.
(B) He was involved in designing the attractions.
(C) He will visit the park from morning.
(D) He has purchased season tickets.

189. Why will the Wipeout Waterslide be unavailable?
(A) It is fully booked.
(B) It is not complete.
(C) Weather conditions are unfavorable.
(D) The admission fee has changed.

190. How will Mr. Bloomfield receive his refund?
(A) By a discount on his next bill
(B) By a cash payment at the gate
(C) By an automatic transfer to his credit card
(D) By a coupon for use at Wally World

Point 1 トリプルパッセージ問題

「2つの文書」問題が「複数の文書」問題に変更され、2つの文書に関する問題(ダブルパッセージ)2組と3つの文書に関する問題(トリプルパッセージ)3組という構成になる。なお、文書が4つ以上になることはないと明言されている。

Point 2 複数の文書の情報を関連付ける問題

従来のテストの「2つの文書」問題と同様、2つの文書内の情報を関連付けなければ解答できない設問(2文書参照型)が必ず出る(この例題では187、188、190番)。ちなみに、「3文書を必要とする設問(3文書参照型)」は、「作るのが非常に難しい」と、Updates発表会においてETSのディレクターが述べたが、「出題しない」とは明言されていない。われわれ著者陣は、実は作るのは簡単で、いずれ出題される日が来るだろうと考えている。

Point 3 英文の量は建前上は変わらない

トリプルパッセージ1題の英文量は、ダブルパッセージより多くなるとは限らない。Updates発表会では「ダブルパッセージと同程度にする」と発表された。リーディングセクション全体の英文量も現行と変わらないと予想される。ただし、「単語や文の理解」に比べて「ストーリーの理解」が重視されるようになるだろう。

Sample 7【Part 7】**186.** (C) **187.** (D) **188.** (D) **189.** (B) **190.** (C)

問題186-190は次のお知らせ、オンライン領収書、メールに関するものです。

[お知らせ]
Wally Worldはこの夏、Funhouse Roller CoasterとWipeout Waterslideという2つの刺激的な新アトラクションを公開します。Wally Worldアミューズメントパークのシーズンチケットをお持ちの方には、先行体験をご提供いたします。体験会は6月9日の夜に予定されています。昼の来場者が帰宅した後、6時から夜のお楽しみのために4時間再開園します。60ドルの入場料には、パーク内のレストラン1軒でのディナーと、他のアトラクション乗り放題が付いています。13才以下のチケットは30ドルです。チケットは300枚限定での販売です。入り口か、またはWally Worldのウェブサイト、www.wallyworld.com/preview で入手できます。

[オンライン領収書]
WALLY WORLD
Atlantaで最も有名な家族向けの楽しいパーク!
ゲスト氏名: Peter Bloomfield
日付: 6月9日
入園時間: 夜
チケット: 大人2枚／子供2枚
割引コード: 82993(15パーセント引き)
合計: 153ドル
購入日: 5月2日
支払方法: クレジットカード
皆様をお迎えできることを楽しみにしています!
領収書を印刷するにはここをクリックしてください。[クリック]

[メール]
宛先：Peter Bloomfield <pbloomfield@whitestar.com>
発信者：Customer Relations <cr@wallyworld.com>
日付：5月27日
件名：お客様のご予約
Bloomfield 様
Wally World は、新しいアトラクションの1つである Wipeout Waterslide が、建設中に起きた困難な事態により、体験会の夜にご利用いただけないことを遺憾に思います。入場料の全額または一部を返金させていただくことをお選びいただけます。チケットをキャンセルされる場合は、6月9日の前であればいつでもウェブサイトで申請してください。チケット販売のセクションでキャンセル方法をお選びいただけます。あるいは、大人45ドル、子供20ドルの割引価格でイベントに参加していただくことができます。現金購入された方は、入り口で返金のご希望をお伝えください。クレジットカードでお支払いされた場合は、返金は自動的に処理されます。
敬具
Gail Nguyen

186. お知らせの目的は何ですか。
(A) 方針の変更を来場者に知らせるため
(B) 準備の支援を要請するため
(C) イベントに来場者を集めるため
(D) 会計上の間違いについて謝るため

187. Wally World について述べられていないことは何ですか。
(A) レストランが数軒ある。
(B) 子供向けの割引を提供している。
(C) Atlanta にある。
(D) 団体割引を提供している。

188. Bloomfield 氏について何が示唆されていますか。
(A) Wally World の従業員である。
(B) アトラクションの設計に関わっていた。
(C) 午前中からパークを訪れる。
(D) シーズンチケットを購入した。

189. Wipeout Waterslide はなぜ利用できないのですか。
(A) 予約がいっぱいである。
(B) 完成していない。
(C) 天候状況が好ましくない。
(D) 入場料が変わった。

190. Bloomfield 氏はどのようにして返金を受け取りますか。
(A) 次の請求書への割引で
(B) 入り口での現金払いで
(C) クレジットカードへの自動振り込みで
(D) Wally World で使える割引券で

[まとめ]
新形式は怖くない。
実践的な英語コミュニケーション力を磨くチャンス

以上、新しい問題形式を紹介してきたが、今回のアップデートの根底にあるのは「文脈理解」である。Updates 説明会において、ETS のディレクターが何度も口にした言葉がある。それは、context（文脈）だ。つまり、与えられた会話や文書の流れを理解したり、複数名による発言の共通点を発見したり、異なるソースから重要な情報を関連付けたりする能力を測ることが、新形式問題導入の主な目的だと言える。

ただし、忘れてはいけない。新形式問題が占めるのは、試験全体から見ればごく一部分である。900 点や 950 点を目指している人は、今回の変化にしっかり備えるに越したことはないが、例えば 600 点を目標とする人にとって、その必要性は低いと言える。リスニング、文法、語彙の力を伸ばす「英語学習」を怠らなければ、600 点を取ることは可能だからだ。

それ以前に、「新形式問題＝難しい」という式は成り立たない。Part 3 を例にとると、ETS の発表によれば、あくまでも問題の難易度を基準に出題順が決められる。つまり、新形式であっても前半に出る問題はあるし、現行形式でも、難しい問題は後半に出る。形式の変化を理由に、必要以上に受験者の危機感をあおる情報に振り回されないよう注意してほしい。

英語に限らず、コミュニケーションにおいて文脈を理解する力が重要なのは当然だ。これまで、「英語力測定ツール」として TOEIC を受験してきた人も、「一定のスコアを求められて」受験してきた人も、TOEIC を意識した学習を継続すれば、実践的な英語コミュニケーション力が高まっていくだろう。

新形式問題に取り組みたい人は…

本冊子の著者3人がこだわりぬき作り上げた至高の模試。
「非公式」だからこそ書ける攻略テクニックが満載！
練り上げられた模試2セットで新形式対策ができる。

新形式問題対応
TOEIC®テスト非公式問題集 至高の400問

ヒロ前田／テッド寺倉／ロス・タロック 共著
模試2セット収録＋CD-ROM1枚付き
（約95分 英語〈米英加豪〉）
株式会社アルク　定価：本体2300円＋税

TOEICテスト研究の第一人者であるヒロ前田氏が中心になって制作した新形式問題集。スコアアップには本番と同じく2時間のテストに取り組める模試がもってこい。
本書は模試2セットがついたうえに、「公式」にはない、スコアアップのための解説も充実している。

非売品

TOEIC®テスト新形式問題早わかりガイド
2016年6月15日

著者：ヒロ前田、テッド寺倉、ロス・タロック
編集：英語出版編集部
デザイン：mocha design
印刷・製本：図書印刷株式会社
発行者：平本照麿
発行所：株式会社アルク
　　　　〒168-8611 東京都杉並区永福2-54-12
　　　　Tel 03-3327-1101　Fax 03-3327-1300
　　　　Email：csss@alc.co.jp
　　　　Website：http://www.alc.co.jp/

・本書の全部または一部の無断転載を禁じます。著作権法上で認められた場合を除いて、
　本書からのコピーを禁じます。

©2016 Hiroyuki Maeda/ Takeshi Terakura / Ross Tulloch
ALC PRESS INC.
Printed in Japan.
PC：9950059